Dancing with the Virgin

Dancing with the Virgin

BODY AND FAITH IN THE FIESTA OF TORTUGAS, NEW MEXICO

Deidre Sklar

UNIVERSITY OF CALIFORNIA PRESS
Berkeley   Los Angeles   London

University of California Press
Berkeley and Los Angeles, California

University of California Press, Ltd.
London, England

All photographs are by the author unless otherwise indicated.

Grateful acknowledgment is made for the reuse of some material from two earlier articles by the author: "'All the Dances Have a Meaning to That Apparition': Felt Knowledge and the Danzantes of Tortugas, New Mexico," *Dance Research Journal* 31, no. 2 (Fall 1999): 14–33, and "Walking with the Grandmothers: Sensual Infiltrations into Writing," *Body/ Language* 1 (March 1999): 21–33.

Library of Congress Cataloging-in-Publication Data

Sklar, Deidre.
    Dancing with the virgin : body and faith in the fiesta of Tortugas, New Mexico / Deidre Sklar ; [all photographs by author unless otherwise indicated].
       p. cm.
    Includes bibliographic references and index.
    ISBN 0-520-07910-8 (cloth : alk. paper) — ISBN 0-520-22791-3 (pbk. : alk. paper)
      1. Religious dance, Modern — New Mexico — Tortugas. 2. Festivals — New Mexico — Tortugas. 3. Tortugas (N.M.) — Social life and customs. I. Title: Body and faith in the fiesta of Tortugas, New Mexico. II. Title.

GV1783.5 .S44 2001
792.8'09789'66 — dc21
                                   00-055968

Manufactured in the United States of America

09 08 07 06 05 04 03 02 01
10 9 8 7 6 5 4 3 2 1

Contents

Illustrations

Acknowledgments

Since this project began, as dissertation research in the department of performance studies at New York University, a great many people have helped me. My chair, Barbara Kirshenblatt-Gimblett, approved my experimental somatic approach and then offered guidance, encouragement, and questioning toward its fulfillment. I am grateful for her wisdom and friendship. At N.Y.U., I was also helped by my committee, Richard Schechner, Jill Sweet, Cynthia Novack, and especially Marcia Siegel, who taught me to see, feel, and describe movement. I was lucky again in California, finding the editor Gwyneth Kerr Erwin. She, too, said yes to the experiment and then held my hand through the submergings necessary to deepen my account. May she be there for the next book. Stan Holwitz at the University of California Press accepted the book and then waited patiently and cheerfully through the years of revision. Laura Pasquale helped me prepare the manuscript, senior editor Sue Heinemann saw it through publication, and Mimi Kusch, copyeditor, fine-tuned its language. I thank them all.

The poet Denya Cascio showed me that words could be living things. Luke Lyon, Los Alamos physicist turned dance ethnologist, introduced me to the Tortugas fiesta, then spread before me his century of news clippings, gathered in the meticulous mode of the scientist he was (Lyon n.d.). His memory is woven through the footnotes of this book. Alfonso Ortiz advised me when I was indecisive about a research site. At the University of New Mexico, Eddie Abeyta and Ted Jojola discussed the fine points of Isleta dancing and also kept me laughing. It was a joy to "talk shop" with Sylvia Rodríguez. Other scholars researching the Tortugas fiesta offered collegial support: Terry Reynolds, Mary Taylor, Andrew Wiget, Terry Corbett, Father Giles Carie, and especially Pat Beckett. The staff of the Rio Grande Historical Collection worked patiently to dig out collections, Xerox texts, and develop photographs. The photographer Miguel Gandert generously opened his collection of Tortugas slides to me and allowed me to publish them. Fermina Paz, too, made available her historical and family photographs. I thank them both.

I am grateful to my colleagues in the dance department at the University of California, Irvine, who insisted on the timely publication of this book, and to the university, which granted me leave from teaching and funds for editorial assistance and travel. Alan Terricciano noticeably improved my notation of *la ese* and *la guadalupana.*

The friends, colleagues, and students who gave of themselves in ideas, editorial comments, and embraces are too numerous to list. Even more than their help, I am grateful for the uniqueness of each one of them. May they forgive me for lacking the space to thank them all personally. From the days when we made theater together in Santa Fe, Denise Chávez has been a sister and *comadre.* She and Daniel Wolinsky have been my roots in Las Cruces. Manuel García y Griego, political scientist, saw me through many crises and did not laugh at my Spanish. Colleagues David Gere, Sally Ness, Michelle Kisliuk, Buck Schieffelin, Mady Schutzman, and Naomi Jackson heated up my enthusiasm for this project with heady discourse in its early years. Friends, both old and new, listened, discussed, and changed the subject. Most persevered with me. Some provided therapy for body and soul. I especially thank Irene Borger, Emily Boardman, Jacqueline West (and Geoffrey, Joshua, and Devora), Robin Goldberg, Jan Cohen-Cruz, Jay Peters, Allegra Fuller-Snyder, Alex Simpson, Debi Davis, Dena Sklar, Marianne Ross, Gail Wexler, and Marcus Ettinger. Most of all, since we climbed trees and made up stories in Three Arrows, I have leaned on my oldest friend, Amy Vladeck Heinrich. For this book, she offered professional wisdom, editorial expertise, and poetic elegance. My love and gratitude to her.

Families in community, their mutual support networks and ways of generating belief, are at the heart of this book. In these pages, my childhood family and community meet the families and community of Tortugas. My grandparents, Ossip and Olya Sklar and Charles and Regina Wiesenberg, are here in their emphasis on education and learning, in their love of words, and in their stories. Most of all, my parents, Elsie and Sam Sklar, and my brother, Rick Sklar, accompany my words, continuing to demonstrate that the best opportunities for learning occur in an atmosphere of love. I have been lucky in my family, which is both contentious and loving, and I am happy to bring them with me to Tortugas. There I met people who also acted on the principle that *unity* and *conflict* are not opposing terms. With generosity, spontaneity, and intelligence, they opened their families and fiesta to me, teaching me how religious faith is generated in community.

This book honors the singular individuals who work together each year to make the fiesta of la Virgen de Guadalupe happen. To the Danzantes and Indios and especially to those who endured my tape recorder and questions—Fred Salas, Paul Herrera, Johnny Peña, Larry Jimenez, Bobby Parra and his sons, Isidro Fierro, Isidro Miranda, and Ernest Misquez—I am grateful. To those I came to know best and their families—Pablo and Marcialla Fierro, Fermina and Frank Paz, Margie Lazos, Robert and Nellie Gonzales, Margarito and Rosalie Fierro, Fred and Martha Salas, Felipe and Katie Chávez, Emma Narvaez, Lorenzo and Elvira Dominguez, José and Andrea Ferrales, Reymundo and Dolores Molinar—I give my love as well as my thanks. I hope they will forgive me for any unintentional misinformation or offense in this book.

This book pays tribute to those who, though gone, still warm the kitchen: Martha Salas, Nellie Gonzales, Ernesto and Elvira Dominguez, Emma Narvaez, Isidro Fierro, Chepa Salcedo, Mary Dominguez, Patricio Gonzales, Bobby Parra, Leo Pacheco Jr., and Francisco (Paco) Herrera.

First Steps

In July of 1986 I moved to Las Cruces, New Mexico. Unlike my Russian and Polish grandparents, who moved to New York City, I was not an immigrant planting new roots, but a scholar, temporarily placed. I intended to do movement analysis of the dances, processions, pilgrimage, and "backstage" work of the annual Tortugas fiesta honoring the Virgin of Guadalupe. But my research was not just academic. Large personal questions of faith, belief, and community prodded me: Who are we? With whom do we walk through life? How should we get along with one another? What is it to believe? What is a good life? The answers would be different in Tortugas than in my childhood community. I wanted to rub up against the differences, paying attention and paying respect.

My Jewish family was committed to humanist ideals but had little connection with religion. My parents found more inspiration in music than in the temple. What I understood of spiritual experience came from nature and from the stories my maternal grandfather told. Walking in the woods, my brother and I would run off and wait for my grandfather's call, a long vibrato he shaped by passing sound through his cupped hands, his fingers quivering against one another: "Deeeee-da-a-a-ww." When we came to him, he would tell stories about a princess who lived in a glass house under the sea.

My grandfather's stories echoed in family visits to the theater. My first excursion, at age five, was to the Brooklyn Academy of Music for the puppet ballet *Love of Three Oranges*. Three puppet princesses emerged from three giant oranges and turned into human princesses who danced. I recognized their world from my grandfather's stories, and I imagined that world to be just beyond my bedroom window in Brooklyn. The brick walls of the Marlboro movie theater around the corner were shaped like the ramparts of a castle. At sunset, when they glowed pink and orange, I was certain if I could get behind them, I would find the oranges, the princesses, and the glass house under the sea. Around the same time I volunteered in kindergarten to imitate a snowflake, spinning until I could see the classroom lucidly, as if from above. This was how to enter the stories: by spinning and dancing. And so, at the age of five, I learned to join dancing to the envisioning of worlds, and I pursued the princesses backstage, into the theater.

Twenty years later I grew impatient with show business and its paucity of mythopoetic images. In the stagings of bedroom, boardroom, and courtroom, no oranges gave birth to humans, and talking heads substituted for spinning. But in the process of training for the theater, I learned the technical skills of making belief, of how to make incarnate what could be imagined. With the American descendants of Stanislavski, I learned the sensory recall techniques of method acting. With the corporeal mime master Etienne Decroux (see Sklar 1985), I learned bodily intelligence: the ability to articulate isolated muscles, to discern the structural and dynamic patterns of performers' movements, and to think/feel the relation between technical manipulation and somatic affect.[1] Through the physically based ensemble techniques of the Open Theatre and La Mama Plexus, I learned to combine bodily intelligence with narrative imagination to improvise worlds in words and movement. During those years, the late 1960s and early 1970s, following the lead of directors like Jerzi Grotowski, Peter Brook, and Joseph Chaikin, theater work came close to spiritual exploration. This shift from making theater to studying ritual made sense for many, myself included. And so I turned from performing and directing to dance ethnology and performance studies.

Qualitative movement analysis, based on the work of Rudolf Laban, provided a bridge between the dancer who learns via kinesthetic sensation and the fieldworker who learns via visual apprehension.[2] Qualitative movement analysis relies on tacking between the two. There is no other way to do this than through one's body, translating from the sight of a movement to the sensation of doing it. This process is neither vague nor mysterious but a matter of developing our inherent capacity to navigate between sensory modalities.[3] More than quantitative details, like the number of steps taken or the angle of an elbow flexion, it is the kinetic qualities of movement that provide clues to the experiential meaning of people's movement knowledge. The meaning of a gesture in the shape of a punch changes if delivered slowly and lightly rather than fast and hard. The first gesture may look like a punch in form, but as experience and communication, it is closer to a caress.

I am playing here on Clifford Geertz's discussion of winking. Geertz discusses the impossibility of determining the message of a wink without understanding the social codes lying behind the gesture. I am suggesting that without also noticing how, in kinetic terms, the person is winking, understanding of the communication is incomplete. Between Geertz's thinly descriptive "rapidly contracting his right eyelid" and his thickly descriptive "practicing a burlesque of a friend faking a wink to deceive an innocent into thinking a conspiracy is in motion" (Geertz 1973: 7), there lies the critical territory of kinetic nuance and experiential depth. Social meanings are embodied not just as symbols but also as kinetic dynamics.

Perhaps qualitative movement analysis was the technique that James Clifford sought when he noted anthropology's "rather meager stock of resources for understanding rigorously how one feels one's way into an unfamiliar ethnographic situation" (Clifford 1988: 37). Clifford hinted at dance, suggesting, "Participant observation obliges its practitioners to experience, *at a bodily* as well as an intellectual level, the vicissitudes of translation" (24, emphasis added).[4] Qualitative movement analysis in particular offers a method for experiencing translation at a bodily level. This was how I worked, stepping into the Tortugas fiesta, in dance scholar Susan Foster's words, "with sternum leading" (Foster 1995: 16).

My interpretations, however, are also infused with an ethnographic perspective. "The sensible is inextricable from the intelligible," dance anthropologist Cynthia Bull wrote (1997: 269).[5] "Sensibility" and "intelligibility" imply mutually permeable cultural processes. Sensory perceptions are molded by cultural epistemologies; abstract conceptualizations refer to culturally specific sensory orderings. All our actions in the world are at the same time interpretations of the world. Drinking coffee outdoors at a mall in southern California, I watch a woman walk to her car. The way she moves in her high heels is a recognition of the pavement as a surface different from the sand at the beach. Her mastery of shoes, her posture in a business suit, her ability to skirt moving cars, are all matters of both sensory and analytical intelligence. Movement, in other words, combines felt bodily experience and the culturally based organization of that experience into cognitive patterns. Ways of moving are ways of thinking.

I postulated that if ways of moving are also ways of thinking, then it would be possible to look for answers to my large questions in the movement of the fiesta. I would attend not only to narratives but also to sensations, not only to the function of dancing but also to its kinetic qualities. If spiritual knowledge is as much somatic as it is textual, then clues to faith, belief, and community would be embedded in the postures and gestures of the fiesta. How does one move here, through what kinds of spaces, constrained by what boundaries? What does the fiesta taste and smell like? What are its sounds? In what rhythms do people move together? My learning, I knew, would begin with my body.

1
. . . . . .
Travels

GOING

In July of 1986, I set out to drive the 285 miles of Highway 25 in New Mexico from Santa Fe to Las Cruces (see map 1). Though I had made the drive before, this time I did it with a conscious effort to pay somatic attention, to weave myself bodily into the landscape of Tortugas history. The journey was like the dancer's preparatory plié before her jump, a gathering of kinetic energy for the launch.

This particular launch intersected hundreds of other migration journeys that had crisscrossed the length of the Rio Grande Valley over time. Some of these journeys traced the ancestral threads of the Tortugas fiesta. Even before the Spanish opened northern New Mexico to Europeans in 1540, trade routes linked the Rio Grande Pueblos with their Central Amer-

6   TRAVELS

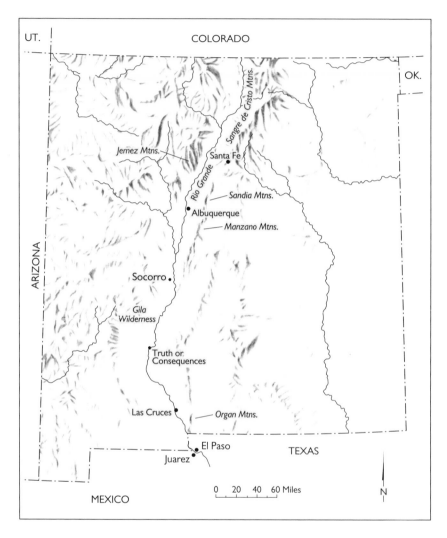

Map 1.   New Mexico.

ican neighbors. After the Spanish *entrada*, a wagon road fed Spanish out-
posts in the north with provisions and news from Mexico City; this was
the original Camino Real, later the Old Santa Fe Trail. Cut through the
hills of piñon and desert scrub, the wagon road was still clearly visible
running parallel to Highway 25. This same road had enabled not only

trade but also the traffic of settlement. From the south, Mexican Indians, displaced, converted, or sired by the invading Spanish, migrated up the Camino Real to start new communities along the Rio Grande. From the north, the Puebloans moved south, sometimes by choice as Catholic converts, sometimes as refugees after the destruction of their Pueblos, sometimes by forced recruitment to the missions of El Paso del Norte. The Tortugas fiesta was born of the changes that moved up and down the road. Its red clay still sticks to the dancers' shoes.

Twenty miles outside Santa Fe, the highway descended steeply at *la bajada,* the "hill," literally "drop-off." The descent marked a transition from the foothills of the Rocky Mountains and the nouveau cosmopolitan center that Santa Fe had become to the arrested space and time of the desert. I had lived in Santa Fe in the 1970s as a participant in its art scene; I knew both that city's urban excitement and the contours of the hiking trails that led into the mountains. But for the Puebloans north of Santa Fe, the mountains marked the boundaries of their world. As I drove, I could see boundaries to the east, south, and west. To the east, the Sangre de Cristo Mountains formed the southern extension of the Rockies. Thirty miles south, the turtle-shaped Sandia Mountains stood guard over Albuquerque. To the west, at the center of the Jemez range, a peaceful and grassy meadow shaped like an inverted dome was once the caldera of a volcano that brewed, erupted, and blew its own neck apart. Cows grazed there now, not far from the Los Alamos Scientific Laboratories, where the atom bomb was perfected. Next door, the Tewa Pueblos of San Ildefonso and Santa Clara danced their own version of energy transfers.

Just south of Albuquerque, the highway dropped and veered west to cross the Rio Grande, wide and shallow with sandbars forming small islands in its flow. The land on the west bank belonged to Isleta Pueblo. Isleta is one of four Tiwa-speaking Pueblos, along with the northern Tiwa Pueblos of Taos and Picuris and the other southern Tiwa Pueblo of Sandia near Isleta.[1] When Francisco Vásquez de Coronado penetrated New Mexico in 1540, there were sixteen to twenty southern Tiwa Pueblos. His exploratory party levied blankets and provisions from the people, molested women, and slayed or burned many inhabitants at the stake. The result was the virtual depopulation of most of the Tiwa Pueblos (Simmons 1979: 178; Schroeder 1979: 242). By the time of the Pueblo Revolt in

1680, Isleta and Sandia had absorbed the entire southern Tiwa population. The Isletans did not participate in the revolt, perhaps because, as Ramón Gutiérrez suggests, they were ambivalent and divided about having to choose between war or peace with the Spanish and rejection of or accommodation to the transformations the Spaniards imposed (Gutiérrez 1991: 64–66). The choice was not simply a matter of ideologies, Gutiérrez writes: the Franciscan friars offered seeds, livestock, meat, manufactured goods, and education in animal husbandry as well as the "immense ritual arsenal" of Catholicism (77).

When the Spanish retreated after the first Pueblo attack in 1680, 317 Puebloans, some Isletans among them, went with them. There are Isletans and academics alike who believe that the Tiwa people who accompanied the Spaniards to El Paso del Norte were not from Isleta but from the abandoned Tiwa Pueblos (Terry Corbett, personal communication; Bandelier 1892: 234). After a Spanish attempt to reconquer the Pueblos failed, 385 more Puebloans marched to El Paso.[2] Were those who went with the Spaniards forced, or did they go by choice? The debate continues in Tortugas, often drawing a line between those who reject and those who embrace Catholicism. In El Paso, the Spanish established the mission and village of Ysleta del Sur for the "Tiguas," as the southernmost Tiwas became known.[3] In 1967, the people of Ysleta del Sur were formally recognized as an Indian tribe.[4]

Driving through the land the Tiguas left four centuries ago, I watched the Sandia Mountains give way to the Manzanos, where ruins of the Saline Pueblos invite tourists. While some of these villages had been home to the southern Tiwa, others belonged to the Piro and Tompiro people. Most Piros and Tompiros were chased out by Apaches or "reduced" by the Spanish before 1660, and all those who remained left their homes by the end of the Pueblo Revolt.[5] Of the 317 Puebloans who first marched with the Spanish to El Paso del Norte, some were Tigua, but most were Piro converts to Christianity. Indeed, in 1657, twenty years before the Pueblo Revolt, ten Christianized Piro families helped the Spanish friar to establish El Paso del Norte's first mission community and church, Nuestra Señora de Guadalupe.[6]

It was from the *barrios*, the neighborhoods, connected with the Guadalupe Church in El Paso del Norte that the first *indios,* as they now call themselves, moved to Las Cruces, bringing with them their fiesta in honor of the Virgin of Guadalupe. The Guadalupe mission, built for the seminomadic Mansos who lived in the area of El Paso and Las Cruces, was, from its beginning, home to a heterogeneous group, including Mansos and Piros, Sumas, Tanos, Apaches, and Jumanos (Hughes 1914: 314). The Mansos proved to be less tractable than the Tiguas and Piros, and after at least five attempts to revolt, most quit the mission to live in the mountains, perhaps joining the Apaches (Hughes 1914: 336; Walz 1951: 143). They did not entirely disappear from the missions, however, for census reports reveal their continued presence into the twentieth century and that they largely intermarried with the Piros and others.[7] In the 1850s, when the land around what is now Las Cruces opened to settlement, some *indio* families from the Guadalupe mission migrated here. Their grandchildren and great-grandchildren are among the only known descendants of the Piro and Manso peoples. In the late 1800s, émigrés from the Guadalupe mission were joined in Las Cruces by Tigua families from Ysleta del Sur and Piro families from Socorro del Sur and Senecú del Sur, two El Paso Piro missions that were abandoned at the turn of the twentieth century. Together, these families now constitute the heterogeneous Pueblo population of Las Cruces.

The base of the Manzano Mountains in early morning was shielded by a rusty haze, and their caps were covered with a wig of graying white cloud. Within the distance it took to pass them by car, the ground cover changed from hay-colored scrub grass and a few dwarfed yucca to tufts of rabbit brush and sage and then back again to grassland. Perhaps it was the grazing cows who were altering the ground cover. At places, the plain was broken with narrow gorges, erratic fissures in the earth. A black mesa appeared abruptly, its volcanic innards exposed by water and wind. Heat rose from the sand when I stopped the car and opened the door. How could a small vulnerable clump of purple flowers grow in earth that seemed to be all sand, in winds that sent the car dodging, and with no water in sight? Water: a subject inherent to the Pueblo dances, its presence and lack, its manifestation in clouds, in snow, in sweat, its visual resemblance to downy feathers and white cottonwood tufts, its gifts to the growth of corn, its life-sustaining properties. The dances celebrate the weaving of dryness and moisture, seeking and finding balance in the way that all plant and animal beings do here. Would water also be the subject of the Tortugas dances?

The landscape itself spoke of the presence and absence of water. As the highway crossed the dry beds of the Rio Puerco and the Rio Salado, a thick line of cottonwoods and several adobe houses nearby announced that the road was closing in on the river. To the west were cracked earth and craggy hills, to the east a green river valley. Irrigation ditches and a sign for the Sandinal Vineyards announced that the farming country had begun. The Pueblo people found ways to move the river's water, and systems of irrigation sustained the people all along the Rio Grande Valley. When the first Spaniards arrived here, starving, the Piros offered them corn, saving Spanish lives for the conquest ahead. A church placard on the main street of Socorro informed the traveler that the town was named for that act of rescue: the word *socorro* means "help" in Spanish.

For the ninety miles south of the Piro Pueblos, the river was unavailable to the Spanish, sandwiched between mountains to the east and deep canyons to the west, impassable on foot or horseback. Highway crews have built I-25 to roller-coaster smoothly up and down the canyons west of the river, but Don Juan de Oñate, in 1598, tried to march on foot through the desert valley beyond the mountains east of the river. As Paul Horgan reports it, after the death of one man, a small dog who led the men to a water source saved Oñate's party. They named the Robledo mountain range after the man who died, and Perillo Spring after the dog (Horgan 1984: 170). The Spaniards called this ninety-mile stretch of desert la Jornada del Muerto, "dead man's march."

The desert symbolized death for the Spaniards. To the outsider, the desert does not yield easily. Unlike the Pueblo dancers, I could not stand for hours on the plaza under the sun without getting heatstroke or go without water on a long walk. My friend the novelist and playwright Denise Chávez, who grew up in Las Cruces, found familial rituals for the hot desert nights. She and her sister, mother, grandmother, aunts, and numerous other relatives used to sleep outside on cots. Each cot was surrounded by watermelon seeds, "the moist remnants of that evening ritual" (Chávez 1986: 55). Like the Piros, who knew the secrets of corn, her family knew the magic of coaxing water-food from the desert. Watermelon in slow desert nighttime suggests a special kind of southern sensuality.

In the heat, my body slowed, edging one notch closer to reptile. I spotted only one other car. There had been no others for an hour. My senses sharpened. I noticed the small movements of lizards in the scrub and the far-off black dot of a turkey vulture. The sky changed again. Puffball clouds gathered and tried to make thunderheads over the great mountains of the Gila Wilderness far to the west, the refuge of the Chiricahua Apaches. Some of the nomadic Mansos who refused conversion and mission life in El Paso joined with the last Chiricahua band of Apaches in the Gila, while some Apaches chose or were forced into baptism at the missions. One of their descendants married a Tigua from Ysleta del Sur and moved to Tortugas. Their grandchildren and great-grandchildren now danced in the fiesta.

On the southern horizon the clouds dispersed in wispy strands, but directly overhead, the sky was clear and blue. There was more sky than land. When the spectacular Elephant Butte Reservoir came into view it was a shock, pools of turquoise water among the mountains of the moon. The dam was built in 1916 to hasten large-scale irrigation in the Mesilla Valley and to protect it from the river's intermittent flooding and drying up. A second storage dam a few miles south at Caballo was completed in the 1930s (Baldwin 1938: 322). These dams changed the heartbeat as well as the face of the Mesilla Valley. From Rincon, the river's bend just east of Hatch, to El Paso, the valley became an agricultural garden. Along with the railroad that preceded them by about fifteen years, the dams were the American equivalent of the Spanish conquest. If Spain transformed local relationships through warfare, livestock, and the ritual arsenal of Catholicism, the United States transformed them through transportation, large-scale irrigation, and industrialization.

The change was latent in the beginnings of nonindigenous settlement in the Mesilla Valley. Until the Mexican revolution of 1821, the territory of Texas and New Mexico was claimed by Spain. After independence and until 1848 when the United States/Mexican border was redrawn under the Treaty of Guadalupe Hidalgo, the land was part of Mexico. For most of those years, there were no settlements in the Mesilla Valley; Mexican activity was concentrated at El Paso del Norte. There, both *vecinos,* or landowners, and mission Indians, the latter often working for the former, farmed orchards and fields and raised livestock along the river (Bowden 1974: 21, 25; Reynolds 1981: 12; Stoes n.d.). In 1836, however, Texas declared independence from Mexico, and the Mexican-American War threw the settlements into turmoil. Complicating the social geography was a change in physical geography: the Rio Grande began to flood and change course in the 1840s. *Indio* land was submerged, in the case of one Piro village, in its entirety, and families were forced to relocate. Relocation was further upset by fraudulent land claims and by government laws that transformed communal land into private property. The Mexican Reform Laws of 1855 effectively broke up the communal lands of the Pueblo villages and inhibited their religious celebrations (Bowden 1974: 60, 98, 108–9; Reynolds 1981: 31–33).[8] Both *vecinos* and *indios* immigrated upriver in large numbers.

War brought the Mesilla Valley to the attention of the Americans, and the Treaty of Guadalupe Hidalgo gave it to them. At the same time that the Las Cruces area was settled by the Spanish-speaking citizens of El Paso del Norte, it was eyed for development by the English-speaking Anglo citizens of the United States. In preparation for the completion of Elephant Butte Dam, there appeared an advertising brochure announcing:

DONA ANA COUNTY in NEW MEXICO

Containing the fertile Mesilla Valley, Garden Spot of
    The Great Southwest, where Modern Irri-
        gation is now being brought to its
            highest development

The town of Las Cruces, the brochure said, was

beautifully situated at an altitude of 3875 feet. Until comparatively recent years Las Cruces was one of the picturesque "show places of the southwest." But the magic wave of development that has swept over all New Mexico within the past five years, has found Las Cruces and has transformed it from a one time sleepy "adobe" town into a rapidly growing, hustling little city of the most progressive type. (McBride 1908)

Within five years of the completion of Elephant Butte, the Americans were producing cotton on an industrial scale for export (Oppenheimer

1957: 39). The homesteaders from El Paso del Norte, including the son of the *indio* cacique, the religious leader, were picking it for seventy-five cents a day (McBride 1908: 54; Curry and Nichols 1974: 115). The slur implicit in the phrase "sleepy 'adobe' town" notwithstanding, it was the settlers from El Paso del Norte who provided the labor that made large-scale development possible.[9]

The waters of Elephant Butte and Caballo Reservoirs lapped against the mountain ranges that the Spaniards once found impassable. The buttes arched up from the lake as if pushed from below, displaying their bones, skeletons of pink and yellow and brown sedimentary rock tilting on a diagonal toward numerous pointy heads. Salt bushes squeezed out of the cracks. On weekends, motorized pleasure boats sliced the water; swimmers bathed at the sandy shore, like aliens enjoying a dip in the moonscape. But just further south, past the Hillsboro turnoff leading to the Gila Wilderness, the practical effects of the dams were visible. Here the valley spoke of fertility through the language of water. After the construction of the dams, the southern section of the New Mexico Rio Grande was no longer a lazy meander around sandbars but a dependably wide and deep alley of moving water. The sinuating thick seam of the Rio Grande held the land together at one life-giving center. Beyond the river was an expansive sloping valley of fields laid out in hundreds of orderly rows. Irrigation was serious and large scale; I could see and smell its greenness. The sky was still blue, but there was cloud activity in profusion, a gathering of humpbacked and bubble-headed beings trading wetness with the river.

Topping a rise in the highway, I glimpsed the landmark mountains that stood above Las Cruces: the Organs. They were unmistakable, with their multiple sharp pinnacles that resembled the stronghold of a fairy-tale king. In actuality the Organs were the last of the San Andres range that further north made up the eastern edge of the Jornada del Muerto. Access to these mountains from San Antonio to Las Cruces was largely restricted; they were within the United States Army's White Sands Missile Range. In the fields of the Mesilla Valley, the farmers grew red chile and cotton; next door in the mountains, the army tested its missiles. Like the railroad and Elephant Butte Reservoir, White Sands, opened in 1945, brought large numbers of American citizens to the Mesilla Valley. It also brought jobs to the local residents, raising the local standard of living.[10]

During the Depression, when Loomis and Leonard interviewed thirty-seven Indian-Mexican Tortugas families, "typical of the other farm laborers living along the Rio Grande in lower New Mexico," they found that the average salary earned by a family was $347 a year, one-eighth the average earned by farm operators in large-scale commercial agriculture in northeastern California and southwestern Oregon (Loomis and Leonard 1938: 1). In these same families, the children now graduated from college, and their parents worked as store managers, store owners, and salespeople, as accountants, office workers, engineers, and teachers. Many of the jobs were at White Sands. White Sands employed as many people as the fields, and those who now worked the fields came up from Mexico, often as illegal migrant laborers. For the local people, the army base was a source of work, not a political issue.

I left I-25 for the two-lane blacktop of Highway 85 that passed through Hatch, the "chile capital of the world." In an apartment window above a storefront on Main Street, I glimpsed through two strips of a faded Mexican blanket a field laborer cooling himself in the darkness of an apartment. There was a brown arm, a white sleeveless undershirt, and a face, young, mustachioed, and barely visible in the shadow. I could feel both his full day of labor and now his rest. A few older workers were outside, crossing the street to look at a display of straw hats for sale on the sidewalk. Except for the men and the hat seller, the street was empty. Were the men up from Mexico for the picking season, living above the storefronts of Hatch? And did they take a quick mental snapshot of my oversized and air-conditioned rental car as I was taking one of them?

South of Hatch, Highway 85 was busier than the interstate, trafficked predominantly by farmers in cowboy hats driving pickup trucks. The back of one truck was piled with onions; perhaps it was onions the men from Mexico were picking. In the fields, the chiles had already ripened to red. There were yellow flowers on the cotton plants and wheels of dried alfalfa tied and waiting to be picked up. Meadowlarks convening on telephone wires declared themselves in flutelike gurgles. A red-tailed hawk in the distance pierced a field to nab a furry prey. Signs of irrigation were everywhere, above all in the muddy water flowing through the neatly dug trenches beside the fields. The irrigation ditches were punctuated with bright orange sluice gates by which the water flow was controlled. By closing the gate beyond his fields, a farmer could control the rise of water in the ditch and hold it at the height of the perpendicular furrows he dug between his rows of crop. The fields were perfectly leveled so that the water flowed down the furrows, irrigating the whole crop. The sluice gates were operated on a carefully organized rotating system so that, in principle at least, every farmer got an equal share of the precious water.

The road crossed the river at Fort Selden State Monument, built during the 1850s to keep the Apaches from raiding the new Doña Ana Bend Colony (Baldwin 1938: 319). Established in 1842, Doña Ana was the first of the new settlements to take hold in the Mesilla Valley. Las Cruces was laid out in 1848, with settlers living there by the following year.[11] After the Hidalgo Treaty divided the valley into Mexican and American sides of the river, those not wishing to be United States citizens founded small settlements on the western, Mexican side. Not knowing what to expect from the Americans, many *indios* moved to Mesilla, choosing loyalty to Mexico. But most moved back and forth between El Paso and the settlements. Two brothers in one family moved first to Mesilla to live with their mother for a year, then to Las Cruces, then back to El Paso, and finally once again to Las Cruces (Reynolds 1981: 33–34). And travel reports from the early 1850s reveal that people returned to El Paso to celebrate the Virgin's feast day (Stoes n.d.). Their citizenship options were cut off in 1854 when the Gadsden Purchase gave Mesilla to the United States. By 1885, about eighty Pueblo families were living in and around Las Cruces (*Rio Grande Republican*, December 19, 1885).

What must it have been like for the *indio* families? Did the men, like the ones I saw in Hatch, move up alone, joined later by their families? Moving back and forth those first years, they must not have brought very much with them, perhaps some clothes, blankets, tools. Did they carry chiles canned in their old homes? Did the children stay with their grandparents in El Paso the way they now came to their grandmothers' houses after school while their mothers worked? Did the women continue to return to El Paso to help out with cooking on feast days, as some Tortugas women still do for Ysleta del Sur's feast day?

Many of the early *indio* settlers worked at the Ascarate family's ranch,

Rancho Viejo, and at Stevenson's silver ore smelter, both near what is now Tortugas. The Ascarates and their Stevenson relatives had been large land-holders in El Paso del Norte before expanding to the Mesilla Valley (Bowden 1974: 97). In El Paso, *indios* from the neighborhoods of the Guadalupe mission had worked for the *vecinos* on their lands and in their homes (Reynolds 1981: 12). Had there been a relationship with the Ascarates and Stevensons in El Paso that continued in Las Cruces? An undated manuscript calls most of the labor of this time "peon bondage, a slavery for debt. In some cases it was a benevolent servitude; in others a cruel condition that lasted for life, and sometimes carried into the second generation. It lasted until 1867 when it was stopped by law" (Stoes n.d.). Bishop Henry Granjon, passing through the valley in 1902, confirmed that the *indios* arrived there "as *peones* in search of better farmlands and room to expand" (Granjon 1986: 5). He writes, "[T]hey possess several plots of land which furnish their subsistence" (37). Likewise, based on interviews conducted with descendants, Alan Oppenheimer found that the early settlers were both fieldhands and subsistence farmers (1957: 24–26, 123–25).

One Tortugas elder, whose grandparents lived in apartments on the Ascarate ranch, called the Ascarates "benefactors." She said the Ascarates let the *indios* use their covered wagon to go to mass in Las Cruces on the Virgin's feast day. This was before St. Genevieve's Church was built on Main Street in Las Cruces. Mass was held "under a tree in O'Hara's Orchard where the Fiesta Drive-in now stands" (Williams n.d.). Later, *indio* families, including her grandparents, built homes near St. Genevieve's Church and Main Street. From Las Cruces, did the men then ride every day in the Ascarate wagon to go to work? There are memory traces of stopping at a sanctuary, a stone niche on the road between Las Cruces and the Ascarate ranch. Did the workers stopping there look up at the Organ Mountains and invite the Virgin of Guadalupe to inhabit this new landscape?

The *indios* were only part of the migration to the Mesilla Valley. Other settlers came from the northern provinces of Mexico, from Chihuahua and Sonora. The father of one prominent fiesta family came from the mountain country of the Tarahumaras. Don Miguel acquired land south of Tortugas and grew chiles and cotton. But only one of his five sons, a leader in the fiesta's dance group, Los Danzantes, stayed on the farm. Whatever livelihood they chose, Don Miguel's children, and then grandchildren, skipped school when the cotton and chiles were ripe and ready to pick. Now the grandchildren study to become engineers and teachers, but they still know how to can chiles.

THERE

I can only imagine what it must have been like to uproot from one country and move to another, gravitating in the new place to the families who had lived next door in the old, seeking out those who knew the rhythms of everyday life, of speech and landscape, knew how to build the right-sized fire for cooking tortillas, knew at what hour to get up in the morning. My grandparents also left one country to start anew in another. My paternal grandfather left his bride and child in Russia while he crossed the Atlantic. Living near Forty-second Street in New York, he earned money hanging wallpaper and then sent for his family. In the meantime, my grandfather caught influenza and lost his hearing, and so I knew him as a man who rarely spoke. I have a picture of him, tall and straight, with the nose of a Roman soldier. He had been in the czar's army, one of the few Jewish men conscripted. The picture shows him in America, in uniform, standing next to a horse on which my father, at age seven or eight, perches. They both have eyes that are big with openness to life but also sorrow. Even in the seven-year-old, there is pain; perhaps it was passed on in the womb.

There is also a picture of his wife, my grandmother, at about forty years old, small and round. She is sitting at a child's desk in a public school classroom in Boro Park, Brooklyn, among other immigrant Jewish women. They are all the same age, in their best dresses that look like housedresses. They face sideways toward the camera. Beyond them I can see the blackboard on one wall and, on the other, wooden doors with calendars and a poster admonishing Drink More Milk. Eight slim young American teachers stand behind the women, sympathetic but clearly different. My grandmother's hair is set in the fashion of the day, tight at the crown with a little roll curled under at the ears. Her jaw is set in determination, but a mischievous smile also plays across her face. Her eyes look off slightly to the side, distant. The look reveals pride in being here. She is learning English. She is learning how to dress and do her hair. She has come out of the house to be a part of the new world.

In Bensonhurst, where my grandparents opened a store to make window shades, venetian blinds, picture frames, and mirrors, they found others whose speech had the same rhythms as their own. The families came from different towns in the pale, but they all knew what to do with a samovar, and they remembered the pogroms and the revolution. My grandmother grew up in Moscow, the youngest of eighteen children, a firebrand who was jailed for handing out revolutionary leaflets. Unmarried at twenty-four, she was considered an old maid. It was the custom of families to invite the traveling Jewish soldiers to Passover dinner. That was how she met my grandfather and gave up her leafleting life. In Brooklyn, they joined the Jewish labor movement, and that became their community. I remember my grandmother sitting with her friends on folding chairs in front of my grandfather's store or Mr. Abeshaus's liquor store. I imagine them making sense of Brooklyn by translating its unfamiliar sights into the cadences and gestures of Yiddish, sitting close together, whispering back and forth, the words not as significant as the rhythms of sound and movement that joined one woman to another, keeping the filament of the old home alive.

Rhythms, in speech and movement, synchronize people. As anthropologist Edward Hall observes, "syncing" is the most basic form of communication, more basic than the content of language. Like language, rhythms are learned and culture specific. People recognize one another as community through rhythmic synchrony. Racism, Hall suggests, may be a matter of incomprehensibility and prejudice across rhythmic differences. "If you want to fit in," he advises, "move to the same rhythm" (Hall 1977: 79). The sound of the Jewish women's language, the gestures that marked the cadences and contours of their thoughts were different from those of the grandmothers in Las Cruces. The rhythms of connection followed different streams of crescendos, diminuendos, and innuendos. They referred to different homes, different sensory details, to grills for slapping tortillas versus samovars for boiling tea. These details are meaningful. They tell what it is to be a person belonging to a community. But the networking was the same. Both groups came together in an unfamiliar place to sing and gesture a home into being.

Anthropologist David Efron, a student of Franz Boas, recognized the symbiosis between movement and verbal thought. "We conceive of gestural behavior as an intrinsic part of the thinking process," he writes (Efron 1972: 105n48). Comparing the gestural styles of first-generation Jewish and Italian immigrants in 1940s New York City, Efron shows that differences in gesture styles embody differences in the process of thinking. Italian immigrants employed gestures referring primarily to the *content* of their discourse, as if carrying "a bundle of pictures" in their hands (123). Jewish immigrants used gestures referring to the *process* of theirs to "link one proposition to another, trace the itinerary of a logical journey, or to beat the tempo of mental locomotion" (98). The gestural embroideries and zigzags were "something like gestural charts of the 'heights' and 'lows,' 'detours' and 'crossroads' of the ideational route" (99). Whereas the Italian immigrants' gestures embodied the "what" of thinking, the Jewish immigrants enacted the "how." Gesturing is a kind of thinking, processing in movement the rhythms, shapes, and sounds of mentation. Thinking is as much an aesthetic process as it is a symbolic one.

But movements and gestures, like language, are not innate. They shape to circumstances. Indeed, Efron undertook his study to refute decisively Nazi notions of an inherent connection between "race" and gesture. He found that the more the second generation of Jewish and Italian immigrants assimilated in New York, the more their gestures grew to resemble each other's and the less they resembled those of their immigrant parents. My grandparents and those in Las Cruces were both in transitional generations, carrying the old rhythms and stretching them to reshape the cadences of thought, language, and gesture to meet a new cultural landscape.

Perhaps it was the Virgin mother, carried by the *indios* from the old place to the new, who enabled them to make the new place home. I can imagine the women carefully packing a statue or portrait of the Virgin onto the back of a wagon. Was there a sigh of relief, unpacking it? Was it a comfort to unpack the trunkful of velvets and laces they used to dress her? Did knowing she was there with them make it possible for a young mother to buy groceries from a man whose language she couldn't speak or send children to a school that would teach them who knows what new thoughts? The trunk and its fabrics were finally discarded in the 1980s after years of debate between the elderly guardian of the Virgin's altar and a younger generation who preferred to dress the Virgin in easy-care polyesters. Perhaps the contents of the trunk were needed at the beginning as proof that there had been a past elsewhere. The Virgin has made her presence felt here for a century now. The smell of El Paso memories is no longer necessary to make Las Cruces home.

Just outside the city, miles of pecan orchards were laid out in rows and leafed out in green, a multidimensional promenade of columns welcoming travelers into the city. The orchards thinned to yard-sized patches shading ranch-style homes, and then they disappeared, replaced by a wide avenue fronted with mobile home lots, car dealerships, and hamburger and burrito joints. I entered Las Cruces by way of its auto strip. Traffic was heavy. No one was walking. Even a drive east into the center of town, past residential streets of painted adobe houses, a central area of tall government buildings, and a small shopping center, yielded few pedestrians. It was in part the heat that kept people indoors, but downtown was no longer the living center of the city. St. Genevieve's Church, which had held Main Street together since 1859, was razed in the 1960s. The bishopric ordered it torn down for financial reasons, and a shopping mall was built there. People still talk about the event as a tragedy. The downtown mall lingered on in a slow death, its lifeblood draining. It was usurped by a newer, larger mall on the mesa east of town.

The *indios* first celebrated the fiesta of Guadalupe downtown, at St. Genevieve's Church, at least as far back as 1872 (*The Borderer*, December 15, 1872). When Bishop Henry Granjon made his pastoral visit to Las Cruces in 1902, they greeted him at the train station, dancing, and led a procession to St. Genevieve's (Granjon 1986: 37). But the church was not entirely comfortable with the *indio* celebrations. In 1904, Father Lassaigne shortened the Virgin's fiesta from a week to three days. As reported in the *Rio Grande Republican* of December 16, 1904:

> They [the Indians] used to spend a week in this service, but, we under-
> stand, that by the advice of the Priest, it is limited now to three days. We
> are told there was a stubborn persistence to doing away with this service
> and they really rebelled and the seceders were forming a church of their
> own, but by compromise and persuasion they were induced to accept
> three days to enjoy the old custom.

There was apparently a public debate on the subject, for five years later a new priest, Father Vandermasen, writes, "Much printer's ink has been applied yearly to describe the 'barbarous' celebration of the Indians in Las Cruces, and not a little harsh criticism has been heaped upon the Catholic church for allowing and even taking part in said ceremonies" (Vandermasen 1909). The only objection Father Vandermasen could imagine was that the annual celebration was "somewhat out of place in a civilized community." It is understandable that in these circumstances the *indios* would want autonomy and their own church as quickly as possible.[12] Not until 1982, when native son Ricardo Ramirez was appointed archbishop of the newly created diocese of Las Cruces, did the church establishment thoroughly champion the *indios.*

From downtown, I set off for Tortugas. It was difficult to find. One had to know which of the side roads led into, rather than around, the neighborhood. Comprising about ten square blocks, Tortugas lay between the southern section of Main Street on the west and the side road of I-25 on the east (see map 2). At the southern edge of Tortugas, house lots backed onto a cement wall, demarcating a new subdivision. To the north, Tortugas Drive was a winding road, in some places dirt, in others paved, between Main Street and the interstate. Another dirt road connected I-25's side road to Tortugas Drive. It was easy to miss the village.

Tortugas actually contains two villages. One, San Juan de Dios, established at about the same time as Mesilla, was a mile northwest of the old Stevenson smelter and only a few feet from the Ascarate ranch.[13]

Though the *indios* did not live in San Juan, other mine and ranch workers did. Still, the *indios* must have had this area in mind from the begin-

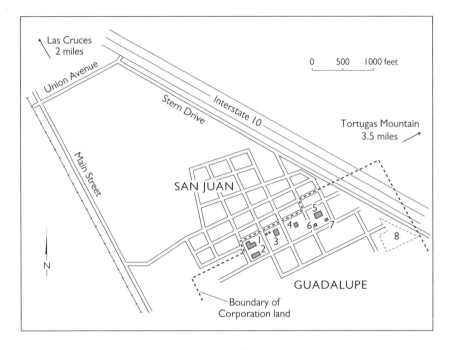

Map 2. Tortugas streets, showing the dividing line between San Juan and Guadalupe. (1) Church of Our Lady of Guadalupe; (2) parish hall; (3) *casa de la comida;* (4) school; (5) *casa del pueblo;* (6) *capilla;* (7) *casa de descanso;* (8) cemetery. (Map based on original drawing by Luke Lyon, courtesy of Rio Grande Historical Collections, New Mexico State University Library, Las Cruces.)

ning, for in 1880 a group of men signed up to help build a church there (Reynolds 1981: 52). Eight years later, a new tract was established adjacent to San Juan. It was called Guadalupe. In January of that year, the *indio* cacique and three other men, together calling themselves the Commissioners of Tortugas Pueblo, petitioned for land in the new tract. They sought house lots for twenty-five families, with enough land to build a church (Beckett and Corbett 1990: 2; Reynolds 1981: 49–50). While some individual families received lots, the commissioners did not get their deed until 1908, with the title cleared in 1910. Construction of the church of Our Lady of Guadalupe began in 1909. The *indios* continued to celebrate the fiesta mass at St. Genevieve's until 1911, but they danced in front of the new, partially built church in Tortugas in 1910 (*Las Cruces Citizen,*

December 17, 1910, and December 16, 1911). Perhaps they were celebrating both the Virgin's and their own arrival in a home of their own.

The path to home was cleared in part by "Colonel" Eugene Van Patten, the only Anglo among the four commissioners of Tortugas Pueblo. Van Patten was a Butterfield stagecoach driver who settled in El Paso del Norte to become an entrepreneur. There he met and married Benita Madrid Vargas, a woman of Piro descent who lived near the Guadalupe mission (Beckett and Corbett 1990: 8). One folk version of their meeting has it that Van Patten was stationed at Fort Bliss and, on a reconnaissance mission, saw the fires from the *indio's* annual pilgrimage on Tortugas Mountain. As the story goes, when he went to the Ascarate ranch to find out about the fires, he became interested in the group, met the "princess" of the tribe, as one account called her (*History of New Mexico* 1907), and married her. Though Van Patten was never actually in the army, and he met Benita Madrid in El Paso del Norte, not on the ranch, the story reveals the mythic dimensions of Van Patten's connection with the group. He became the first land commissioner of Doña Ana County and in this capacity was able to help the *indios* obtain a land base.

It was probably also Van Patten who conceived the idea of incorporating as a nonprofit organization to receive the land. In 1914 Los Indigenes de Nuestra Señora de Guadalupe filed articles of incorporation. The four commissioners sold the forty acres of land in Guadalupe to the new corporation for the sum of one dollar (Beckett 1982: 97; Commissioners of the Town of Guadalupe 1914a). The new corporation was a heterogeneous group, including *indios* from the Guadalupe mission, Tigua and Piro immigrants from Ysleta del Sur and the El Paso Piro villages of Senecú del Sur and Socorro del Sur, Mexican residents of San Juan de Dios, and the one Anglo man. The mestizo Virgin had overseen a new blending of tribes, this time through the American corporate system.

Articles of incorporation established guidelines for the future. The corporation's purpose would be "to secure the moral, physical, and intellectual development" of its members and their families, to make and secure "improvements" in the vicinity of the new Pueblo, to encourage and assist in the building of new homes there, to "cooperate" in construction and improvements to benefit the whole Pueblo, including a "club meeting house," "to secure, own, maintain and support a suitable Roman Catholic church," to provide and maintain a cemetery for the Pueblo, and to establish guidelines for carrying out cooperative work (*Los Indigenes de Nuestra Señora de Guadalupe* 1914).

There was no mention of the fiesta, but in deeding a parcel of its land to the Catholic archdiocese that same year, the corporation retained the right to "keep their old customs provided there is nothing in them immoral, disorderly, superstitious or contrary to the laws of the Catholic Church." The corporation also maintained the right to collect alms at the fiesta from which a priest would be paid for delivering masses, the right to "dress the image of Our Lady of Guadalupe," and the right to bury corporation members in the Tortugas cemetery (Commissioners of the Town of Guadalupe 1914b). Thus, from the beginning, the corporation conceived of itself as a combination of cooperative land-owning society, church-centered community, and guardian of tradition.

Over the years, the corporation distributed house lots to its members, but many continued to live in Las Cruces. Some families built houses in the Guadalupe section of Tortugas, others in the San Juan section. Except for the distinctive red ceremonial buildings built by the corporation for celebrating the annual fiesta, nothing distinguished Guadalupe from San Juan. From its founding until the 1950s, the corporation erected four ceremonial buildings: a meetinghouse, the *casa del pueblo;* a community kitchen, the *casa de la comida;* a small chapel, the *capilla;* and most recently, a small resting house for the dancers, the *casa de descanso* (see map 3).

Stopping my car near the red ceremonial buildings, I got out to walk around. I had visited Tortugas twice before, in 1984 and 1985, flying out from New York for the fiesta. On my first visit, I had knocked on the door of what I thought was simply a red adobe house to ask where I could find Benny Sandoval.[14] Luke Lyon, a Los Alamos physicist turned dance ethnologist who had written about the fiesta, told me to look up Benny Sandoval, corporation president in the 1970s. The red house where I knocked turned out to be the *casa de la comida,* and the man I questioned was Benny Sandoval himself. This coincidence was my first encounter in Tortugas. Now in July, a year and a half later, the ceremonial buildings were as if asleep. A hot breeze and patches of summer greenery sang to their hibernation. A group of teenagers rode by in a pickup. I wandered on foot,

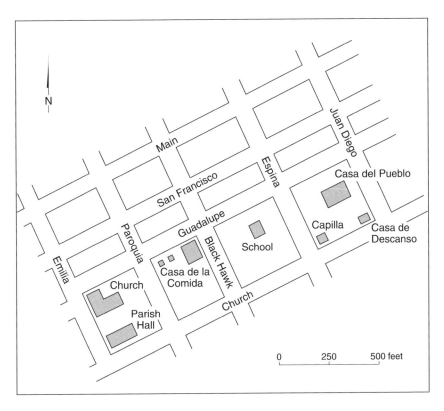

Map 3. Ceremonial buildings. (Map based on original drawing by Luke Lyon, courtesy of Rio Grande Historical Collections, New Mexico State University Library, Las Cruces.)

enjoying the mountain view, the narrow dirt streets, and the small well-tended gardens. In one front yard, someone had cemented together an altar of rocks. In its niche was a statue of Our Lady of Guadalupe and, surrounding her, two dark-skinned priests, several other saintly figures, plastic roses, and a burning candle. Flanking the niche on both sides were two tall *quiotes,* the staves of yucca that people make on Tortugas Mountain during the fiesta pilgrimage.

Driving around after my walk I spotted a woman I thought I recognized, Elena Sandoval, Benny's sister-in-law. Elena was laying out laundry on lawn chairs next to a large adobe brick house surrounded by lawn and a few shade trees that sheltered patches of iris. Her five-year-old grandson rode his bicycle in the dirt parking lot next to the house. Elena invited me in and led me in the back door, through the kitchen, and into the dining room. We sat at her long dining table drinking iced tea, smoking, and speaking English.

Elena was close to sixty, short and full like my Russian grandmother. She wore a red sweatshirt and worked in her kitchen with the propriety of someone who enjoyed the environment she created but wasn't overly finicky about it. I was just over forty, taller and more muscular, but dressed as casually as she. We were comfortable with each other immediately, both of us liquid in the way we moved. When we got to know each other better, we were as likely to sit curled on the carpet as straight backed in dining room chairs. For a scholar who depended as much on the subtleties of movement as on words, these were the kinds of communications I appreciated. After my five hours on the road, Elena's house and welcome were like a cooling drink.

Getting to know each other gently, we discussed the relative merits of Las Cruces, Los Angeles, and the East Coast. Elena had traveled widely, following her seven children. I talked freely about my Jewish background, my years in Santa Fe, and my desire to learn about the fiesta, the dances, and Catholicism. Elena told me her whole family was involved with the fiesta and related how much work it took. "We probably take it for granted," she said, then added that the bishop had said that in all his travels he had never seen the devotion in Tortugas matched anywhere else. Finally Elena told me that the fiesta "does something," it "has an effect." That effect was what I hoped to experience and understand.

Elena and her husband Raul were *mayordomos* in 1986; in whatever ways I would be participating in the fiesta, it would be under their supervision. The *mayordomos* were in charge of the smooth running of the fiesta, including dressing the Virgin, cleaning and decorating the ceremonial buildings, and ordering supplies. During the year they maintained the church building and the *capilla* and supervised two fund-raising enchilada dinners. Unlike *mayordomo* systems further south, in Tortugas *mayordomos* had no financial responsibility: the corporation raised money and food donations from local businesses. Most important, the *mayordomos* "took care" of the Virgin. They were her stewards vis-à-vis the hundreds of people who came to the fiesta to be with her.

In the next few weeks, I looked for a place to live. At summer's end I would be joined by my fiancé, who had found an intern position at White Sands. The late summer was hot in Las Cruces, sometimes staying at 105 degrees for weeks. It was not a piercing or humid heat, but dry and everywhere at once. I felt it in my swelling hands and scratchy throat. The brightness, too, of an enormous vaulted sky was pervasive. I bought an old black Volvo whose heating system, I discovered, remained permanently on and whose engine didn't start when it was overheated. By September I found a house in Mesilla, a mile from Tortugas. It was close enough for me to be a neighbor and far enough for mutually respectful privacy.

In the coffee shop where I read and wrote in the mornings, I listened to the farmers discussing the weather and the current state of their crops. Out the window I watched the day-to-day changes in the cotton field across the road and the minute-by-minute cloud and light progressions over the Organ Mountains. Gradually, I began to develop a visceral sense of place. I became familiar with the shape of the mountains, the feel of desert dust in my mouth and eyes, the sound of English inflected with Spanish, the smell of red chiles cooking, and the pace of a walk up and down the irrigation ditches. All this, I knew, would feed my work, grounding me in the sensual particulars that were familiar to those who lived here.

An irrigation ditch passed behind my house. It was part of a network of ditches that dissected Mesilla, San Miguel, Mesquite, Vado, La Mesa, on and on down the Rio Grande Valley to El Paso. Until the flooding, which began in 1865 and lasted until after 1900, shifted the path of the river, the Rio Grande flowed along the edge of Tortugas. Displaced by over two miles, it now flowed a mile west of my house in Mesilla. One day, hot and short-tempered from a week of hunting for used furniture in the temperamental Volvo, I cooled off with a walk down the irrigation ditch behind the house.

The orchards of pecan trees, at ripeness, were thick with green fruits among green leaves. I picked up a pecan. It looked like the fruit of a cactus, about two inches long with four ridges that divided it neatly into four lengthwise sections. I dug my nail into one of the ridges and pressed inward toward the center. My nail was stopped by the nut only an eighth of an inch in. I began to rip away the fleshy covering. Though the fruit looked pale and dry, like tree fiber, it was surprisingly moist. A dark greenish brown juice ran down my fingers. The green pecan flesh now turned the same metallic brown from being exposed to the air. I worked away at it with a stone, chipping off bits of the flesh, staining my hands with a dye that would not come off for weeks. The exposed yellow shell of the nut sat on the dashboard of the Volvo for the next two years, drying. It served as a reminder of this first initiation into southern New Mexico, my eager impatience and ignorance about pecans, the nourishment in the outer covering, and the inviolability of the shell that protected the core.

2

. . . .

From the *Capilla* to the *Casa del Pueblo*

On December 10, 1986, it snowed three or four inches. By afternoon the ground was still white, unusual in the southern New Mexico sun belt, where snow sometimes fell but usually melted immediately. At sundown, when I drove to the *capilla* for the beginning of the fiesta, the roads were icy, and it was almost dark. Ten or twelve people waited outside the double metal doors, shifting to keep warm. In the light of a single bare bulb above the *capilla* door, the group was a shadowy conglomerate.

The two *mayordomo* couples arrived to open the doors. The interior space seemed tiny, its light bright white and warm. Beneath high windows on each side, a row of empty folding chairs was placed in front of a row of wooden benches. The floor was covered with a green shag carpet. Opposite the doors, a tiered sideboard held plaster statues of the saints, gilt lamps, and, unifying it all, vines of plastic flowers. At the top was a statue

Photograph 1.   Mayordomas with the Virgin's altar, December 6, 1987.

of Our Lady of Guadalupe. But the statue was not the focus of people's attention. A few feet in front of the sideboard, an altar table supported a framed portrait of the Virgin. This picture was the centerpiece of the fiesta (see photograph 1).

The portrait was not honored for its aesthetic value. It was a faded color reproduction, donated in 1913 when the Guadalupe church was completed. Its significance was evocative and invocative: through it, the Virgin's presence was invoked and her story evoked. About four feet high, the Virgin's portrait rested on a papier-mâché mountain half its size. On a lower ridge of the mountain was a statue of a kneeling man in a hooded yellow robe and sandals, cast in plaster. The man's size was equal to the mountain's, so that his head reached the Virgin's knees. The overall effect was one of the Virgin on high looking down on a tiny mountain and a larger-than-life man. It was the opposite of traditional images of Mary looking up at Christ on the cross. Here, the man looked up from below at his mother.

The Virgin in the picture was dressed in a long pink shift that fell in folds. She wore a dark green cloak trimmed in gold, dotted with gold stars. It was draped loosely, covering her back and shoulders but revealing her face and hands. She tilted her head to the right and downward as if to hear better. Her eyelids were half closed, but her eyes were focused. Her palms were cupped together in prayer, her fingers tapering to a point and touching, sensuous. Although the robe concealed her body, the way she stood hinted that she might be pregnant. She rested her weight backward, her body slightly curving in an arc toward the right. Her left knee, pressing forward, left its imprint in the fabric of her robe. There were no sharp edges anywhere; she was all welcoming softness. The Virgin seemed to invite the man, or the viewer, to rest in her attention.

Looking up at the Virgin, the kneeling man met her gaze. His back was rounded, humble, but he leaned forward. Poised at the uncomfortable midpoint between sitting back onto his right foot and lifting himself up onto his left, his lower body appeared taut with urgency. Even the toes of his right foot curled up, signaling that he was ready to stand. By contrast, his upper body appeared limp. His right arm hung at his side, his shoulders were collapsed, and his head was tilted back. Whereas the woman's softness suggested solicitude, his slackness announced surrender. The man's contradictory qualities of melting and eagerness gave the impression that, in the presence of the woman, he was both submissive and inspired to action.

The first time I saw the diorama in 1984, I felt the intimacy and force of this relationship between supplicating human and divine mother. Many times during the three days of fiesta, when people said, "We do it all for her," tears came to their eyes. This *indio virgen* was not the far-off Mary I remembered from the ornate Italian churches of my childhood neighborhood in Brooklyn. She was closer, of the flesh. I felt her underground reserves of both dominion and physical warmth; she seemed less like a gilded young woman than like an experienced mother or grandmother. If, as Paul Horgan writes, the *santos* of the Rio Grande Valley were actually self-images (1984: 383), then the scene on the altar offered a clue about how people approached the Virgin. This Virgin would be available directly and intimately, as she was for the man who knelt before her.

The women enacted this intimacy when they came together the week before the fiesta to clean the *capilla* and dress the Virgin. They brought Windex, rags, a vacuum cleaner, satin fabrics, plastic flowers, and straight pins. When I arrived at 10:00 A.M., several women were already vacuuming the carpet, washing the windows, and dusting the plank benches. The two *mayordomas* were pinning white satin polyester into one-inch folds along the edge of the altar table. They intertwined the stems of peach-colored plastic roses onto more white satin that was tufted onto a wire arch above the portrait. They shaped and reshaped a rhinestone tiara on the frame above the Virgin's head. Relaxed, though not irreverent with the sacred image, they fussed over its details.

During this intimate task, the women kept up a steady stream of commentary on the aesthetics of the arrangement. They praised it, compared it to last year's, made plans for next year's. They shared information on where to get the best buy on fabric and sympathized with one another's medical problems. I felt held by their talk, as if a place had been made for me in the Virgin's company. One woman assured me, when I was precariously balanced on a ten-foot ladder, that the Virgin would take care of me and make sure I didn't fall off. I slowed to the rhythms of the work and let myself slip into its humming. It was like being a child in a safe space, body smiling. There would be strictness later on, but these moments were light. The Virgin became part of the conversation, so much so that the roles were reversed. The women mothered *la virgencita*, "the little virgin."

I asked Elena Sandoval if the fiesta was for the Virgin alone or for Christ as well. "He is always there," she said, "but the Virgin is more available." We were in her home and, as she spoke, she leaned against the sofa and opened her arms against its back. The gesture spoke of the mother as behind Christ, holding him. It was an ideal of motherhood that I found easy to appreciate. I have had dreams about my own Russian grandmother walking across a cold expanse of the Siberian steppes, holding generations of children under her cloak and against her body. Elena, as the mother of seven and grandmother of many more, had tended children for over forty years. Her grown, married, and independent children still came to her for meals, advice, and companionship. She knew from experience what it was to hold children.

Now, at the start of the fiesta, while the small crowd waited outside the *capilla*, Elena and the other *mayordomos* took their places of honor behind the altar table. The *mayordomos* were always two couples, most often husband and wife, but sometimes sister and brother or parent and child. Incoming *mayordomos* were chosen by the outgoing from among the forty or so members of the corporation, taking into consideration members' experience with the fiesta, their ability to work long and hard hours, and a policy of balancing the workload over the years. The pool of suitable *mayordomos* changed as older couples grew too weak to take on the physical responsibilities and younger ones learned the choreography of the fiesta scenario. This year, both couples, Elena and Raul, with Luis and Lena Alvarez, were elders who had worked together many times.

Erect in the hard-backed metal folding chairs, they maintained a strict decorum based on a lifetime of instructions to keep still in church. Elena told me that when she was a girl, no movement was allowed in church. You couldn't turn around, and you couldn't cross your legs. "I hit my three girls when they cross their legs," she said. I could imagine it, her hand shooting out to slap a thigh, or her head turning for a quick reprimanding look. I confessed to her that at the monthly rosary in the *capilla*, I was the only person with crossed legs and that I had uncrossed them fast. She laughed with me, perhaps imagining the scene, twenty people in prayer with straight spines and uncrossed legs, and the gringa quickly uncrossing her legs. It was not just that I didn't know the rules of decorum. My body had no habit of being in a church, with uncrossed legs and straight spine, listening to the prayers and smelling the incense.

I had had only sporadic brushes with the postures and rhythms of religious spaces. Though we lived across the street from a synagogue, on the night before holy days my family parked the car around the corner and slipped out in the morning to drive out of the city, unnoticed, to our upstate summer community. Rosh Hashanah was not the indoor space of the synagogue but the smell of an apple orchard, a body full of running, tumbling, and breathing hard, and the intimacy of an indoor fire. No straight spine and uncrossed legs. I learned from my father's bird-watching and gardening a different direction for the spiritual impulse, though, as an agnostic, he himself would never have called it that. The strange sounds and rocking moves of the synagogue where my grandfather sometimes prayed held a different mystery, musty and dark. The old men in beards evoked pictures of a past I somehow belonged to, their rituals connected to rocking in my grandmother's arms. The discipline and decorum of religion, its words laced with the habits of body posture, were new to me in Tortugas. I stood before its doors and waited.

One at a time the people waiting outside entered the *capilla,* taking the few steps across the shag carpet to kneel before the Virgin's portrait. Raul and Elena's oldest son, Robert, took his turn. He was a big man, physically strong. I hold an image of him from one of the corporation's winter rabbit hunts. Cherished as part of the community's Pueblo legacy, the rabbit hunt was a ritual day spent in a wilderness field of twisting brush, chasing after, cornering, and clubbing rabbits. Brandishing sticks, someone would call out when a rabbit was spotted, and the run, accompanied by piercing ululations, would begin.[1] In my memory, I watch Robert determined to unearth a rabbit that had eluded the people's sticks and escaped into its burrow. Robert sprawled on his belly and shoveled into the hole with willful thrusts. Next to that picture, I place the softer picture of Robert kneeling at the altar in the *capilla.* He held his knees close together, clasped his hands, lowered his head, and drew in. He seemed to make himself smaller; his eyes closed, as if in private conversation with the Virgin.

I listened. Praying, the people said, was a way of "talking with the Virgin." The cacique, Lorenzo Serna, taught me that praying was a full-bodied engagement, that in praying, one entered the mysteries, the sorrows, and the beatitudes. He spoke of visualizing the miracle of Christ dying and rising up. Lorenzo could see a light, he said, and then Christ "went up." As we talked, I could see Lorenzo seeing this, his face muscles easing and his eyes changing focus, as if he were opening a hole within our conversation, which widened and into which he entered. He spoke, too, about the holy ghost, how he could see the doors shaking and feel the holy ghost entering him. He mentioned meditating on the sorrows of Christ, when they refused Him, hung Him up, threw stones at Him. These narratives were palpable to him. In the living room of Lorenzo's home hung pictures of Christ and the saints. I understood that, through prayer, they had become familiar presences, like family members he had recently left but would see and feel again soon.

I first met the cacique in 1985 outside the doors of the church. The church bells rang as the *mayordomos* carried the Virgin's image out for the final procession of the fiesta. We came face-to-face, tears in our eyes. The next year, I asked Lorenzo if he remembered me. "Sure," he said, "you're the person from New York. You cried last year." I was surprised that he remembered our brief meeting. Had he found in my tears a mutuality, a recognition of the capacity for feeling the Virgin's presence? For me, the tears were a remembering after forgetting, when, after being engulfed in the busyness of fiesta preparations, expansive awareness returned. The tears came as the release of reconnecting.

Tears also came to one of the grandmothers while we were dusting the pews in the church. She asked if I expected to get so involved in the fiesta. I replied that I felt welcomed here. She must have understood my words to mean that I felt welcomed by the Virgin, for she said, "Yes, she calls you," and tears came to her eyes. In that moment, as when Lorenzo saw Christ rising up, had the good grandmother heard the Virgin calling?

A call: that was how the Virgin of Guadalupe made her presence known to the man kneeling before her on the altar. The community knew her story so well that there was no need to tell it during the fiesta. The story was in the air, evoked in an instant by the Virgin's image on a dancer's outfit or simply by mentioning the name of the man at her feet, Juan Diego. I heard the story told as a play for voices at a Las Cruces conference on Our Lady of Guadalupe, discussed it with others in small groups at the bishop's annual Day of Recollection, watched it as a Mexican television program in a grandmother's home, and read encapsulated versions in the

local newspapers at fiesta time. During the fiesta, names and events from
the narrative were dropped like pinches of salt into soup. I asked people
to tell me the story, and they seemed surprised at the question. "Everybody knows it," one woman replied, as if to say, surely I already knew it,
why would I ask? Others agreed to tell it for the sake of my research, and
then did so in a few sentences, omitting the names of the characters and
referring to them only as "he" and "she." But there is an official version,
in texts, that can be culled, with commentary interspersed.[2]

Juan Diego was a middle-aged Nahuatl-speaking Indian who lived near
Mexico City at the time of the Spanish conquest. Convinced by the friars
that Catholicism was the true religion, Juan Diego accepted baptism and
became a member of the church. On December 9, 1531, ten years after the
last decisive battle for control of Mexico City, Juan Diego was stopped by
a sound on his way to church, just as he passed Tepeyac Hill. Amid a
choir of birdsong, he heard his name called: "Juan Diego! Juan Diegito!"
Without thinking, he followed the voice to the top of the hill, where he saw
a lady of glowing beauty, radiating like the sun. She was a "dark Virgin,"
part Indian and part Spanish, and she spoke to Juan Diego in his own
Nahuatl language. Since the story was told locally, in Spanish, she said:

> ¡Juan Diegito! ¡El más pequeño de mis hijos! ¿A dónde vas? Sabe y
> ten entendido, tu, el más pequeño de mis hijos, que yo soy la siempre
> Virgen Santa Maria, Madre del verdadero Dios, por quien se vive.
> (Chávez 1987)

> Little Juan Diego! Smallest of my children! Where are you going? Know
> that I am the Virgin Mary, mother of the true God through whom every-
> thing lives.[3]

The Virgin told Juan Diego that she wanted a church built there on Tepeyac Hill so that she might, through her love, remedy the pain and suffering of the people of the land. Would he go on her behalf to Bishop Zumaraga in Mexico City? Juan Diego never doubted her presence or
questioned her wish; he simply obeyed.

Bishop Zumaraga kept Juan Diego waiting and finally told him to come back another day. Disappointed, he returned to Tepeyac and confessed his failure to the Virgin. "Why don't you send a nobleman who will have more influence?" he asked her. "My beloved son," she answered, "I have many messengers I could send, but it is you I need and want for this purpose" (Paola 1980). As one Tortugas woman put it, she wanted "the little guy."

Juan Diego went back. This time the bishop gave him an audience but asked for proof, a sign to show that the woman he had seen was indeed the one true mother of God. When Juan Diego reported this to the lady, she gladly agreed to provide a sign and instructed Juan Diego to be on the hill the next morning to receive it.

But when Juan Diego got home that night, he found his uncle Juan Bernardino dying. No doctors could cure him, so the next morning Juan Diego was sent to get the priest to perform the last rites. As he was running, aware that he was missing his appointment with the Virgin, she intercepted him. He told her he hadn't come to see her because he was at that moment running to get a priest for his dying uncle. The lady immediately reassured him, "Am I not here, I who am your mother, and is not my help a refuge?" (Demarest and Taylor 1956: 47). Or, in the words of one of the women, "Don't worry about it. He's not sick anymore."

The Virgin sent Juan Diego to the top of Tepeyac Hill, telling him to gather the flowers he would find there. On what had been a cold, wintry hilltop of rocks and cactus, there was now a lush garden of Castilian roses. Juan Diego gathered as many flowers as he could hold in his *tilma*, his farming apron. He brought these to the lady, and she rearranged them in his *tilma*, tying its corners around his neck. She then sent him off to the bishop.

The bishop's guards kept Juan Diego waiting all day—it was now December 12—but finally, when they caught a glimpse of the flowers in his apron, they let him in. Juan Diego opened his *tilma* before the bishop, and the roses tumbled to the ground. Everyone in the room fell to his knees. All could see that the *tilma* was miraculously imprinted with an image of the Virgin. This was indeed a sign from the mother of God, and the bishop agreed to build her a church on Tepeyac Hill.

Accompanied by the bishop and his retinue, Juan Diego returned home. His uncle, in good health now, came out to greet them. On his deathbed he, too, had seen the lady. She instructed him that the name of the temple was to be her name, Santa Maria de Guadalupe.

I would not have entered the *capilla* while the others were praying had not one of the men pushed me to do so. I found myself following the others to the altar. Without thinking, I knelt before the Virgin's portrait. Unlike the others, I did not cross myself. But I could feel time slowing down. Humming thoughts separated and broke apart, then stopped. Although I had never before knelt to an image (it is forbidden in Judaism), doing so came easily at this moment. My body simply went down. I became aware of several things at once: people's eyes on me; the effort to keep my spine erect, maintain dignity, and not fall over; and a sense of melting into connection with the lady in the picture. We seemed to be face-to-face, a small person enveloped in a larger person's presence. I could smell her centuries-old cloak and feel the weight of her larger body in front of me. The physical sensation of being on the ground before a divine woman who palpably embodied compassion and wisdom was profoundly agreeable. It was a pleasure to experience my own smallness, humility replacing academic distance. Abruptly, at the thought that I was in the *capilla* in the midst of a crowd, a shiver moved up and down my spine. I stood, my private moment of "conversation" with the Virgin over. I went outside to wait for the procession that would officially open the fiesta.

The chords struck in me were not the same as those struck in lifelong members of the community. How could they be? I grew up in a New York Jewish family. We lived in Bensonhurst during the school year and spent summers at Three Arrows, a Utopian Socialist community forty miles outside the city. The land was held in common, a farm on a small mountain, traded in the late 1930s for a piano. It was divided into home sites for seventy families. Norman Thomas, the Socialist candidate for president in the 1940s and 1950s, visited every summer. We children serenaded him in the old barn with songs of the labor movement. Our wet bathing suits rolled up in towels and tucked under our arms, our hair still stringy with lake water, we sang, "There once was a union maid / Who never was afraid . . ." Among these seventy families who shared a common idealism, discussed the issues of the day in weekly "shmoozes," and treated each other's children as their own, I, too, grew up with a sense of belonging. But it was different from the sense of belonging experienced by the people I was now among. No worship or deities were involved in our rituals. The feeling of meeting a deity whose presence was a communally recognized event was new to me.

Down the street, inside the *casa de descanso,* the *danzantes* finished the last-minute details of adjusting their clothing. Perhaps it was their *cupiles,* the high headpieces shaped like bishops' miters, that made me see the dancers as large men. The *cupiles* hid their faces. A silky dark fringe attached to the front edge of each *cupil* covered the men's eyes. A bandanna across nose and mouth concealed the rest of their faces (see photograph 2). Colored ribbons, ironed smooth, were attached at the back of each headpiece, fanning down the men's backs to their knees. The *cupil* was like a horse's mane that enlarged and stood for the creature. The men's collective presence was forbidding, but also potentially protective. Softening the effect, on the front surface of each *cupil* was a portrait of the Virgin, speaking for the man behind: "I do this for her. This is who leads me." Each portrait was customized, surrounded by scallops of pearls, dots of gemstones, little mirrors, and curlicues of rickrack framing the Virgin's portrait.

Her image was also imprinted on a large silk scarf tied around each man's waist like an apron. Below the scarf, from knee to ankle, the pant legs were covered with white lace leggings, called *polainas.* Finally, over a sports jacket or sweater they wore a wide red ribbon, a *tercieau,* pinned diagonally from shoulder to waist like a bandoleer. Under these coverings, the father who managed a paint store, the young man who worked behind the counter at a chicken take-out restaurant, the lawyer who commuted from Albuquerque, the two brothers, one about to join the border patrol, the other about to be married, were unrecognizable, their individualities hidden beneath the signs of their purpose.

I have a picture of the two Trujillo brothers in their dance outfits taken in their home in 1985. Their parents, Eddie and Donna Trujillo, were *mayordomos* that year, the second year I visited the fiesta, and I stayed at their house, sleeping in the bed of the daughter who had moved to

Photograph 2. A *danzante's cupil* (photo by Miguel Gandert).

Albuquerque when she married. The other daughter lived at home and worked. The youngest son was still in high school. Donna and I had just finished sewing the *polainas* onto her sons' pant legs when I took the picture.

Ever since Billy was born, his parents had been mainstays of the fiesta. They were part of the small group at the center of the corporation who knew its scenario well enough to be *mayordomos.* As a teenager, Billy had danced with the Danza group. Then the corporation allotted him one of the last plots of land on their original forty acres. This was a weighty matter, the giving of land. It represented the future of the community and the fiesta, a trust that the recipient would give of himself in return. Each one of the younger generation was needed, each one worried over. Billy might take the land and disappear from the corporation. He might sell it, as one woman had done recently. After he married, Billy stopped dancing. He was building a house, a plumbing business, and a family. Ten years later, he returned. Now, for the first time, he was a *mayordomo.*

Standing in the doorway, Billy described his happiness at dedicating himself to the Virgin, the corporation, and the fiesta. He talked about his plumbing business, how he instructed his workers that whenever a corporation member called, the workers were to drop whatever they were doing and respond. Even if it were in the middle of the night, he said, corporation members knew they could call him and that he would come. This story was an indication of how much he had come "home," of the dedication he now felt. We beamed at each other because of his happiness and the rightness of his return. There was no need for us to talk about what was on both our minds: his mother's health. Everybody knew that Donna was in the hospital, when she would want to be working in the community kitchen. Instead of mentioning her, Billy said, "Do you remember the time you stayed at our house and we took pictures in our dance outfits?" The memory was an anecdote, but even more, it was a tribute to Donna. The story brought her back into the kitchen.

We worked the story and Donna's presence together into that year's fiesta. Those who were remembered deepened the fiesta with their blessings. Like the others in the *casa de la comida,* I watched Billy and saw his mother. But from the corner of one eye, I, with others, watched Billy's infant daughter. We saw in Billy a way for the past to move into the future, carrying mother and daughter. The movement of building memories did not stop. And our conversation, there in the doorway, like the tears shared with Lorenzo, would also become a piece of fiesta memory. The story of the photograph, the image it called up, the door frame, united us as sharers of memory and also as builders of new memories. All the people who had ever worked behind the scenes were still at the fiesta, sewn into the lace leggings on the *danzantes'* outfits, copied in the lean of a back against a door frame. Collective memories were bodily memories, incorporated as gestures and inflections, rendering the meaning of the fiesta itself.

Another fiesta was about to be set in motion. For the moments of waiting before the *capilla*, the space of memory opened. Once the fiesta started, there would be no rest until it was over. In silence and single file, the dancers walked the hundred yards from the *casa de descanso* to the *capilla*. They entered one by one to kneel before the Virgin's portrait and then lined up again on the street outside, double file. The four *mayordomos* lifted the handles of the palanquin that held the Virgin's altar and brought it outside. The guards delivered a burst of rifle fire. Shorty, the violinist, scratched out the opening bars of the Danza music. Its rapid notes pierced the sliding chant of the walkers. The people sang the "Alabanza Guadalupana," the birthday hymn to the Virgin (see below).[4] Its refrain would rise and fall throughout the fiesta.

Music for "Alabanza Guadalupana." (Notation by the author and Alan Terricciano.)

The *mayordomos* led the procession in the dark, carrying the Virgin's palanquin down the dirt road, turning at the corner of Juan Diego Street toward the *casa del pueblo*. Before them, in two lines facing the Virgin, and one couple at a time, the *danzantes* skipped up to the palanquin, bowed, and then peeled off to the sides so that the next couple could take their place. The road was icy, so the men had to take small sliding steps, but they did not compromise on the energy of the dancing. In that year's wet weather, they wore plastic coverings over their *cupiles*. Drops of rain caught the light from the *capilla* roof; watery sparks danced over their masked forms. The spectral figures bobbed in time to Shorty's violin.

Outside the doors of the *casa del pueblo*, the two lines of *danzantes* formed a passageway for the *mayordomos*, who carried the Virgin between the lines, through the doors, and into the empty hall. Its cement floor was newly painted in high-gloss gray, the red curtains on the two long walls freshly laundered, and the hearth cleaned out and covered with a lace silhouette of the Virgin. The fireplace was superseded by an oversized heater, buzzing and rattling. Two portraits on the wall, one of Colonel Eugene Van Patten, responsible for organizing the corporation, and the other of Don Francisco Sandoval, responsible for modernizing it, looked down on three rows of wooden benches lining each long wall. The *mayordomos* advanced down the wide center space in measured steps, leading the people. They placed the Virgin's palanquin on the satin-covered table at the front of the hall, then took their seats behind it.

Until dawn, periods of prayers recounting the nine Catholic mysteries would alternate with dancing, with short breaks between. At the beginning of the century, before the Church insisted that the *indios* shorten their fiesta, the nine days preceding the feast day of December 12 may have made up a novena, one day for each mystery. Now the mysteries were condensed into a one-night *velorio*, a wake for the Virgin. The *velorio* was one of the few Catholic ceremonies in Tortugas still conducted by lay leaders rather than by clergy. The responsibility belonged to the cacique's family. I have a singular memory of Lorenzo's elderly sister, Lupe, as a bent woman in a long dress and kerchief, gliding around the altar keeping the vigil candles lit. Lupe did this work for as long as anyone in Tortugas could remember, but by 1986 she was too ill to serve. Her daughter, Grace Serna, now led the prayers. She was the opposite of her mother, large boned and wearing a short-sleeved sports shirt and slacks. Grace would place herself squarely at the altar and fill the room with her operatic vibrato. She said leading the prayers was the job she was born to do. Until her death in 1993, she flew in from California to do it.

The people filled the benches and crowded four and five deep against the back wall. There were perhaps one hundred worshipers, sleepy, cold, and calling on the mother. Many were elderly, some accompanied by grandchildren. There were families, prepared for the night with piles of coats and blankets. There was a group of young men in black leather jackets standing against the rear wall. A woman from the corporation sat alone, choosing not to work in the kitchen this year so she could pray for her ailing father. Some here tonight would also make the next day's pilgrimage. They believed that their actions—reciting the prayers, staying awake all night, forgoing comfort—made a difference. The sacrifice people made to the Virgin was ongoing, the connection renewed again and again.

Praying and singing to an image that was both within them and in front of them, they neither questioned the reality it represented nor mistook the image for the reality. From my outsider's perspective, the people's power of belief, and the multiplication of it through community, did indeed bring the Virgin's presence, although the people would not interpret their actions this way. The Virgin embodied the prayers offered to her. She was the locus of memories and of hopes for the future. She accumulated potency through the words, actions, thoughts, and emotions that comprised her honoring. And she incarnated not only "values," that word dried out from overuse, but the immediacy of desires too strong to voice. She gave them back as blessing.

Years ago, during a retreat in the mountains near Taos, New Mexico, I heard Shlomo Carlbach, the New Age rabbi, tell a story about the Psalms of King David. King David heard the music of the spheres, which was all the prayers of all the people throughout all time. David gathered the music and brought it down, shaping it into words. These were the Psalms. This is how I heard the prayers at the *velorio*. The Virgin was the keeper and caretaker of the changing news of people's everyday lives. As Robert Plant Armstrong said of all "affecting presences," she was "ever in the process of being enacted" (1971: 5).

I was not intimate with the mysteries of Catholicism, nor could my body claim the rhythms of Catholic prayer. I had little experience of liturgical texts at all. In my few childhood visits to the synagogue in Brooklyn, it was the cadences of the Hebrew and the intensity of the davening that I found most compelling. As an adult, when I went to synagogue at all, I preferred the orthodox ones, where Hebrew was the language of prayer, because English translations provoked my intellectual distrust. Words had too often lied and misled. Not to be trusted in any absolute sense, they were to be kept at a wary distance. Only recently have I understood that the knowledge of cells and synapses could be invoked in speech and how the spoken prayers of others could harmonize my body, thoughts and all. At the time, though, my experience of connection came through movement and sensation rather than words. So I reached toward the *velorio* through the dancing. The Danza was my point of access. I could ride the repetitive patterns of the dance and contemplate the way they marshaled all I had learned about the Virgin, about devotion, and about how to be present. Though I struggled to find humility in relation to the hierarchy of the Church, I had no resistance to offering up humility when the *danzantes* honored the Virgin.

Once everyone was seated, and before the lay leaders took over, the *danzantes* filed into the hall and knelt in two lines down the open center. Sitting nearby, squeezed together on a bench in the first row, were the *malinches*, nine little girls who would take turns dancing, one or two at a time, with the men. They were dressed in white communion dresses, rhinestone and pearl tiaras, white stockings and shoes, and blue, rather than red, *tercieaus*. None was younger than five or older than thirteen. To dance, the girls had to have taken first communion but must not have started to menstruate. They would lend their innocence to the men's weighty presence.

I can only dimly imagine what it must have felt like to dance as a *malinche*, to be a child staying up all night among strangers. Did they even comprehend the activities swirling around them? The dancing was a responsibility. The girls had to come to practices, stay in step with the music, sit quietly through the dances they weren't called to do, and follow the commands of the leaders. At the same time, dancing as a *malinche* was the first time they would be putting aside the everyday to enter bodily into the spiritual world of their elders. To dance as a *malinche* was to participate in the work of the fiesta, to call on the Virgin. Surely, they would feel themselves caught up in the immediacy of the night walk in the procession, sitting through the droning of prayers, surrounded by so many people, the intensity focused on them, shepherded with the other girls in a group, shepherded by the *monarcas* in the dance, their feet sometimes unable to keep up, all of it passing by, themselves moving through, dazed with lack of sleep. One of the grandmothers who had been a *malinche* told me it was an experience she never forgot.

Did the *malinches*, too, as I had, learn to know themselves through the appreciative gaze of their elders watching them dance? Was their experience like the dissociation I experienced in kindergarten, spinning as a snowflake and seeing the world as if in a dream? Was it like the time I watched the puppet princesses emerging out of the three giant oranges and saw how people could cross between worlds of sensibility and worlds of imagination? The *malinches'* experience, however, belonged to a religious world that made sense of such crossovers.

Some *malinches* squirmed, others sat glassy-eyed, while the parish priest, Father Giles, lowered himself onto a velvet footstool before the speaker's stand at the Virgin's altar. He prayed silently, then stood to give the opening talk. He was a large man in a gray monk's cowl, and his presence spoke of authority. Father Giles was a Franciscan friar who had directed the Holy Cross Retreat House a few miles to the south before being assigned to the Tortugas parish. Since 1981, the Franciscans had provided priests for the Tortugas parish. In a rotating system, each priest served two or three years and was then replaced. Unlike the others, and unlike most of the ecumenical priests preceding the Franciscans, Father Giles built a lasting rapport with his parishioners. From the Midwest, he had researched his Miami Indian and French ancestry. He was equally passionate about Tortugas history and shared that research with the people. After a few years' absence, Father Giles was reassigned to the Tortugas parish permanently. The corporation elected him to honorary membership and reserved him a plot in the Tortugas cemetery, the only time a priest was so honored. Now he told the people in fluent academic Spanish that the tradition of an all-night vigil was not Mexican, but Indian. The Puebloans, he said, used to have all-night community meetings whenever they needed to make an important decision.

During the forty-five minutes that Father Giles spoke and prayed, the eighteen dancers remained kneeling on the concrete floor. Some of the men were more than sixty years old, and forty-five minutes on their knees could not have come easily. Moises Sandoval, Raul's brother and one of the Danza leaders, had difficulties with his spine that limited his arm and leg movements. When he danced, his struggle was evident. Yet, almost immediately after Moises lowered himself, stiffly and with the help of his arms, his body eased, and his eyes ceased to register the sights of the room. He had made a *promesa*, a vow to the Virgin, during the Second World War, standing in the Rhine River up to his knees in mud, with German bombs exploding around him. If he survived being buried alive, he would dance for her for the rest of his life. He was fulfilling that promise.

Like a religious obligation, a *promesa* is a personal sacrifice made in thanks for the Virgin's blessings. *Promesas* could be onerous, involving voluntary endurance or physical sacrifice: some people vowed to make the pilgrimage up Tortugas Mountain without shoes. Sometimes the sacrifices were basic, as when Lorenzo's granddaughter vowed to go to confession every week for three years. According to Father Giles, a *promesa* should not be made as a deal—"I make this sacrifice, then you fulfill my request"—but people did make promises in appealing to the Virgin for help. Parents could make a vow on behalf of their children. A mother's promise started the dancing life of Rico Bernal, the leader of the Danza. He got sick frequently as a child, and his mother vowed that if he got well, her son would dance for the Virgin for one year. Rico fulfilled her promise when he was sixteen years old. But then, as Rico said, "I got so much in love with the thing I danced for another year, and that's the way it's been going until the present. . . . You could say that I fell in love with *la danza*, or I liked dancing with the *virgen*" (Bernal 1986).[5]

When Danny Amador, a nineteen-year-old dancer, was ten years old, he wanted to join his father as a *danzante*. But according to the rules, ten was too young to understand the reasons people danced. Now his younger brother wanted to dance, and Danny repeated what his parents told him:

Photograph 3.   Two lines of *danzantes,* December 12, 1986.

> Physically, you could be ready—you can dance all night, you can stay
> up all night, that's not hard for you now. You won't get tired, but . . .
> mentally, you know, why are you gonna dance? Are you gonna dance
> just for fun, or because I'm there, or are you gonna make a sacrifice
> to the *virgen* and then, in turn, see if she grants your promise? (Ama-
> dor 1987)

The first year that Danny danced, it was for his grandfather who had just
died. The second year he danced to "take care of" his parents and all his
relatives. The third year he decided to "make it for life," thinking "if I can
dance for as long as I can, she'll take care of me for the same amount of
time. . . . We'll keep interacting with each other" (Amador 1987). Each of
the men was there in fulfillment of a promise, not only to dance *for* the
Virgin, but also to dance *with* her.

I once asked Rico what the opening moments of dancing in the fiesta
felt like. "It can't be described," he said. "You have to do it. It's the mo-

ment you've been waiting for all year." Some experiences, he seemed to be saying, were simply unavailable to language.

How then is the ineffable to be made available in words? How shall I draw out the effects of the dancing? Bit by bit, building fragments of sensation and association so that its pieces lock in with sensory memories like a jigsaw puzzle. Dance manipulates energy, and every dance can be apprehended as a particular play of vitality. So can everyday movements. The click of high heels on pavement has a different effect than the slide of bare feet on grass. Imagine everything in the world moving, changing rhythm, slowing down and speeding up, drifting, hobbling, intensifying, building up steam, coming to a head, exploding, dissipating, regathering as a new eddy. Looking, it is possible to apprehend the vitality. And apprehending, it is possible to evoke it in words. We have until dawn to fill out the contours of the dance. We will build it slowly. For now, we need only a beginning. After forty-five minutes on their knees, stiff and awkward, the *danzantes* stood to dance (see photograph 3).

3

. . . .

Dancing with the Virgin

Hear now the first sounds of the violin exploding, scratchy and squawking, seeking smoothness.[1] It calls in high register:

(da)-YA-ta-da, da DA-a/ (da)-YA-ta-da, da DA-a[2]

Music for *la ese*, first phrase. (Notation by Alan Terricciano.)

A staccato call to action, repeated like a reveille. And then, deeper, a more lilting figure eight of sound, like the melody of a nursery rhyme:

(da) YUM da da, YUM da-da-da/ (da) YUM da da, YUM da-da-da

Music for *la ese,* second phrase. (Notation by Alan Terricciano.)

And again from the beginning:

(da)-YA-ta-da, da DA-a/ (da)-YA-ta-da, da DA-a
(da) YUM da da, YUM da-da-da/ (da) YUM da da, YUM da-da-da

No Brahms violin this, no Russian vibratos. This is an upbeat violin, closer in musicality to an Irish jig, a quick, winding melody, repeated over and over, calling out in notes that excite and mesmerize, calling feet, calling for skipping and pounding, repeating again and again until there is no notice of the repeating, just a ride in the multiple windings and un- windings of the dance.

The *danzantes* did not learn to dance by breaking down the steps, as I do here. I did not sit as a child on the benches in the *casa del pueblo* watch- ing an older brother or father or uncle dance, as Danny Amador's brother did. Though the dancers practiced once a week for six weeks before the fiesta, there was no dance instruction, no words for remembering the steps. The new men learned by doing. They got into line and followed along. But my kinesthetic sensibilities were honed in the dance studio and classroom, synthesis following analysis, and that is how I broke down the steps and counted them out. Then I had them in my body.

Six beats to a measure. Three steps in place, stamp, and kick. Skipping the uptake on the first beat (da), start on the second, taking three steps in place: YA-ta-da, da. For the downbeat on count five (DA), drop in the knees and make a strong stamp. Just before count six on the held note, let the stamping foot shoot forward into a low kick. No need for fancy pointed toes here, just a flick from the knee, bringing the kick back in time to take the three steps in place again on the second beat of the next measure. Three steps in place, stamp, and kick. A lightly bouncing triplet of steps in place, slow and heavy for the stamp, catching the momentum off the re-bound to propel the kick forward, and a quick recovery to begin again. Three steps in place, stamp, and kick. And for the second melodic phrase, the same step is repeated, skipping the upbeat on count one: (da) YUM da da (three steps in place), YUM (stamp), da-da-da (da) (kick and recover).

The steps themselves are simple, but coordinating them against the melody takes practice. And there is more. Imagine carrying the *guaje,* a rattle covered with colored tinsel, in the left hand and the heavy *palma,* a stick supporting a cross within a circle, made of wood and wire and also covered with tinsel, in the right. Keep the elbows in and carry the *guaje* and *palma* in front of the chest. Keep the beat with the rattle, small, light, even knocks, one for each of the first five beats, but with the last knock coming in syncopation after beat six. At the same time, pass the *palma* up and down, smoothly, slowly, in an arc, up on three counts, down on three. Do not, of course, stop the three steps in place, stamp, and kick. It is an exercise in coordination.

Feet and arms marry the beat while the center, the torso, stays firm. This is no West African get-down body with its serpentine segmentations. Nor is there any balletic airiness, no jumps or leaps. Only the small re-bound, close to the ground, like a boxer's, the stamp a grunting explosion, echoed in the knocking of the *guajes.* The Danza is like a steam engine working at full boil, the pressure condensed to fit through a sole steam pipe whose shape is the steps and figures of the dance. Imagine the day a small crew of corporation men pickaxed the packed clay dirt in front of the *casa de la comida* to unearth a burst water pipe. Imagine the cacique in his pith helmet, a bandanna tied under it around his forehead to absorb the sweat. Take the cacique's effort, the swing of his pickax, and pass it through the choreography of the Danza, its figures precise, its patterns symmetrical, its steps small, and its moves far more restricted than a man with a pickax would like. The power of the swing, full body arching back and coming down, is measured out in small doses in the dance. The momentum is held, and held even longer, through the next measure and the next.

Each of the ten dances in the repertory created a different *figura*, a design in space. In *la ese*, the "S," the men traded places across the hall, drawing the shape of an S back and forth between the lines. In *la mudanza*, the "exchange," they traded places diagonally across from one another, working from the ends of the lines to the middle and back out. In *los arcos*, the "bridges," couples made arches under which the rest of the lines filed, as in the game of London Bridge. In *los paños*, the "handkerchiefs," couples linked, each holding the corner of a handkerchief, then turned under the handkerchiefs and stepped over them in procession. *El son de la malinche*, the "malinche's song," was all processions in different floor patterns, with both lines filing outward, then filing in, then each line passing around the other. In *la entre tejida*, the "interweaving," the men formed into phalanxes of three that braided together from the corners of the hall. And in *la trenza*, the "braid," they wound and unwound ribbons on a maypole, changing places. Two dances introduced the rest, like ceremonial offerings: *la entrada*, the "entrance" and *la batalla*, the "battle." One dance, *la procesión*, the "procession," framed the beginning and end of each dance set.[3]

Imagine now the large presences of the eighteen men, nine to a line, their faces hidden under their bandannas and the *cupil's* fringe. Between the two lines, three named characters dance: the *monarca*, or dance leader, the *malinche*, the young girl dancer, and the *abuelo*, also called the assistant *monarca*. Imagine the small girl at the back between the lines, standing next to the *monarca*, and up front between the lines, the *abuelo*. "*¡Vuelta!*" the *abuelo* calls, and all the dancers turn to the right, quickly. "*¡Vuelta!*" again. All turn to the left. It is an introductory framing of the dance.

Beneath the sound of the violin, for the dancers' ears alone, the *abuelo* calls out, "*¡Por fuera!*" Taking up the beat, in an everyday walk, the two lines of men cast out to the sides and back (see figure 1). Not stopping, they turn the back corner and file down the center, picking up the *monarca* and *malinche* between them on the way, leading them forward, in one smooth progression (see figure 2). Halfway down the hall, there is a slight pause while the last of the men finish rounding the corner and file into place behind the leader of each line. Between the two leaders, *monarca, ma-*

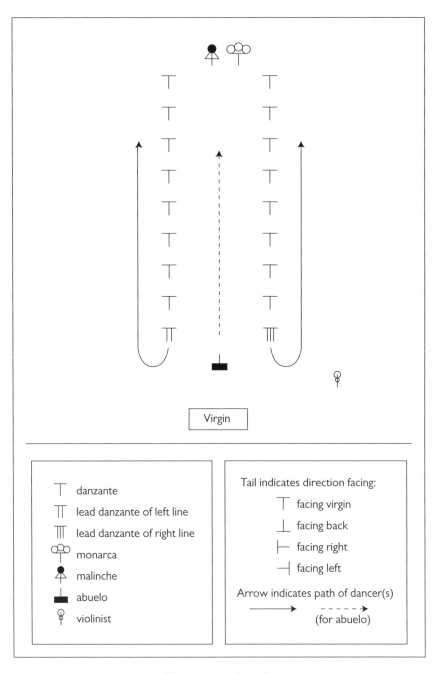

Figure 1.   Casting off.

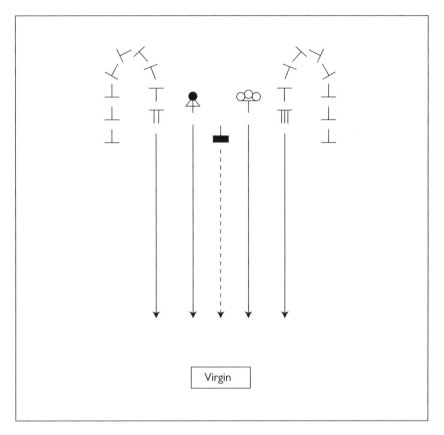

Figure 2. "Picking up" the *monarca* and *malinche.* (See keys in figure 1 for explanation of symbols.)

linche, and *abuelo,* now together, also pause. Then, everyone breaks from everyday walking into the dance step, moving forward, as one, in step, presenting themselves: an army of the Virgin. This was the opening of the dance, a flourish, setting off the mazelike complexity of the *figura* to follow.

Slow down now to follow the choreographic design in space. The steps unfold quickly, but the *figuras* unfold slowly, and thus two designs are superimposed: the step a quick circling in time and the choreography a slow circling in space. The *abuelo* will lead the *malinche,* his shepherding invisible, a light touch on her shoulder or merely a presence by her side. Imagine *monarca, malinche,* and *abuelo* up front between the lines,

Photograph 4.   Monarca and *malinche* circle with the first *danzante,*
December 10, 1986.

one small girl between two large men. Three steps in place, stamp, and
kick. Watch the *monarca,* followed by the *malinche,* approach the lead *danzante* in the left line, "picking him up" and circling with him.[4] While
monarca and *malinche* dance forward into the small circle, the *danzante*
pivots and backs out of his place to join in (see photograph 4 and detail,
figure 3).

Completing the circle and returning the *danzante* to his place, *monarca*
and *malinche* cross the hall to the lead dancer in the right line. They circle
with him. Leaving him in his place, *monarca* and *malinche* cross again to
the left line, where they circle with the second dancer. A pattern emerges:
approach, circle, and cross over to the opposite line, back and forth, moving up the lines and weaving S shapes across the hall until all eighteen
men are exchanged (see figure 3). "*¡Vuelta!*" the *abuelo* calls, and all the
men turn left. "*¡Vuelta!*" again, to the right. And the pattern is repeated
in reverse, unwinding what has been wound. This is *la ese,* the S.

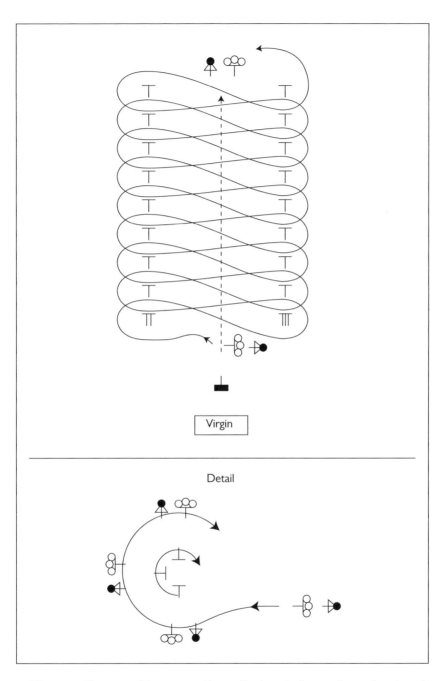

Figure 3. Choreographic pattern of *la ese*. (See keys in figure 1 for explanation of symbols.) Detail: *monarca* and *malinche* circling with the lead dancer of the left line.

Imagine the pattern emerging with painstaking slowness. Take each step with the men, three steps in place, stamp, and kick. Stay with the violin. Move back and forth between the lines with *monarca, malinche,* and *danzante,* never getting ahead. There is no efficacious travel here; each step is a piece of the geometric pattern of exchanges, layered above the driving and mesmerizing three steps in place, stamp, and kick. Like a sigh, the pattern comes to completion in a sequence that matches the opening curtsy, closing the design off properly and symmetrically. It brings the dancers out of the *figura* and drops them off with turns again. ¡*Vuelta!* Turn. ¡*Por Fuera!* File out in procession. This time the procession is broken into two parts. First the left line marches forward around the right one, while the right line eases back to make way for them. Reaching the back, the left line marches behind the right and comes forward beside them, pausing midway down the hall to pick up the right line. All dance forward into place together. Turns again, and the procession is repeated in reverse, right line marching in front of left to the back of the hall, all coming forward together. The dance ends with an elongated bow. Continuing the basic step, three times the men retreat a few steps then advance a few steps, with a final deep bow to the Virgin.

The *figuras* unfold and refold in symmetrical scrolls, the dancers etching out the loops and filigrees like the designs in a Moorish painting. The metaphor is appropriate; the Spanish Christians came to the New World on the heels of military victory over the Moors. The Franciscan fathers superimposed European violins and the story of the Moors' conversion onto Aztec dances to teach the people in Mexico City the new religion.[5] The Yaquis, who do a similar dance, still call their dancers "good soldiers" of the Virgin (Spicer 1980: 88, 1962: 510).

The danced message of conversion spread outward from Mexico City on the backs of missionaries and settlers, west to the Pacific Coast, north through the Sierra Madres and the deserts of Sonora and Chihuahua, and up the Rio Grande past El Paso del Norte into the Pueblos and new mestizo villages of northern New Mexico. Among the Yaquis, Mayos, Ocoroni, and Cora in the west; among the Huichols and Tarahumara in the Sierra Madre Mountains; along the Rio Grande in the Pueblos of San Juan, Taos, Jemez, Santa Clara, and Cochiti; and in the Hispanic villages of Alcalde, Bernalillo, El Rancho, and San Antonio, the meeting of American native and European was enacted.[6] In anthropologist Sylvia Rodríguez's words, "[T]he Matachines dance communicates symbolically and metaphorically about the history and character of Indo-Hispano relations in the community that performs it" (Rodríguez 1996: 10). The dance bent and shaped around the different local truths it encountered.[7]

Embedded in the dance names *monarca* and *malinche* is a story of confrontation and conversion. When Hernán Cortés and his small Spanish army marched from the Atlantic toward the inland Aztec empire, they were introduced along the way to a chief's daughter who knew many local languages. Her name was Malintzín, or Malinche. She converted to Catholicism and accompanied the Europeans as their translator. It was Malintzín who persuaded Montezuma, the Aztec monarch, to convert, opening the way for the capitulation of a large nation to a small army. Some call Malinche a betrayer, the *chingada*, the violated one (Paz 1961: 86). Others honor her for being the instrument of conversion. In several Rio Grande Pueblos, Malinche is called the daughter of Montezuma, and it is said that Montezuma will return (*Santa Fe New Mexican*, August 19, 1918; Parmentier 1979). In other Pueblos, no reference is made to the historical narrative of Malintzín and Montezuma at all; only the names remain as abstract characters in a dance.

This is how it was in Tortugas.[8] The names had become abstractions: *monarca, malinche,* and the vestige of a third character, the *abuelo,* grandfather, who in other places represented devil, clown, animal, or conscience. In Tortugas, this dangerously pagan character was eliminated in the late 1950s along with the two narrative dances in which he once appeared (see photograph 5). In one, *el toro,* the *abuelo* played the role of a bull who tried to gore the *malinche;* the *monarca* killed the bull at the end of the dance. In the other, *la malinche escondida,* the "hidden *malinche,*" the *abuelo* tried to keep the *monarca* from finding the *malinche,* who was hidden inside a circle of *danzantes* (Miranda 1988).[9] The Tortugas *abuelo* officially became the "assistant *monarca,*" but people still called him by his old name. Now he acted as a shepherd for the dance, announcing the changes in step, leading the *malinche* through the complicated choreographic patterns, and ensuring, in general, that the dance flowed smoothly.

I once asked Rico why the Danza group no longer performed the nar-

Photograph 5.   Danzantes with *abuelo,* ca. 1916 (photo courtesy of Rio Grande Historical Collections, New Mexico State University Library, Las Cruces, RG84–7).

rative dances with the *abuelo*. Before 1955, when he became *monarca*, Rico said, there was an *abuelo* who was strict to the point of cruelty. As part of his dance role, he used to carry a whip. But he also used the whip to discipline the men—the *abuelo* was responsible for keeping them awake and away from drinking during the *velorio*. Every time he would find somebody with a bottle, Rico said, that *abuelo* would break the bottle. "It got so bad that people just didn't want to dance anymore. He was pretty rough with them." When the *abuelo* died, he was never replaced, and the narrative dances were discontinued.

Rico continued, talking about the Chichimeca Aztecas and the Guadalupanos Aztecas, two neighborhood *matachín* groups that also danced in the fiesta but were not sponsored by the corporation. They performed an Azteca or Chichimeca variation of the *matachines,* and their dances still included masked characters. The corporation didn't permit the masked ones to participate in the final procession when all the groups danced together. When I asked Rico why not, his wife, Graciella, answered, "Religion."

"Religion," Rico repeated. "In my belief I don't think we're dancing or dressing ourselves up to make a show for anybody." As another member said, the corporation didn't think the fiesta was something "to be made fun of" or "for entertaining people."

"I'll tell you about the *abuelo*," Rico went on. "I guess it's something that they put there themselves. As far as I know . . . that is not part of the story. Because in no way, if anybody reads the story of the apparition of the Virgin of Guadalupe or the celebration, they never see an *abuelo* there."

"The apparition?" I asked, lost.

"That's when she talks to Juan Diego," Rico said.

"That's the Danza's story?" I knew the men were dancing *for* the Virgin, but was Rico suggesting that the dance also told the story of her appearance on Tepeyac Hill? When I questioned the other dancers, they said only that they were dancing for the Virgin, and they referred me to the *monarca* for more information.

"All the dances, somewhere along the line, have a meaning [going back] to that apparition," Rico said. Different parts of the men's dress referred to different people and actions in the story. The *polainas*, the leggings, were what Indians like Juan Diego used in the fields, Rico said, so they wouldn't get their pants dirty. The scarf tied around each man's waist was like Juan Diego's *tilma* where, Graciella added, "she grew the roses." The red ribbon, the bandolier, was where each carried his little bag of food. The bandanna covering the dancer's face referred to Juan Diego's bashfulness. Rico was quoted in the local paper as saying, "Scarves cover the dancers' faces to symbolize Juan Diego's reluctance to recount his vision. . . . The Virgin appeared to him and told him to go and see the bishop and have a chapel built. He was just a regular old Indian and he was bashful to go before the great man" (*Albuquerque Journal*, December 23, 1979). Bashfulness was a quality Rico valued; he was looking for a man with this quality to succeed him as *monarca*.

"Now the corona, of course," the crown the *monarca* wears instead of

a *cupil,* "that represents the bishop. . . . He's the bishop, and we're dancing now to show that he has understood what she wanted."

"Do you represent a combination of Juan Diego and the bishop?" I
asked.

"In the full story, yes," Rico answered.

"It's not as if one person represents one thing?" I pressed.

"No, no," he said.

"And everybody just represents the whole story?" I asked.

"The same thing, yes," he agreed. Rico had elaborated a hermeneutics
of the Danza the way a scholar or ritual specialist might, drawing correspondences between elements of the dance and pieces of the narrative.
The dance and the story were mnemonics for each other.

To illustrate further what he meant by the dances "having a meaning to
that apparition," Rico discussed the *entrada* and the *batalla,* the slow and
ceremonial opening dances. First, he dismissed the steps as unimportant:

> It's the thing that we do on that particular time, or that particular thing
> that he's playing on his violin, that changes. That is what expresses what
> we are doing. Take, for instance, the first tune we have or when we start
> dancing, we have what is called the *entrada.* Now that particular tune,
> of course, the man is playing, we have one *malinche* playing with—danc-
> ing—at that time. She's way up in the front. Now every time the violin's
> talking, she's gonna come back to where I am standing at the back of
> the line.

The music for this dance contains two melodic phrases. During the first
phrase, the *malinche* and *abuelo,* starting at the front of the hall, advance
one couple at a time, moving toward the *monarca* at the back. At the same
time, the *danzantes* do the basic step in place in their two lines. At the second melodic phrase, all the dancers, including the *malinche,* turn, once to
each direction. "Every time the violin's talking" refers to the transition
back to the first phrase.

> Now, she gets there, we're gonna change bows. And then she's gonna
> take my—*palma* . . . I'm gonna pass it to her.

"Change bows" refers to a unique exchange performed when the *malinche* reaches the *monarca.* The *monarca*'s hand holding the *palma* and the

malinche's empty hand held flat, circle each other several times. Rico had once called this a "gesture of respect," and at another time, an offering of Juan Diego's prayers.

> And she's gonna go dancing back to the front of the line. Now when she gets there, she's gonna come back again and she's gonna give it to me.

When the *malinche* gives back the *palma,* they repeat the hand-circling gesture. Rico later said that the *palma* is "something like the fathers use to spray holy water. . . . She's bringing it to the bishop."

> Now she has completed that tune. She has permission [from] me to enter, to come to the temple. So that's what I mean by it's what goes on between the dancers, but our step is still the same.

On my audiotape, it is difficult to hear whether Rico said "she has permission *from* me to enter" or "she has permission *for* me to enter." If it is "from" me, then it would mean that here Rico represents the bishop, who agreed to build a temple for the Virgin. If it is "for" me, then he would represent Juan Diego, who has the bishop's permission to enter into the temple.

> Now our second tune is what we call the *batalla,* or the "battle." At this time all the dancers are kneeled down except me and the *malinche.* Now we are coming forward.

The *monarca,* starting at the back between the two lines, performs a slow pivoting step while he gestures in a sweeping arc toward each man (see photograph 6). Rico described this gesture as a "blessing of the ground" leading to the temple.

> There's a click [in the music] that I know that any *monarca* would know. Every time I hear that click, of course, I move a little farther, until I get to the front.

The tune changes for the *batalla,* slower and with a lead-in of four sustained notes. The *monarca* moves forward on the fifth note, the one that begins each repeat of the melody. The *danzantes* are kneeling.

> Now I'm at the front of the line. Now he's still playing, but he's gonna change to another way of playing that tune. So I'm gonna come back, and every time he gives me that click, I hit my foot and two of the *danzantes* get up.

Photograph 6.   La batalla. The *monarca* gestures in a sweeping arc toward each kneeling *danzante,* while the *malinche* follows the *monarca,* December 10, 1986.

"Another way of playing that tune" is a return to the quicker melody of the *entrada.* The *monarca* dances up the center, stopping between each pair of *danzantes* and stamping. On his stamp, the two men rise. The click is the pickup note for the second phrase of the melody.

> Now when I get to the back that means that I have already entered into the temple. And we are ready for whatever is to come. I mean we go into the building—we dance it anywhere—that's part of the tune. That's just our expression that says we're entering. The other dancers just come around with me, and then we come in and dance three times and then we have already entered.

When Rico said they "dance three times," he might have been referring to the three dances that are performed in each Danza set.

"You see, every tune has a different meaning," Rico concluded.

I understood that the *entrada* and *batalla* referred to the apparition story and the three visits Juan Diego made to the bishop to ask that he build a church for the Virgin. While the dance *represented* the story, Rico and the dancers were also *entering* the story, "entering the temple." Rico's description joined the sacred time of the Virgin's appearance with the durative time of the present.

When I asked if they were dancing for Juan Diego, Rico said no, not *for* Juan Diego, but "trying to follow in the steps of Juan Diego."

> Each *entrada* is one of Juan Diego's visits to the bishop. We're trying to say that Juan Diego went to see the bishop and we have to have something to show that it was the bishop involved with it. The *monarca* is not both Juan Diego and the bishop. That he's wearing the crown shows that he went to see the bishop. . . . We're trying to get the whole story to one picture, one dance. We're trying to show the Virgin Mary, we're trying to show the holy water, we're trying to show the bishop. (Bernal 1987)

"We're trying to get the whole story to one picture, one dance," summarized Rico's interpretive strategy. A one-to-one correspondence between dance moves and narrative wasn't what he was after. Rather, his strategy was global, allowing for alternative readings of the same dance action. He juxtaposed pieces of the narrative with pieces of the dancing so that the dance as a whole referred to the story as a whole.

Rico's flexibility of correspondences permitted a meditation in which the experience of dancing evoked images from the story, and together dance and story invoked the Virgin's presence. Once, during a conversation with one of the women and a priest who had served the parish and retired, I asked if people could *see* the Virgin. The Virgin only appears at times of historical crisis, they agreed, so it was unlikely that people would see the actual Virgin. But they agreed that people can *feel* her presence. When Rico danced, he felt himself to be within the story, entering the Virgin's presence. He used the first-person pronoun ambiguously. Dancing and story merged in the person of the dancer.

What Rico described is the way that sensory, rather than merely verbal, memory works. It enables current sensations to be alive with meaning, because they engage with accumulated associations both somatic and symbolic. It is the same way I remember the fiesta, its images, sounds, words, and meanings interpenetrating in an associative play that refers back to and deepens its own tapestry. My image of Robert at the altar suggested the bodily memory of him on the rabbit hunt; my description of the Danza outfits called up the conversation in the doorway with Billy. The words I write join with the remembered sensations so that, eventually, the rhythm of my sentences becomes part of my fiesta memory.

At the end of the *batalla,* the *danzantes* got up from their kneeling positions, and the first *figura* could begin. After the static exchange of *palmas* between *monarca* and *malinche* and the *monarca's* slow-moving "blessing of the ground," the *danzantes'* eruption into vigorous movement came as an exultant celebration. Feet came off the floor for the first time. Knees lifted. Steps were larger, with weight and bounce. There was a feeling of running, charging.

It was easy to imagine, as Rico said, that "they're getting the people together. Now they know it. The Virgin Mary's gonna come. Juan Diego's already seen it." At this point, by Rico's understanding, the *monarca* was leading the people into the Virgin's temple. Rico, as both dance leader and narrative character, was now in her presence, dancing with the Virgin, bringing the *danzantes* and the people with him.

On a break after the first *figura,* the dancers shuffled and looked out over their bandannas through the fringes on their *cupiles.* It was as crowded as before in the *casa del pueblo,* so I was having difficulty seeing the dancers. Surrounded and pushed, I was experiencing a moment of "frayed nerves," as the women called it. Later the crowd would thin. This early in the evening, although there were many who wanted to hear the priest and see the first rounds of the Danza, they would not stay the night. I stepped outside and smoked a cigarette, then walked to the *casa de la comida* two blocks away.

Electric *farolitos,* little lights in brown paper sacks, lit up the tiers of the church tower. Above these a single cross in blue electric lights announced the mystery of faith, the authority of the church, and the solidarity of community. The walk was a liminal moment, a time to step back, but not away, to feel the air, check the sky, and reflect. Throughout the night, people repeated this unofficial processional route, alone or in small groups. They left the kitchen for a few minutes to watch the dancers in the *casa del pueblo* or, in the other direction, came from the *velorio* for *dulces*, sweet breads, served in the kitchen at ten, or for hot stew at midnight. Though walking and eating were a change of activity, they were not a break from meditation. Many people held the silence and slowed their pace to stay in sync with the rhythm of the *velorio's* purpose.

I walked with different thoughts. Where did I belong in this community? Two years earlier I had flown in from New York and retreated regularly from the fiesta's intensity to eat cheese and crackers in the privacy and anonymity of a Motel 6. The following year I stayed with the Trujillo family and helped pin leggings on their sons' dance outfits. I was welcomed as a daughter. This third year, when I moved to Las Cruces, I stepped into the community as a volunteer worker. It began at the *casa de la comida* the week after I drank iced tea with Elena.

Driving through the village, I spotted her husband, Raul Sandoval, outside the parish hall of the church. He had been introduced the year before as someone who knew the history of the corporation. I parked next to his old turquoise pickup and got out to say hello. Since his retirement in 1984, Raul volunteered as all-around handyman for the church. It was a labor of love. Raul was happy to engage Father Giles in talks about the history of the *indios*. He pored over old deeds, maps, and photographs and collected newspaper articles about the fiesta. He kept his archive in cardboard boxes in the parish workroom. Later, when we knew each other better, Raul pulled from one of those boxes a Xeroxed page covered with hand-drawn squares, a name in each one. It was his family tree. He pointed to the square showing his mother's ancestors. Her grandfather had been a Tarahumara Indian. It was the only time I heard Raul discuss his family genealogy, and he spoke of it with delight, as if unraveling a mystery.

The *indios* from El Paso del Norte were not the only families who built the corporation. Many others came from the northern provinces of Mexico, from Sonora and Chihuahua. When Raul's father, Don Francisco Sandoval, moved to New Mexico, he secured land south of Las Cruces and grew chiles, apples, and cotton. His children skipped school when the chiles and cotton were ready for harvesting. Only one of Don Francisco's five sons continued farming, the assistant *monarca* who made his *promesa* in the mud of the Rhine River. The other brothers, and their children, moved into other worlds. Raul went to work checking in explosives at White Sands Missile Range. Benny trained to be a barber and opened his own business in Las Cruces. Two brothers each built plumbing businesses, one frequently donating plumbing services to the corporation. Among Don Francisco's grandchildren, there were now an accountant, a businessman, an engineer, and a schoolteacher. His family history is not unlike my own. My grandmother sat at a child's desk in a public school learning English. Her son was a detective for the New York City Police Department. Her granddaughter became a university professor.

When I drove up, Raul was unloading boxes from the pickup into his parish hall "office." He worked with a tall man's gangly grace and an abstracted demeanor, as if the physical labor provided an accompaniment to his thoughts. Raul immediately announced that the men would be building an addition to the *casa de la comida* that weekend, and I volunteered to help. Having second thoughts about working with the men, I asked if the women would be there too. No, Raul said, they would only bring lunch for the men. He invited me to come for lunch. But because I grew up with cooperative labor, men and women working together, I told Raul that I would help out. Construction became my introduction to the "back region" (Goffman 1959: 112) of the fiesta.

When I arrived on the following Saturday, Raul was on the flat roof of the *casa de la comida* pouring tar. Below, two men were stirring it in oil drums on improvised fires. One was Luis Alvarez, a *mayordomo* with Raul. The other was the cacique, Lorenzo Serna. Lorenzo was slighter in build than Raul, older, and more subdued. Eyeglasses accentuated his serious face. Wearing an old dress shirt and a red bandanna with a construction worker's hat over it, he was flushed and mud smeared.

This was the moment when I asked, "Do you recognize me?"

"Sure. You're the person from New York. You cried last year."

Lorenzo invited me on a tour of the *casa de la comida*. The men had poured concrete floors and built the wooden frame of the extension themselves. It would be covered with plaster and painted to match the red adobe of the original building. They would next tear down the wall between the old and new dining halls to make one expanded space to accommodate the growing numbers of people who came to feast on December 12. Lorenzo told me he was proud of these changes and confident that the corporation and fiesta would continue. The old people, he said, had told him to be sure to keep changing things—but not a lot.

The next weekend, even though it was raining, I appeared again for work. Raul drove up in his pickup, leaned out the window, and said there would be no work that day. They would be back tomorrow. "Bring a hammer," he instructed. "There's lots of work for you to do."

I arrived the next day with a hammer. Raul and several young men I didn't know were nailing up lengths of chicken wire over the tar-papered wooden frame of the extension; this would hold the final layer of plaster. I waved my hammer in greeting. "You should have brought two," Raul joked. Luis Alvarez's brother joined the joking, flailing his arms to demonstrate what it would be like to work with two hammers. Among men who worked and conversed with a minimum of unnecessary movement, his physical outburst was unusual. Luis Alvarez could lean over the edge of the roof, holding a piece of chicken wire in place for five minutes, while the man below hammered, holding nails into place. He watched a group of boys at batting practice on the neighboring lot. The stillness seemed comfortable.

Raul motioned me to follow him inside the *casa de la comida*. He picked up a cloth construction apron and tied it around my waist.

"You don't mind, do you?" he asked.

"No, it's all right," I said, though I felt uncomfortable with being dressed. He dropped a few handfuls of nails into my apron pockets and told me to follow him. Outside, Raul stretched a piece of chicken wire taut over the tar paper with a crowbar and instructed me to hammer in the nails to hold the wire in place. He showed me how to locate the solid beams under the outer wall. Once I had the first holding nail in place, Raul moved off to the next spot. We continued this way in silence around the building. The younger men were doing the same job. They worked in a contagious rhythm, unhurried yet efficient, and I moved into synchrony with it.

At the end of the day my hands were shaking from the unaccustomed hammering. Raul repeated twice, "You're a good worker."

"Yes, at first, but I wear out soon," I joked.

Raul then showed me a list where he had calculated the hours each worker donated. He had me down as "lady." I realized he didn't know my name. It was the hours of labor I contributed that he noted, not my name or my reason for being there. Eventually the story about the lady from New York who slung her hammer around with the men turned into a joke.

I entered the community on my muscles. Physical labor was part of my Three Arrows inheritance. Indeed, the two communities felt alike in their cooperative dance. People worked together. They hugged and told jokes. They got angry with one another and moved in and out of agreement. They took care of one another's children. In Tortugas, as in Three Arrows, working was a customary way of participating. The cooperation felt similar, but the premises of the two communities were different. Three Arrows was unified by an egalitarian political ideal, Los Indigenes de Nuestra Señora de Guadalupe by a spiritual one. No one joined the corporation without a personal relationship with the Virgin. Laboring for the fiesta was a form of sacred work.

What started as a personal religious choice also brought social obligations. When people joined the corporation, they knew what was expected. Before the fiesta, the phone calls came: the *casa de la comida* had to be cleaned from top to bottom, including dishes, cupboards, bathrooms, floors, tables. During November weekends the women made *biscochos,* cleaned and decorated the buildings, and dressed the Virgin. The men cleared brush on the procession route and on the mountain and gathered supplies for the pilgrimage. The phone calls came, too, for the fund-raising enchilada dinners, one in October, another in April. There might be a rabbit hunt in the winter, and someone might call for a traditional Pueblo social dance, the *baile de olla.*[10] Every day for the week before Palm Sunday, people met to make hundreds of *ramos* (literally "branches"), the local version of palms, fashioned out of cactus fronds and juniper branches tied to a cross of twigs. There were monthly business meetings and weekly church services. People were called on to act as *mayordomos* and as corporation officers. Most unifying, and most consistent, however, was the kitchen work: cleaning, cooking, and serving.

One woman who helped out with only some activities told me she had not joined the corporation because she knew she could not meet the people's expectation that she work in the kitchen. She knew she would be criticized for not fulfilling the responsibilities that went along with membership. The continuity of the corporation, and the fiesta, depended on the balance between the autonomy of individuals acting out of a personal experience of faith and the negation of that autonomy in their choice to take on an obligation to the community. Work was both a service to the Virgin and an expression of allegiance to a human community. Voluntary obligation held the fiesta together.

I knew little about work done as religious devotion. I had come to learn, to understand the way belief was born and kept alive, the way community, which I knew, could be woven with religious faith, which I did not know.

The week after the joke about the hammers, I asked Raul if he knew what I was doing there. He stepped back, laughing, and said, "No, do you want to tell me?" I started talking about my research and the connection between dance and religion. In passing, I mentioned a conversation with a scholar who was also writing about the fiesta. Raul interrupted. He told me that the corporation didn't like that this man was applying for a big government grant to publish a book and get lots of money for it at their expense. The corporation allowed photography and videotaping of the fiesta dances, but they reprimanded a local couple for selling copies of the videotapes they made. Before giving a cameraman permission to shoot footage for an Albuquerque television station, the corporation wanted to know what the man would do with the film. Using the fiesta for financial gain debased its religious nature, and several people expressed resentment at having their religion used in this way.

There was a related political reason for being suspicious of the scholar's big government grant. Members insisted on the importance of their independence from government control. Following the Tiguas of Ysleta del Sur, who were granted federal recognition in 1963, the corporation looked into the possibilities of attaining tribal status. In the 1970s they hired a lawyer and requested an investigation of what it would mean to become a reservation.[11] But they decided against it. As Raul said, "The people of Tortugas don't want to be under anybody. We want to do things our own

way." Others echoed Raul's argument. Rico said they preferred autonomy to tribal status. Benny said the corporation wanted to be left alone
and have no connection to government agencies or to anyone who would
tell them what to do. They simply wanted to keep their religious celebration and pass it on to their children. Instead the members chose to function as a nonprofit corporation within the economic and political mainstream. Corporate status gave them more freedom than tribal status.

The corporation's objection to outsiders profiting from the fiesta was
an aspect of this larger insistence on retaining internal control over what
the community did. From this perspective, the fiesta itself was a form of
resistance, based on choice, mutual obligation, and what social scientist
Carlos Vélez-Ibánez calls "reciprocal exchange." In Mexican-American
border communities, he writes, extended families, usually several related households, provide mutual help with baby-sitting, godparenthood,
or *compadrazgo*, putting up visitors, and giving emotional support.[12] They
share recreational and religious activities and exchange information
about jobs, housing, and dealing with the government. These networks
act as a "safety net" against the mainstream's economic appropriation of
their labor and destruction of their culture (Vélez-Ibánez 1993: 120, 123,
125). The "template" for these exchange relations and the "cultural glue"
that holds them together "are the repetitive yet syncretic series of sacred
and secular calendric and life-cycle rituals that operate throughout the
year" (125). Ritual events, like the fiesta, measured whom one could
count on.

The corporation organized this exchange dynamic on a scale larger
than family and *compadrazgo* networks. It brought together families who
were otherwise unrelated, families who might then choose each other as
godparents. Lorenzo and his wife, Magdalena, were godparents for Raul
and Elena's daughter. They continued to give her gifts and advise her
even when she entered motherhood herself. The corporation, because of
its large scale, visibility, and local popularity, also drew into its sphere the
very economic and political forces that might have co-opted the people's
labor. Local businesses and politicians found it advantageous to support
the corporation with donations of food and money and with appearances
at the fiesta. By adapting, from the beginning, the methods of the larger so-

ciety, namely corporate structure, the corporation widened its exchange network and established its relation to the larger society as one of equality rather than dependency.

The complex of choice, obligation, connection, and network was more than a sociological schema. It was animated by spiritual purpose. The choice to participate was grounded in faith, and people's obligation was to the Virgin as well as to the community. The connection between people was spiritual as well as social, informed by the narratives of the Virgin and holy family. Their stories were the models of and for choice, obligation, connection, and network.

The Virgin was mediatrix both within the holy family and between the holy family and humankind. One day, while working construction at the *casa de la comida,* Lorenzo offered what he called my "first lesson in local Catholicism."

"The first miracle was the Annunciation," he said. "The angel told Mary that she would have a child and Mary said, 'So be it.' She didn't question its probability, she just accepted it."

In other words, Mary chose to give herself. She didn't debate the existence of God or consider the feasibility of becoming pregnant with His child. Hers was a choice based in faith, echoed in Juan Diego's choice on Tepeyac Hill to obey the Virgin's wishes.

Later in the day Lorenzo repeated the lesson. "The first miracle was when the angel appeared to Mary and told her she would bear the son of God. Then Mary said, 'but I have no husband.' The angel told her that her husband would be God, and she accepted it, making herself an instrument of God's will. The Virgin mediates to God for the people. How can a son say no to his mother?"

I heard the same phrase often in the community kitchen. The women asked me questions about Judaism, and I, in turn, asked about the Virgin Mary. "She is the mother of God," one woman said. Another interrupted, "Not God, Jesus." Acknowledging the distinction, the first said that the Virgin was chosen by God to be Christ's mother. The women all agreed, however, that the power of the Virgin comes from the fact that "a son can't deny his mother anything."

The comment seemed to erase the distinction between Father and Son.

In becoming the mother of God the Father's divine child, Mary enabled Him to be doubled, as both Father and Son. Becoming the instrument of God the Father's will, the Virgin gives Him life on earth as the Son. She is the bridge between God and humanity, and also the bridge between the divine and the human within God Himself. She first enables God's differentiation, and then, as mother, enables His connection to His created Son. She also embodies obligation. Both Father and Son are obligated to her. How can a son say no to his mother?

Though many in Tortugas said they felt closer to the Virgin than to God, in the hierarchy of the holy family, God is "higher." The saints, including the Virgin, are "down here," as one woman said. Another clarified, "It is not the Virgin who answers prayers. She only intercedes. It is always God." The Virgin did not take the place of God the Father or Christ; rather, she was the entry point for the whole network. When I asked if the fiesta was for Our Lady of Guadalupe alone or for Christ as well, the answer came, "He is always there, but the Virgin is more available." Unlike God the Father, who is distant and abstract, the mother of God is close and familial. She gets involved with the quotidian details of life. She arranged the roses in Juan Diego's *tilma*. She watches over baby-sitting, cooking, dressing the altar, clearing brush, and exchanging news, all the work that sustained both her fiesta and the social networks that made the fiesta possible. These chores were acts of faith, the yes-sayings that made connection with the Virgin possible, just as her yes made the connection between humankind and God possible.

Faith and service were inseparable. By serving, one brought the Virgin closer, regenerating faith. Faith was expressed through service. One corporation member complained when he thought others weren't doing their share of the work, saying, "They just don't have it." I understood him to mean that devotion not expressed in participation was not true devotion. Working in the kitchen was a way of serving the Virgin, and so was going to church or climbing Tortugas Mountain. Service was the blessing itself. It took one into both the human and the divine network. This, I understood, was why Raul noted my work, rather than my individuality.

"Everyone wants to write about us suddenly," Raul said. He had thought to write up his memories from the 1940s and 1950s when the corporation passed through a transition toward modernization. "Maybe you can help me." I said I'd be glad to tape-record his stories and help him write them down. Then I asked whether I needed to get permission to do my writing. I didn't want to go ahead if nobody wanted me to do it. He laughed, "No, you'd be wasting your time." After debating whether or not I should make my request at a meeting of the board of directors, he finally said, "We'll have to play it by ear." This was what we continued to do. No one said stop. No one said go. We played it by ear. I heard in Raul's words both a welcome and a hesitancy. As a woman volunteering for men's work, I had brushed against a boundary. As a scholar who might betray the community, I was given a warning about limits.

My response to those limits was a vague fear. The kind of discipline I encountered in Tortugas was unfamiliar to me. It began with the way children were raised. As in my own community, children grew up in "thick networks" (Velez 1983), but parents were more strict here. A woman my age said that when she was young her father taught her how to offer a guest a glass of water. First, she must ask if he would like some water. Then she must get the water and bring it to him, standing next to him with her arms folded across her chest while he drank. Finally, she must take the empty glass back to the kitchen. One grandmother friend scolded her grandson, albeit with loving sternness, when he interrupted our conversation to tell me a story. "Stop talking. Leave the lady alone. She doesn't want to listen to you." Children were loved differently in my family. There was less tough edge, more permeable boundaries, and more encouragement of creative expression. I remember my grandmother, not the one who sat with the women in front of the store in Brooklyn, but the storytelling grandfather's wife, with her Breck blond hair and bright green dress-up suit. She sang for Hadassah. And when I sang in the living room, she smiled throughout my performance. I can still feel her patience, her happiness at a child's expression of life and *simcha*, joy.

Once I was invited to help a Tortugas grandmother, Mireya Ruiz, make clay animals for her Christmas nativity scene, and her grandchildren were there. We spread newspapers on the patio table and dipped into wet clay to pull out chunks for shaping. Mireya made a cow, and I made a donkey. Her seven-year-old grandson, Jorge, made something that didn't resemble a nativity animal at all. It had a huge pancake snout and short legs on a dumpy body, looking like a cross between a dinosaur and a rhinoceros. It made Mireya laugh, unsuitable as it was for the scene in the manger. She grabbed it up to throw it back into the clay stew, but I protested and salvaged it from oblivion. I like to think now that my seriousness about Jorge's "art" struck Mireya as funny as his misshapen animal. She had the tact not to say anything, and I later saw that the creature had been included in her crèche on the mantel, a clumsy figure next to my acceptable donkey and Mireya's fine cow. What grace the grandmothers had, keeping silent about my transgressions, allowing liberties they would not allow their own children.

4

. . . .

Choreography of the Kitchen

For the grandmothers, freed of children and work, coming together in the *casa de la comida* was like being at home in a shared public space. I, too, felt at home there, like a small girl learning from her mother the secrets of mixing and blending food—and the secrets of relationships. Stepping into the kitchen I stepped back into my childhood, comfortable among the elders, warm within the exchange of news, learning how to be. My father's parents from Russia lived with us until I was four, and the adults spoke Yiddish when they didn't want the children to know what they were saying. In our kitchen, Yiddish held the smells of roasting chicken, just as Spanish in the Tortugas kitchen held the smells of roasting chiles. As at home in Brooklyn, the combination of language and aromas beckoned me into an older generation's world, especially in the women's kitchen.

The women's kitchen was the second oldest of three kitchens in the *casa de la comida,* the oldest, for the most part, being men's turf. The men's kitchen was a narrow passageway between the other two, crudely appointed, with steel sinks along one long wall and a deep stone hearth flanked by two huge gas-fueled cooking pots opposite. During the feast on the twelfth, the men stirred red chile stew and meatballs in these pots. In a line of three at the sinks, they took turns washing and drying dishes. They took breaks to tilt back in folding chairs or to lean, standing, against the hearth wall, telling jokes to keep the dishwashers company and teasing the women who passed through. Perhaps because of the room's spatial arrangement, the men all faced the same direction when they washed the dishes. But this arrangement reappeared when they sat at the long tables in the main dining hall sorting stones out of the beans. It was the same configuration the men took when they nailed up the chicken wire, side-by-side in a line facing the same direction.

By contrast, the women worked in a circle. Around the perimeter of their kitchen were several sinks—used for washing food, not dishes—a refrigerator, two stoves side-by-side, and cabinets that held aprons, dishcloths, and the women's coats and purses. But the heart of the space was the central worktable. It was rectangular, covered with a red-checkered oilcloth. The women stood or sometimes perched on high stools, barely sitting at all, while they chopped onions or lettuce, pared and sliced tomatoes, patted and rolled out dough. The circle of bodies and talk infused the food they labored over. They cajoled and scolded onions, tomatoes, and dough into place, then fed this wisdom-steeped food to the community. It was a reversal of the transubstantiation ritual of the Church, where spirit is made flesh; here flesh was made spirit.

When the women traded stories and jokes, it was not just small talk. They adjusted the boundaries of belonging, revised outdated rules, introduced and evaluated newcomers, recommended measures for keeping people healthy, shared information about resources, and kept connections alive. Stories leaned toward the ideal and made exceptions for the real.

The first time I sat with the women in the *casa de la comida,* hidden among the talk about the best buy at Dillard's and the most recent family illnesses was a joke about a woman who called her boyfriend a friend. At the time I didn't get it: the joke was on me. My situation could not have been comfortable for them; I was a single woman asserting her presence with far too much exuberance, living with a man to whom she was not married. Jay and I had agreed to become engaged, but we had not set a date for marrying. Later, when the women knew me better, they debated what to call Jay, deciding finally and simply on "Deidre's Jay." Two of the women joked that we should marry in the *casa de la comida*. It would be a first, and they would hold the reception. The men were more forward, teasing from the beginning. When I said I would be driving halfway across the country to pick up my fiancé, one joked, "You won't be doing a lot of driving." And if I mentioned that I was going home for a nap, someone was sure to say, "Alone?" Another asked, each time we greeted, "So, are you married yet?" His wife finally had to tell him to keep quiet, that he was embarrassing her.

After the joke about calling a lover a friend, the conversation turned to annulment and divorce. The women agreed that the Church was more lenient than it used to be. Now, one woman said, you could get an annulment even four years after being married. They explained that second marriages were not permitted for Catholics, so it was more acceptable to be sleeping with a man than "cohabiting" or remarrying. I had learned from Father Giles, who served as an ecumenical judge in El Paso, that the clergy tried to make it possible for Catholics to stay within the Church, and to that end they applied the marital laws with flexibility. Talk about annulment and divorce led to talk about raising daughters. The women agreed that they wanted to give their daughters more freedom than they themselves had known. They also wanted to be sure that their daughters "knew how to take care of themselves." As one woman said, "In just a few seconds, you can ruin your whole life." When this would happen, though there might be criticism, the network of grandmothers would close around the woman.[1]

When I visited Magdalena, the cacique's wife, she, too, talked about mothering. She and Lorenzo had raised a niece and two of their niece's children. Magdalena was angry about mothers going out to work when they didn't have to. "No one's teaching the next generation," she said. "A baby-sitter doesn't care." Magdalena insisted that a mother's place was in the home. "She should be teaching her daughter the important things— what good food is and how to make tortillas." She was upset that her granddaughter preferred pizza to beans and tortillas. My Russian grandmother, too, worried about what we ate, advocating for vegetables. "Wienies and hamburgers," Magdalena repeated twice. "I hate the smell."

In the community kitchen a joke went around more than once about a new bride who could not make her tortillas round. She made them in the shape of states—like Texas, California, and Florida. At first, when the bride served her misshapen tortillas to her husband and mother-in-law, the mother-in-law made fun of them, and so the bride stopped making tortillas. But after the mother-in-law passed on, the bride practiced making tortillas until she learned how to make them round. If the women don't know how to make tortillas, how will the next generation know who they are?

The connection between raising daughters and knowing how to prepare food was not incidental. Both were women's work and both were bodily transforming. On the day the women prepared *biscochos*, crisp cookies flavored with anisette and sprinkled with cinnamon sugar, one of the grandmothers came in and announced that she would not be eating anything that day, since she was having stomach pains. Another woman joked that it wasn't her digestion that was the problem but "little feet." The suggestion that a sixty-year-old grandmother must be pregnant was absurd. But the intentional linking of two kinds of bodily events that feel similar and that occur in loosely the same bodily space made sense and depended on an experience unique to women—having babies.

Childraising and cooking also worked bodily transformations in another way. Childraising turns "raw" newborns into "cooked" adults (Lévi-Strauss 1969), and cooking domesticates foodstuffs. Both kinds of work are culturally perpetuating. Raising children, especially daughters who can teach the next generation, and knowing how to cook the right foods fed back into the community resources and knowledge that might otherwise, in Vélez-Ibáñez's terms, be co-opted by the American market. Women's work of cooking and raising children was a subtle form of resistance to assimilation. Indeed, Vélez-Ibáñez writes that it is the women, and especially the older women, cooking together for the ritual feasts, who sustain the mutual support networks that enable border communities to survive (1993: 120, 125, 128).

Many of the jokes in my own immigrant community were also about food, but it was my father who told them. Food in our community was also about physical and cultural survival, negotiating between old and new worlds. The joke that stays with me most is about Bessie and Sam, first-generation immigrants. They were poor, with seven children. Perhaps they lived in Boro Park, Brooklyn, or on the Lower East Side of Manhattan. At dinner, Bessie always found a way to have seven chicken legs for her seven children. But when the relatives came with their seven children, there weren't enough chicken legs to go around. Sam told the children, "When I say, 'Who wants chicken?' don't raise your hand. When I say, 'Who wants tuna fish?' everyone raise your hand." Everything went as planned. When Sam asked who wanted chicken, none of the children raised their hands. When he asked who wanted tuna fish, they all raised their hands. There was enough chicken for the cousins. When it came time for dessert, Sam said, "Now who wants apple pie?" And all the children raised their hands. "Oh, no," said Sam, and here my father demonstrated how Sam shook his finger at the children. "All those who didn't have chicken can't have apple pie."

It was a tricky joke. Our family was not like Bessie and Sam's family; we weren't greenhorns, and we didn't need to scrimp. But we were also like them. In a pinch, we were to put our desires aside for others in the family and community. Taken to the extreme, the message is like the riddle "How many Jewish mothers does it take to change a lightbulb?" "None," the answer goes, "Don't mind me, I'll sit in the dark." Though these jokes could be painfully uncomfortable, the kind of self-sacrifice they taught and also mocked was a means of survival: people in the community were to take care of one another.

In the *casa de la comida*, too, people told jokes about cultural survival. One was about a black man and a white man who argued about whether God was black or white. It just so happened that they died at the same time and met at the pearly gates. "Now we'll find out who was right," they agreed. St. Peter came to meet them. "So, who's right? Is God black or white?" they asked him. "Just wait and see," said St. Peter. "Here He comes." God walked through the pearly gates. "*¿Qué pasa?*" He said. It was not hard to imagine the *pachuco* swagger. Holding onto vernacular language may inspire derision in the assimilated, but it also asserts a refusal to be robbed of cultural identity.

Benny's wife, Rita, who told the joke, was trim and impeccably groomed, her black hair coifed, her skin smoothed with makeup. She was one of the corporation leaders. She and Benny lived "in town," in downtown Las Cruces, near Benny's barber shop, not in Tortugas. Benny told me that when he was young, he and his brothers spoke only Spanish. Skipping school to pick chiles and cotton on Don Francisco's farm made it even harder for the children to catch up. He and Rita chose to speak only English at home so that their children would not be stigmatized as he had been. There was no contradiction between delighting in a Spanish-speaking God and wanting the children to assimilate into English-speaking schools. As the New Mexico anthropologist Sylvia Rodríguez points out, it is a popular Anglo misconception that maintaining Mexican-American identity is inimical to modernization and progress (Rodríguez 1987: 365, 388). The goals of cultural preservation and upward mobility are not mutually exclusive.

The *casa de la comida* was the place that held these stories. The church may have generated faith, but the community kitchen generated the dance of social belonging. It was the "backstage area" (Goffman 1959: 112) that the public didn't see. Fiesta visitors came into the *casa de la comida* only once for the feast on December 12. Corporation members, and the family and friends who volunteered to help, spent the majority of fiesta time there. For those intense three days, the *casa de la comida* was a second home.

Its choreography was like a postmodern dance score in which a set of tasks is repeated from one performance to the next. In Tortugas, these tasks could be enacted by any permutation and combination of the participants. The kitchen score included distinctions between men's and women's work, but these were neither permanent nor rigid. Washing dishes was men's work and chopping onions women's, but dishwashing was once women's work, and men sometimes helped chop the onions. Everyone knew the score well enough to improvise on it spontaneously.

Working in their own informally designated space, standing in a circle curved over their cutting boards, the women handled the food with small and precise gestures, pushing and patting it like grandmothers scolding and caressing unruly children. Even when they were resting or waiting for the next round of chores, talking and drinking coffee, the women maintained their loose circle, connected by intricate, fine-tuned verbal and gestural filaments.

Now, from a coffee shop in California, holding memories in the bowl of my body and savoring their mix, I sit with the women again, dicing images, sensations, and words. Roll up your sleeves. Put on an apron, the red one with the armholes, like a jacket worn backward. You know what to do. Pick up a cutting board from under the sink and a knife from the drawer in the main dining hall. Bring a few extra knives for the other women. Find a spot around the table and pick up the conversation, and an onion.

We sliced off the stems and peeled the skin. Rita cut her onions in half lengthwise, laid the halves flat on the board, and sliced down to make moon-shaped slivers that she then chopped. I halved the onions at their wide middle and checkered the two surfaces, cutting off thin layers afterward. Everyone had her own technique for slicing onions. But after slicing, we all chopped the pieces yet finer, pressing down on the knife handle and moving the blade back and forth among the bits. It was better, the women said, to chop onions by hand than with a food processor; the processor drew too much water. And the sound of the knife on the board satisfied. We swept the chopped onion into big plastic mixing bowls and dipped into a box of tissues to wipe the tears from our eyes. "How many more onions?" I once asked. "Don't be such a baby," was the answer. We worked until five bowls were full.

There it was, that edge of strictness. Sometimes I felt too large, too liquid, with too much chutzpah and not enough of the sharp slap of discipline. My coloring went outside the lines. I complained and questioned. Late on the night of the *velorio,* when I was debating whether or not to go on the next day's pilgrimage, the man who joked about the two hammers advised me that everyone does what he wants to, but if you want the rewards, sometimes you have to do what you *don't* want to. "It's like a dog who wants a bone," he said. "He can't just lie there and wait for it to come to him. He has to go and get it." His sister-in-law overheard him, and teased, "What lies has Joe been telling you?" But there was truth in his advice. Following the rules without complaint was a principle of belonging. In Mary Douglas's schema of "positional" versus "personal" value systems, Tortugas listed toward the positional pole. People valued and made choices based on a strong sense of social pattern. Three Arrows, my family's Utopian community, tended toward the personal pole. Choice-making was looser, more situational, based on valuations in the moment (Douglas 1970: 20–36, based on Bernstein 1965). Douglas's schema was oversimplified, but it helped me to think about our differences.

In spite of these differences, the grandmothers befriended me and took me in, perhaps trying to be alert to any trouble I might cause. When I visited them in their homes, they gave me canned chiles and jalapeños, with instructions on how to cook them, and herb tea to settle an upset stomach. But friendship consisted not so much of these gifts as of permission to trade answers to the question, "Will you tell me who you are?" The trade was not so much the functional, "I am a grandmother who has raised seven children" for "I am a graduate student who wants to be a scholar" as it was the personal, "I have always been surrounded by my family, never alone" for "I have a hunger for the world and need to be alone a lot of the time." Friendship meant spending time together because we liked one another, because we were curious about one another's lives, and because we agreed to trade secrets. The pact we made was delicate. As with any intimacy, it held the danger of loss.

It was 8:00 when I left the *velorio* and walked to the *casa de la comida*. Since 1:30 in the afternoon, food preparations had been continuous, along with the usual cleaning, mopping, dishwashing, and talking. Now the floors were swept and mopped again, the tables and benches washed down, the cups, sugars, and creamers in place on the tables for the 10:00 *dulces*, with coffee and hot chocolate. The kitchen seemed brightly lit and expansive after the subdued and enclosing space of the *velorio*. Elena's five-year-old grandson, dressed in a mouse suit, and his older sister, dressed in a Pueblo manta like the *indio* dancers wore, had just come from a school play. They ran up and down the aisles between the dining room tables. A loving uncle caught the boy and turned him upside down. The women stirred the green chile stew that would be served at midnight. Everything was in order.

I looked for a place to write up notes on the Danza and chose a spot next to the kerosene stove on the far end of the dining room away from the kitchens. One of the men said, "She's writing a book about dirty jokes. Just don't publish it. No names, no names." Two ten-year-old girls who helped me sweep the floors that afternoon sat with me. They had the same subject on their minds. Had I ever been married? Did I plan to get married? Wasn't I embarrassed about it? I don't remember what I answered, but now I think of the women around the table and a piece of gossip one told. It was about an elderly woman. "Did you see her when that young man came in?" The words stopped, and the storyteller stood and imitated the walk of a petite eighty-year-old woman, a self-effacing curled-in posture and tiptoeing mincing steps. Then the storyteller straightened up and puffed out her chest, flaunting and wiggling it like a young girl. We laughed at the transformation and the storyteller's "artistic license."[2] Should I have told the young girls that they would still be asking their questions when they were eighty?

I finished writing up my notes and went back into the women's kitchen. It was early in the fiesta, the intensity still on a low boil, the workers fresh, happy to be there, greeting one another and catching up on the news. A woman complained about her new haircut and set. She felt that the back was too short. Her son joked that she'd just have to walk around with her shoulders hunched up to her ears, and he mimed the posture. Rico's wife, Graciella, who would be signing people up for the pilgrimage at dawn, showed me her warm long underwear and I showed her mine. Benny paced, stopping only to peer out the windows. The three or four inches of morning snow was still on the ground. Should the pilgrimage be canceled? The war captains would be meeting at 10:00 this night to decide. As Benny moved the red kitchen curtains aside to squint out into the dark, he checked the clouds for signs of tomorrow's weather. Ambivalent about making the pilgrimage, I asked whether it was important to go. Rita said that the fiesta was made by a lot of people: the women who worked in the kitchen, the dancers, the people who went up the mountain. The pilgrimage had to happen for those people to fulfill their part. In twenty-three years it had never been canceled.

Talk was interrupted by the arrival of the *danzantes,* still held by their meditation, filing into the *casa de la comida.* I could smell the cold they brought in, picture their walk in silence from the *casa del pueblo.* But it was not quite silent. There were jokers among them. Sometimes, during rehearsals, the men whispered jokes to one another while they danced. Perhaps jokes were the underbelly of devotion, the banned clown-devil *abuelo* asserting himself. The men were trailed in the door by the nine small girls in white, the innocent, teasing ones who could have asked the same questions about marriage my young interlocutors had.

The workers scurried to serve the dancers, in silence, respectful of their vigil. As part of the fulfillment of their *promesas,* the men were expected to discipline themselves throughout the night. In the *casa de la comida,* they had to keep silence. They had to wait, one dancer told me, for the *monarcas* to sit down at the dining room tables before they could sit and then wait again for the *monarcas* to stand before they stood to leave. They had to ask permission to go to the restroom. They were expected to be respectful of and obedient to their leaders.

The week before, at a practice, Rico had instructed his dancers on discipline. At 7:00, the men were waiting outside the *casa del pueblo* in their pickup trucks. The *monarca* had not yet arrived. The *malinches* were already inside, dropped off by their mothers or older brothers. The girls sat on a bench behind a long folding table at the front of the hall, hunched together in winter coats. When Rico's car pulled up, the men left their cars and trucks to enter the hall. They greeted one another with subdued nods, then sat in silence, spaced unevenly on the benches. Tired perhaps after a day of work, some leaned forward, bracing themselves with their forearms on spread knees. Others slouched back against the single wooden crosspiece of the benches. Rico took off his dungaree jacket. He was dressed casually, like his men, wearing a plaid shirt, blue jeans, and crepe-soled shoes. The oldest man there, he was also the shyest. He moved with a light grace, silently motioning the men to sit together in a group. Standing no more than two feet in front of them, Rico addressed his dancers.

There was no question where the authority in this group lay. The quiet command in Rico's voice, the spatial relationship between the seated group and the one standing leader, and the bowed heads of the younger men attested to the older man's authority. Rico's approach was gentle; he himself possessed the humility he looked for in a *monarca.* Helping them to fulfill their obligations to the Virgin was part of his obligation. Because this was understood, Rico's leadership was respected rather than simply tolerated.

He spoke to the men quietly and firmly in Spanish, telling them that they could miss two rehearsals at the most, but if they did miss one, they would have to find a stand-in. They were expected to help clean the *casa de descanso* before the fiesta. If they had made a *promesa,* it would not be fulfilled until they escorted the Virgin back to her *capilla* on New Year's day. Last, he hinted that there had been complaints from the corporation about the *danzante* tradition of drinking in the breaks during the *velorio.* The drinking and joking from the days of the *abuelo* had lessened, but not stopped.

The rules Rico gave the men were strict. He expected protest from those who considered drinking to be part of the tradition. But there were neither questions nor complaints, so Rico told the men to take their positions for the dancing. They lumbered into their lines to wait for the violin to signal the beginning. Shorty, the violinist, stood up, and the *monarca's* three assistants waited up front, but no command came from Rico. He had lost his car keys. While he searched without hurry under the benches, through his jacket pockets, outside on the ground and in his car, the men waited. Deference to the *monarca* was part of the contract they made when they took on a *promesa* to dance. Strictness was expected as part of the sacrifice they made for the Virgin.

One of the dancers, Frankie Valdez, talked about this strictness and why it was important. Frankie once belonged to one of the two neighborhood dance groups, the Guadalupanos Aztecas, before joining the Danzantes:

> When I was dancing with [the Guadalupano leader], the first year, back then, he'd hit you behind the legs and whip you. . . . If you weren't shaking the *guaje* loud enough or hard enough, he'd hit you. When you're supposed to turn and you don't turn, it's right there—whhht. He'd hit you behind the legs. He'd keep everybody in order and we'd dance real good, real strong. And now it looks like everybody just goes with the flow, just drags themselves through the dance. I noticed that. They don't really dance with . . . emotions. (Valdez 1987)

"And you're supposed to in that dance?" I asked.

"In every dance," he answered. "You're dancing for her. . . . [The leader] wants you to . . . that whole day is for her, so you give it all."

This did not make sense to me. Connecting emotion and disciplinary strictness bucked up against my experience. The dance groups I belonged to had created their works collaboratively, through improvisation. In that format, emotional richness came from encouragement, patience, explanation, exploration. In both family and theater work, I was taught that to experience performance in depth, one did, indeed, sometimes have to "go with the flow." For Frankie, and perhaps for all the dancers, "going with the flow" implied a half-hearted commitment and a superficial experience.

I asked Frankie if the Danza leaders were also strict. "They're real strict," he said. "We don't really mingle before practice. He says you get in line, you get in line. You stand there, you know. You don't cross to the other side of the room with a cigarette. You just stand in your spot until—"

"How do they make it clear that's what you're supposed to do?"

"They'll tell you that right off, right as soon as you get in. This is what we want. . . . And you learn it as respect. You do it as respect. I mean, you don't cut in the middle of a dance to go get a drink of water."

I finally understood that for the *danzantes,* the strictness and rules were opportunities. They provided a container for each individual. Within it, the men could make the connection to what they found most sacred. The discipline imposed from without was an aid rather than a barrier to emotional expansion, and they chose it voluntarily. This took a faith I lacked, faith that the order of creation was reflected in the rules and roles instituted by humans.

The *danzantes* and *malinches* finished their midnight supper, waited for the dance leaders to stand, and then returned to the *casa de descanso* to wait for the next round of dances. The men moved through the night as they moved through the dance, as a group, from the *casa del pueblo,* to the *casa de la comida,* to the *casa de descanso,* and back to the *casa del pueblo* to dance again. After helping to clean up the kitchens, I returned with them.

Now, at 1 A.M. in the *casa del pueblo,* people were no longer crowded against the walls. Only those who had made a promise to stay the night were still there. I entered through the back door and sat with the cacique's family, letting go of my earlier difficulties. I moved into the slowed rhythm, felt under layers of clothing the small space of warmth that one needed to create at this early morning hour. I heard the thickness of tired voices in prayer, no one talking any longer. The benches were still filled, but I could see the dancing. This was the time to let its effects do their work.

When I first heard the scratchy violin and saw the repetitive patterns of the Danza, I found them tedious. By the time of the 1986 *velorio,* after long immersion in the winding *figuras,* the Danza had become a deep and familiar cave that I, too, could drop into and there ride its echoes in my own synaptic byways. I could slip easily into a sharp awareness of the details of the dance and a feeling of compassion for the dancers' discipline on behalf of us all. The men brought to mind another "army" of dancers, the *fariseos* at Yaqui Easter.[3] At the climax of the Yaqui Easter ceremonies in Tucson, the *fariseos* shed their concealing black cloaks and ran full out down the plaza toward the church ramada. Many of the men were in late middle age and, like the *danzantes,* struggled to overcome their physical limitations for the sake of their faith and their community. It was said that those who fell during the run would not live out the year. I thought, too, of a film I'd seen of middle-aged and elderly men dancing all night for a Pomo girl's puberty ceremony. The sight of grown men in the contemplative state of the circle dance, honoring a girl's passage into womanhood, stunned and moved me. Needless to say, such demonstrations of male humility in dance were absent from my childhood and academic milieu.

Humility gave the men's dancing an elusive quality of softness, even vulnerability, in spite of the dance's driving force. But I could not locate the quality of softness in the dancing itself. In part it came from the contradiction of large men struggling to move quickly and precisely. Especially at early rehearsals, I could see their struggle, the men clumsy and breathing heavily, perspiring after a few dances. In part it came from the contrast between the men and the *malinche.* Among the large masculine presences, the one small girl was clumsy in a different way. She could not get her feet to catch up with the tune; she could not keep her mind on the step and the choreography at the same time. She could not manage the *guaje.* She didn't need to. It was not expected. Because she was a child, she was allowed a certain leeway. If she made mistakes it was only natural. Her girlish awkwardness was charming. It spoke of her otherness.

I once asked a *danzante* who the *malinche* was.

"A little girl."

"I know, but . . ."

"She's a pest."

"A pest?"

"When everybody's resting, the little *malinche*, she's keeping everybody awake, you know, playing games. She's just a pest."

The cacique's sister, Isabel Cruz, who danced as a *malinche* in 1916, said that the *malinche*, dressed in white, was a symbol of innocence and peace. According to Rico, she represented the Virgin Mary. "They have to show a character of a child. Innocence is the word I want." As I watched the men dancing beside her, they seemed alternately protective, honoring, instructing, distant, in awe, patronizing, and sometimes resentful of her naïveté. She seemed less her own person than a contrast to the men. While I imagined what it might feel like to dance as a *malinche*, from a more distant perspective I also saw her as a mirror, reflecting the vulnerability that lay beneath the surface of the men's imposing presences.

I gradually understood that this appearance of vulnerability was related to the men's focus of attention. At practice without their *cupiles*, their faces were exposed, their eyes revealing that they were not performing for an audience the way a stage dancer might. Nor were they watching themselves dancing. Although they occasionally looked around to see where the *monarca, malinche,* and *abuelo* were in the choreography, the men's focus was not primarily material. Rico confirmed this:

> When I'm dancing as the *monarca*, I don't see nothing of the people that are standing around. All I see is the dances and the vision to the holy Mary. That's all I see. I don't even know who is around me, if anybody's around me. That's the way I feel. . . . Soon as I get the music, I know what I'm gonna do next. And I never lift my head up. I shouldn't lift my head up. I'm there for one purpose. I'm there because—maybe I'm saying the rosary when I'm dancing. Who knows? I have to be all by myself. (Bernal 1987)

It was as if the men were already under the *cupiles* that during the fiesta would separate them from the rest of the world.

At rehearsals, the men faced a portrait of the Virgin that hung on the rear wall of the *casa del pueblo*. During the *velorio* her altar was before them.

On the twelfth, in the church courtyard, they danced toward her altar within. Rico was clear about the spatial focus of the dance. "I always tell them, I guess I shall until I die, that if they want me to dance—somewhere, in the church, in any church, for the Catholic religion—that we must have the Virgin Mary in front of us all the time, the Lady of Guadalupe." The image the men faced was the image they carried within. The softness that contradicted the driving power of the men's dancing, reflecting off the mirror of the *malinches'* innocence, was not a structural element of the dancing, but a manifestation of the men's offering of themselves to the Virgin.

The Virgin's story made it clear that she called on each individual, personally, to serve her. In exchange for that devotion, each would receive her blessing. Perhaps the most significant part of that blessing was the feeling of her presence, the bliss of giving oneself over, like Juan Diego, to her solicitude. And perhaps Rico spoke for the others when he said, "When you're dancing it's the same as dancing with the Virgin. It's something like if I were talking to her, expressing our gratitude for what she had done. . . . Every time we're dancing there, it's like we were saying thank you and just talking to her, giving her our thanks."

To dance with the Virgin echoed the message of Juan Diego's posture on the altar. It was specific and revealing. His legs were at the ready, with action imminent, but they were matched, even driven, by the yielding of his upper body, as if giving himself to the Virgin was the condition propelling him to action. Like Juan Diego, the *danzantes* worked the potent territory of this contradiction, where surrender becomes kinetic force. The vulnerability I saw was the Virgin's space. It was the open and receptive energy core of the dance, its ineffable subtext of belief manifested as a quality of energy.

Consistently, when I asked the men what made a good dancer, none answered with technical details or with an explanation of how the dancing should look. Rather, all spoke of the spirit in which one must dance. Danny Amador insisted that a good dancer was

one that isn't just there for the dance, one that's really there for the sacrifice to dance for the *virgen,* not just to dance because it looks good or it's fun to be in. 'Cause that's what I learned as a kid. I wanted to dance at first because my dad danced and because they just looked neat at night—you know, the costume. But later I found out that's not why you're there. . . . You're dancing for the *virgen*. (Amador 1987)

To sacrifice oneself was to give oneself over. And Rico again, "You have to have a big belief and big faith in order to dance and do it right" (Bernal 1987). "Doing it right" meant filling one's whole awareness with the Virgin.

I saw the effects of the dancers' sacrifice when I entered the *casa de descanso* for the first time. Without being told that it was off limits, I sensed that the resting house was the dancers' private place, not to be carelessly invaded. In 1989, a bolder male scholar led me inside. He led a *matachín* group in Albuquerque and said he was a guest of the *danzantes.* It was 3:00 in the morning, between the last two rounds of dancing.

The inside of the resting house was stark white, repainted each year by the dancers as part of their obligation. It was divided into a main front section for the men and a back alcove for the *malinches.* There, two women, mothers of *malinches,* had spread blankets out on the floor. They sat with the girls while they played jacks. Some girls were lying down on the blankets. It was like a lair, warmed and made comfortable by the two women who were taking care of the children.

In the larger front room the only furnishings were painted wooden benches along the two side walls. The men rested several feet apart on these benches, each one quiet, with head bowed. At first it was difficult to tell whether fatigue or meditation governed their leaning bodies. But when they looked up I saw that the stillness was not owing to lethargy; their eyes were charged with the brightness that comes with long meditation. Though they were without their headpieces, they were still "dancing with the Virgin," and their inward focus was outwardly visible.

After about ten minutes, the men stood, moved about the room, and joked with one another. The transition happened without comment. None of them spoke of their experience; they simply moved on with the night's business.

The *casa de descanso* worked for the group the way the headgear worked for each individual, as a boundary that sequestered a space. Set aside for their sole use, the room protected the men against disturbance from the outside. Like the rules of strictness, decorum, and obedience, the space focused the dancers inward. The boundary was intentional. Mask, resting house, discipline, and rules worked similarly, setting limits to delineate a protected space. The boundaries expedited an inward focus on the Virgin and intensified the sacred work the men were there to do.

The last round of dancing began by 4:00 A.M. When it was over, the dancers had completed five rounds. The small church choir arrived to sing a medley in honor of the Virgin. The *mayordomos,* the few hardy kitchen workers who stayed awake all night, and the priest who was roused from his bed converged at the *casa del pueblo* to hear the singing. After a sleepless night, the slow *mañanitas* and dreamy guitar loosened my mind and muscles, making it difficult to stay awake. But there was one more obligation, to accompany the Virgin's palanquin to the church. The *mayordomos* lifted it from the altar table, and the people took up the votive candles that were placed around the Virgin's altar during the night. Led by the dancers, all filed out the doors and into the predawn dark for *el alba,* the dawn procession.

The way was lit by the candles. We progressed slowly down the street toward the blue lights of the cross on top of the church. Inside, the *mayordomos* placed the Virgin's palanquin amid red roses set up before the red velvet steps of the priests' platform. Father Giles would give a 6:00 rosary, marking the end of the *velorio* and the beginning of the second day of the fiesta.

5
. . . .
Pilgrimage

Before the dawn rosary was over, people began arriving at the *casa del pueblo* to sign up for the pilgrimage. Though not everyone signed up, two to three hundred people climbed Tortugas Mountain every year on December eleventh. Mostly they were locals for whom the annual climb was a tradition and an obligation, like going to mass on Sundays. But relatives, friends, and former locals also flew or drove in from other parts of the country. Many climbed in fulfillment of a *promesa*, like the elderly man who grew up in Las Cruces, lived in California, and returned thirty years later to complete a vow made for him in his youth. Some *danzantes* prolonged their sacrifice to the Virgin by climbing after a sleepless night. They returned home briefly to pick up lunches and change clothes before setting off up the mountain; there would be plenty of time to nap later. Some Tigua dancers, who would gather in the evening for their final rehearsal, prepared by first climbing during the day. Others from the neighborhood Guadalupano and Azteca dance groups climbed before dawn so that they could be back in town for their noon practice.

I did not go on the pilgrimage in 1986. Instead, I stayed up all night with the Danza group and kitchen workers, then went to sleep at 6:00. My feelings about the pilgrimage are still ambivalent. During the rest of the fiesta, the connections I made with people enabled me to overcome my fear and open my sensibilities. I grew to trust the people with whom I worked. Among the large and anonymous crowd of the pilgrimage, however, I did not feel safe. In 1985, when I did climb, I went through the motions, watched and listened, but I was closed to its depth. This disengagement altered my perceptions, and later my writing about the pilgrimage. My voice was more distant.

In 1985 I stayed with the Trujillo family, *mayordomos* that year. Their house was full with family and guests, their married daughter visiting from Albuquerque, a son's friends sleeping on the living room couches and floor. Yet the house still felt spacious. People were careful to sidestep one another. Family members were on the move, running errands back and forth to the *casa de la comida* or gathering pieces of the sons' dance outfits. We worked at the *casa de la comida* through the *velorio*, then took an hour's sleep before the dawn procession. One daughter drove at 3:00 A.M. to the all-night supermarket for frozen fried chicken to microwave for the next day's lunch on the mountaintop.

The family's grace, including me in their rhythm, helped me through a newcomer's bewilderment and the fiesta's sometimes overwhelming intensity. Distracted and grappling with the dynamics of an unfamiliar religious devotion, I have little memory of the morning activities. I compared my lack of discipline with the people's sacrifices and self-inflicted hardships. The willpower that came of their devotion was beyond my own. I wanted to slip off alone to a coffee shop, go back to being an outsider who could come and go as she pleased. Yet I remained, and signed up for the pilgrimage.

At the *casa del pueblo* at 6:00, two corporation women sat at a table at the front of the hall, taking the names, and the one-dollar contributions, of those arriving for the pilgrimage. About ten people sat on the wooden benches, exhausted vigilers who had spent the night with the Virgin and were now waiting to be picked up and taken home. A single police car, with its rotating blue light, waited to escort the pilgrims down the side road of the highway. At 7:00 A.M., in the diffuse light of dawn, the *capitán de la guerra*, the first war captain, called the people together in the empty lot across from the *casa del pueblo*. While the *mayordomos* were in charge of the Virgin, the kitchen, and church-related activities, and the corporation took care of business matters and paperwork, the war captains, under the cacique, ran all the Pueblo ceremonies, the Tigua dance, and the pilgrimage.[1] There were five captains. The *capitán de la guerra* was first captain, the others second to fifth. The *capitán de la guerra* told us that the men and women must now separate into two lines. We were to walk up the mountain in formation.[2]

I see his face now in my mind's eye. He looked at me coolly, saying, "The girl from New York." He was carrying a *vara*, the tall willow branch that symbolized the war captains' power. I did not want to set out. The separation by gender did not disturb me; the more concrete reality of being part of a mass, herded into lines, was far more difficult. I saw, not the kind people of Tortugas, but another march in another time and place, the people separated, men here, women there, on the road to a concentration camp. Tricks the senses play. I froze on the road and let the other pilgrims pass me by.

The specter of those other marchers, people trudging and bent with effort, settles in my back as I write. The Tortugas pilgrims evaporate into those others, and I am among them. They are not the Jewish emigrants, like my grandparents, who traveled by choice out of ghettos and cities, full of ferocious will and purpose, determined to start anew elsewhere. They are travelers I know only in imagination, shamed into submission and ordered into lines. I see them carrying meager sacks of belongings. They have lost the feeling of desire, and so they simply move along, dazed. I feel their confusion and fear in my body, shoulders and neck tightened against stopping, against feeling. I am trying not only to understand why my body rebelled against moving with the pilgrimage but also to bring to light some deeper knowledge of events that happened before I was born. How does it come down to me, this knowledge? Through my mother's body? Through fragments of stories heard and images seen? Through nuances of body language picked up within my childhood community? My body knows what it was like to be blinded by a fear that swallows rage, the desire for resistance turned to self-hate. It is a fear that leaks only meek grumbles of protest having neither clarity nor direction. Perhaps you've seen old women and men who grumble this way, in subjugation. When there is fear, hatred is not far behind. Fear and hate thrive in the unbreathable air of frustration.

There might be those who do not understand my association to the Nazi concentration camps, viewing it as not logical, and my terror as not rational. My associations were not a response to any real threat from the Tortugas war captain, but to an inner wraith of frightening vividness. It was not a vision of death that held the terror, but a vision of compliance and therefore death in life. Fog. Perhaps these buried images were the reason I could not embrace the orderly structure and discipline that gave my Tortugas friends such freedom. I needed to keep a different hard edge, one that protected agency and autonomous judgment. Perhaps this was why I left the crowded *casa del pueblo* at the start of the *velorio*. Large anonymous crowds held the danger of compliance, of getting caught up in the emotional momentum of a mass.

This association of the pilgrimage with concentration camps had been with me from the beginning, from my first visit in 1984. That year I had signed up for the pilgrimage but did not join the crowd leaving from the *casa del pueblo*. I drove away, circling the streets until I found the back road past the university that dropped me at the base of the mountain. From there I climbed the same road as the pilgrims, but apart. I climbed again in 1985, with resistance, and I descended early. My failure as a pilgrim nagged at me for twelve years. Now, a thousand miles away in California, it bursts out like water spewed by the Leviathan, asking to be looked at. I do not want to write about this. Send the monster back down.

But secrets must be brought to light. Wars depend on secrets, Susan Griffin writes in *A Chorus of Stones* (Griffin 1992). Hidden family stories seep through the cracks of decorum and get enacted as the bombs of wars. Were there secret places for the Tortugas people too? One of the men once pulled me aside and for no apparent reason whispered, "Oh, there are many skeletons in the closets." Surely there are: old historical secrets, from the Spanish conquest, the battles for Mexican independence, the international wars over borders. But also more familial secrets of sexuality or violence, most unknown to me, a few not mine to reveal. Were these emergent in the shootings that had increased in the streets of Las Cruces since I left in 1988?

I can tell the story of a young *indio* dancer who was shot and killed in his backyard. He was no more than twenty, the only son of a corporation elder with many girl children who was so proud to have at last fathered a boy. A cheeky boy with a compelling grin, he was teasing his neighbor; it was something about a dog. The neighbor, a grown man, grew enraged, took out a gun, told the boy to dance, and began shooting at his feet. The boy refused. He was shot in the head for it. Was the boy refusing to pollute his Tigua dancing? Was he, like me, not afraid of death so much as loss of choice? Did he choose resistance over fear? So small a resistance, so much to pay.

In 1985, while I was standing in the road, letting the other pilgrims pass me by, a scholar came along, chatting and friendly, unheeding of the injunction to separate into lines of men and women. I hung onto my colleague's words and let them carry me forward until I was in step with the stragglers. Had he not drawn me out, engaging in pleasantly out-of-place academic conversation, I would not have continued. As it was, perhaps I got a small taste of the experience of self-sacrifice. Perhaps it was not easy for the participants to put aside feelings of doubt or fatigue, anger or fear, to respond when called upon. A young woman who married into the community said she went to the priest when she was struggling with doubt. He told her that belief required doubt, that faith was meaningless without struggle. That was a wise priest. Belief and faith cannot be enforced; only acquiescence can. But faith can be nurtured and grown. Not so that one can then join the crowd and follow the leader, but so that one can have a reference point for making choices and a basis for participation.

My friends in Tortugas demonstrated this. The rules and rituals offered a sanctuary of order inside of which self-knowledge and self-discipline could grow. They did not accept blindly. The debates they struggled with around the kitchen table engaged minds as well as hearts. They talked and chose. They knew how to convert restrictions into backbone. But the opposite could also have been possible. What would make the difference between rules that strengthen and rules that subjugate? When would loyalty and responsibility to community usurp moral judgment? When would keeping private thoughts become hiding secrets that fester and turn violent?

Over the first hurdle, I began to enjoy the walk to Tortugas Mountain, called "A" Mountain locally. "A" stood for Aggies, the sports teams of New Mexico State University, once called the New Mexico College of Agriculture and Mechanical Arts. The path to the mountain snaked along a sandy-bottomed arroyo under the highway to El Paso. It crossed an expanse of scrub desert, with sagebrush, juniper, several varieties of spiky yucca, and squat barrel cactus. The action of walking, one foot after the other, over flat ground, with an open vista for the eyes' wandering, was calming and invigorating.

While the walk across the desert generated an easy stride, the climb up the mountain forced a broken pace. Climbing steeply eight hundred feet to the top was a struggle, especially for the elderly and those few who made *promesas* to climb barefoot or in socks. The wide path was a mixture of jagged exposed rock, loose dirt, and small stones (see photograph 7). It took spurts of effort, followed by rest stops, and careful maneuvering among the easily dislodged stones. The year before, in 1984, there had been freezing winds with rain that turned the dirt to muck. People lit smoky fires on the mountaintop and huddled against the concrete-block walls of a ramada to change wet socks. Briefly, I joined a group of workers from the local L'Eggs factory; they were drinking beer and treating the pilgrimage as a picnic. I then crouched against the concrete wall next to a woman who once climbed barefoot when her mother had cancer. The mother got better, and her daughter had made the climb every year since.

In 1985, the eleventh was sunny and brisk. At the foot of the mountain, I met a woman who was convinced she could not make it to the top. Rosala was afraid of being left alone. Her husband had left her, and she was raising their children. She was "cleaning up her life, paying debts, and seeking payments." Her daughter's hiking boots hurt and blistered Rosala's feet, and she hadn't brought enough clothing to keep warm. Her

Photograph 7.   The terrain of Tortugas Mountain.

physical struggle matched my emotional one as we helped each other up
the mountain. We met a group of middle-aged women, strangers to one
another before the pilgrimage, who had joined up to carry one of the car
tires the *capitanes* had distributed at the foot of the mountain. These tires
were to be placed in piles along the path. The captains and their helpers
had already been up and down the mountain, placing similar piles along

two subsidiary trails. Runners descending the mountain after dark would set these piles of tires ablaze, making three strings of light down the mountain. The women passed their tire back and forth to ease the burden, joking about their aches and pains and stopping frequently to rest.

Near the top the rough surface smoothed out and became a road; a last switchback emerged into a relatively flat plateau. Vegetation was sparse, small clumps of scrub hugging small outcrops of rock that jutted out from dry earth. A three-sided ramada made of cement blocks held a pile of stones, a shrine to the Virgin. People placed votive candles upon this miniature mountain. At 11:00, the bishop would give mass here and later in the afternoon, a *velorio*. About fifty yards north of the ramada stood a cement dome, a receiving station for the university. Several four-wheel-drive army trucks were parked between the ramada and the dome, their beds piled with sotol cactus and juniper branches. These would be used in the afternoon for making *quiotes*, the ritual walking staves the pilgrims carried down the mountain.

The *capitanes* had gathered the foliage from Las Uvas, the flat-topped hills northwest of town. Helpers now unloaded the plants on the mountain, separating the long spiky fronds of sotol from their fibrous roots. People would come to the trucks at their leisure to pick up the materials. They trimmed the pointed tops off the sotol fronds, leaving only the spoon-shaped waxy white bases. These they layered and tied, along with the juniper branches, onto a staff, the sotol's long flower stalk. The "string" for tying was made from the cut-off tops of the sotol fronds, pounded out into fibers, separated, and tied together into long lengths. Some people attached small pictures of the Virgin among the juniper, others carved and painted their stalks. The final design depended upon each individual maker (see photograph 10 below).[3]

I wandered across the mountaintop, watching people set up camp. The youngest Trujillo son, Petey, found me and took me to the family's camp. Petey and his two older *danzante* brothers had arrived early and claimed a comfortable hollow formed by an outcrop of rock surrounded with low bushes. It was on the south slope of the mountain, in the sun and sheltered from the wind. The brothers struggled to keep a blaze going with odds and ends of foraged roots and green wood. The elder dancer dozed, and the rest of us tackled the fried chicken, though it was still only 10:00 in the morning. Spread out on the summit, and next to other rock outcrops on the slopes, fires were in progress at similar camps. People would stay on the mountain through the bishop's 11:00 mass and the afternoon activity of making ritual staves. For now they wandered, slept, and ate. Except for a warning against denuding the mountain of its already sparse plant life, there were no restrictions on where people went or what they did. The response to the unbounded space was slow and celebratory.

Las Cruces was spread out below like a miniature diorama. It was possible to trace the path of the pilgrimage backward through the desert, under the highway, and to the red ceremonial buildings of Tortugas, the church steeple visible above them. The city center, with its chunk of office buildings, rose up from the valley to the north. To the east, acres of pecan orchards, in orderly rows, advanced all the way to the Rio Grande. The spikes of the Organ Mountains were close by above us to the west, and in the far southern distance, tracing the path of the river and the road to El Paso, sporadic humps of hills roller-coastered. Contours of land and sky dwarfed the work of humans.

During the preceding and succeeding days, fiesta events were centered in Tortugas village, flowing among the *casa del pueblo,* the *casa de la comida,* and the church. The fiesta spaces were circumscribed, contained within buildings and along the streets between them. Chairs, tables, and pews shaped posture. Street corners and doors determined paths. On December eleventh, however, the ritual bonds solidifying that center loosened; on the mountain time and space became more expansive. Town was a place, the mountain a space. "Place is security, space is freedom," Yi-Fu Tuan writes (Tuan 1977: 3). If place is a "calm center of values" (54), space is the open-endedness of possibility. Leaving the containing walls of *casa del pueblo, casa de la comida,* church, and home, the people set out for a mountain with no buildings, no objects of routine, and none of the habitual movements around those objects that make places familiar.

But even wilderness can be tamed when the orienting values of place are applied to it, the mental landscape transforming the physical (131). Puebloans, for example, conceptualize the world spatially, with the "place of emergence," the *sipapu* or earth navel, at the village center. Concentrically outward to the four directions, there are echoing earth navels in the surrounding hills and, at the farthest boundaries of the Pueblo world, four named mountain peaks. At each orienting point, the *sipapu*, the center, is reproduced. As Alfonso Ortiz notes, "Since all space is sacred and sacred space is inexhaustible, these models of the cosmos can be reproduced endlessly around them" (Ortiz 1972: 142).[4] Men from the Pueblo ritual societies make pilgrimages to the orienting points for prayer, joining center and periphery. Wilderness space is made sacred through its connection to socialized place.

Vestiges of a Pueblo worldview were still apparent in the Tortugas pilgrimage, which was under the authority of the war captains, themselves vestiges of Pueblo warrior societies, traditionally connected as much to healing the disruptions of fighting as to fighting itself. When, years before, at the College of Santa Fe, I staged a script calling for a "war dance," I consulted with a traditional Tewa Puebloan. We do not do war dances, he told me; we do not celebrate the taking of life. Upon setting out and returning, he said, the warriors purify themselves and pray for harmony, acknowledging in gesture giving out and taking in. The war dance was a healing after taking life. It was also a return from the periphery, the outside, to the center, and to order.[5] Like the Pueblo warrior societies, the corporation war captains, as guardians of the pilgrimage, held the responsibility of managing activities at the periphery to protect the center.

Before dawn on the day of the pilgrimage, they met in the *tuh-la*, a small ceremonial chamber off the northeast corner of the *casa del pueblo* behind the altar. Like a northern Pueblo kiva, the *tuh-la* was a ceremonial center, used for preparations, like smoking the drum every three months and rolling corn husk cigarettes for the rabbit hunt in winters when there was one. When the *casa del pueblo* floors were cemented in the late 1940s, only the *tuh-la* was left with a dirt floor. Both the dirt floor and the five-sided construction were considered ritually prescribed. On the morning of the eleventh, the captains built a fire of greasewood there. A man designated as *humero*, or smoke maker, would carry the live coals up the mountain. With them, he started the flameless greasewood fire he was required to maintain all day.[6] Smoke, for the northern Puebloans, though not necessarily for the *indios* in Tortugas, is associated with clouds, cloud-beings, and life-giving moisture. Smoke rising works as a bridge between earthly and cloud worlds.

When the *indios* first came to Las Cruces, no clergy and no masses of people climbed Tortugas Mountain. According to Oppenheimer, only the cacique's council, called in Tortugas *principales* or *abuelos* but unrelated to the *abuelos* of the Danza, made the pilgrimage (Oppenheimer 1957; Tessneer 1973).[7] The *velorio* was held the night before at the house of the cacique in Las Cruces. In the morning, the *abuelos* set out from there, climbing from the northeast rather than the west as they now did (Williams n.d.). On the top, they prayed and set bonfires, *luminarios*. Oppenheimer writes that these represented the Pueblo four directions (1957: 105–6). According to the *Rio Grande Republican* of December 15, 1888, they were made in the shape of the Christian cross. Perhaps both theories are true. Half a century later, the bishop told the Tortugas congregation that the *humero's* smoke was similar to the incense of church, wafting prayers to heaven, making a bridge. Perhaps the fires set to the four directions were also a bridge—between cosmologies as well as between earthly and spiritual realms.

In the early years, the *luminarios* on the mountain were signaled by those in the plaza and on the church of St. Genevieve (*Rio Grande Republican*, December 19, 1885). In the 1920s after the town of Guadalupe was built, the fires were lit before the *casa del pueblo* and the village houses. The lights "guided the virgin to the Pueblo" (*Las Cruces Citizen*, December 11, 1926) and "to the homes of the faithful that she might bestow her blessings on the households" (*Rio Grande Farmer*, December 15, 1927). Although there were no house bonfires in the 1980s, a string of *luminarios* burned before the *casa del pueblo* from late afternoon, and a huge bonfire of yucca greeted the pilgrims upon their return.

According to an Albuquerque journalist, the cacique's council was disbanded, probably in the early 1940s.[8] At about the same time, the period of preparations for United States involvement in the Second World War, relations between the corporation and church began to smooth out, and the number of people doing the climb grew.[9] Did the growing integration of the *indios* into the Las Cruces Catholic community open the fiesta to greater local participation? As Terry Reynolds suggests (1981: 85), did a

spate of magazine articles and a sociological study on Tortugas, all published in the 1930s, draw the state's attention to Tortugas, inviting participation?[10] Did Las Cruces now see in the fiesta a valuable tourist attraction? Perhaps, too, the hardships of the Depression and the Second World
War impelled local Catholics to renew their faith through pilgrimage.
After the war, servicemen did climb in fulfillment of vows, like Moises's,
made to the Virgin during their ordeals. Perhaps, as more local non-
Indians participated, what had been an embarrassing "pagan" custom at
the turn of the century became a source of pride to both city and church.[11]

Increasingly, church-related practices were incorporated into the fiesta.
The corporation instituted a rosary on the mountaintop in 1951, led by
the "members of the procession" (*Las Cruces Sun-News,* December 9,
1951). The new *capilla* was blessed in 1947 (Narvaez 1959). The first mass
was said on the mountain in 1959 (*Las Cruces Sun-News,* December 12,
1958), during the same period that the Danza group stopped the narrative dances and banished the *abuelo.* In 1962 the corporation completed a
permanent ramada on the mountaintop (*Albuquerque Journal,* December 7, 1962). It was scaffolded with lights and speakers for the bishop's
morning mass and afternoon rosary. Priests offered confession in niches
temporarily partitioned off with steel poles and canvas against the back
wall. Though there were vestiges of Pueblo traditions woven through the
pilgrimage, Catholicism was now the major cosmology transforming the
mountain from space to place.

"You'll come back a different person," the bishop told his congregation at a Day of Recollection a month before the fiesta. Bishop Ricardo
Ramirez had been climbing A Mountain since his appointment in 1983.
A native son, he had served in the Philippines before returning home to
become the first bishop of the Las Cruces diocese. He had a grasp of the
vernacular in relation to the spiritual: the pilgrimage "is not like walking
to the Circle K," he said; rather, *"es un camino sagrado,"* a sacred walk.
"We're on the way. We walk. We pray. We meditate about Jesus. We're reminded of things that happened in the Bible." He compared the pilgrimage to the exodus and the way of the cross, both of which led to "something good": a meeting with God.

The bishop encouraged the people to think of the panorama as a vista from heaven. "We can look over the valley and say, 'Boy, Jesus, you sure are good to this valley . . . *algodones y uvas y vino y un río muy bonito*": cotton, grapes, wine, a beautiful river. "We see things the way God sees them, in a way. We think about God, and how he made this world, and how he made it so beautiful." Seeing panoramically was a way to switch focus away from oneself and onto God. "The words I want to use are these, and I hope you won't forget it. A pilgrimage is supposed to be an experience of conversion." He paused and appealed to the people. "What is it?" he asked. "Conversion!" they chimed in. "*¿En español?*" he questioned. "*¡Conversión!*"

In my family, the natural world was an alternative to organized religion. I often hiked, either alone or with friends, and early on discovered that in mountains, deserts, and ocean, I could join "the rhythm of nature's body." This brought me closer to a sense of creation, the numinous. For many of those on the pilgrimage, the situation was reversed; the mountain was sacred because of its association with the church. Elena once told me she came closest to God in church. She mentioned communion, in particular, and that you can't take communion without going to church. I sought to understand this, creating the sensation of taking into my mouth wafer and wine and imagining its transformation, through the priest's sacred words, into the body and blood of Christ. I could step into the experience and feel the transformation, the assimilation of presence into my body. It is immediate and visceral. The action merges with the memory-rich thought of Christ. The thought infuses the action. I could also understand the connection between that transformative experience and the church space. In the intimate but public place that is God's house, He could be experienced personally and directly through communion. In that particular place and through the agency of the priest, God who was outside comes inside as well.

Understanding that the church building and the priest were essential to Elena, I asked her if she ever felt close to God in the mountains or anywhere else besides church. She said she'd never been to the bishop's mass on A Mountain, but perhaps if there were a mass there it might be possible. "Maybe it's the place, the enclosed space," she said, illustrating with a self-enclosing hug; "maybe it's the mass." After pausing, she added, "I guess if I prayed hard enough anywhere else, I could experience God there too." The church as place, God and Jesus as its informing presences, and the mass as its transformative scenario: one could carry this center up the mountain.

The pilgrimage had historical as well as spiritual undertones. Like that other journey centuries before, from the northern Pueblos to El Paso, it reiterated the confrontation between cultures. Now, as then, the outcome was ambiguous, a balance between conversion to Catholicism and retention of Pueblo memories. The historical was expressed in the mythic: the Virgin of Guadalupe embodied both the confrontation and the continuous unfolding of its outcome. The link between Tortugas Mountain and Tepeyac Hill was latent within the pilgrimage.[12] As Rita said, "Having the mountain makes it as if the Virgin is right there, right here." The link was made overt in 1987 when the corporation replaced the papier-mâché Tepeyac that rested on the Virgin's altar. While the old Tepeyac had been crowded with the houses, people, and scrub of the real Tepeyac outside Mexico City, the new Tepeyac was a miniature version of Tortugas Mountain. There was no attempt to show the concrete ramada, the university's dome, or the poles and wires that actually stood on A Mountain, but the representation of bare brown earth, a single outcropping ridge, and three pathways leading to the top was unmistakable. Only the miniature cacti from the old model were kept. Now Juan Diego kneels and sees Our Lady of Guadalupe on Tortugas Mountain.[13] The epiphany takes place locally.

At about 4:00, those who have stayed all day gather for the descent. First, one of the *capitanes* or a helper paints the pilgrims' faces. He dips into a small jar of *almagre,* a local ochre pounded into a paste of pigment, and applies dabs of it with his forefinger. The men get a chevron stripe drawn from the bridge of the nose across their cheeks, the women a dot on each cheek and one on the chin. The women then descend first, down the main trail. The men wait until sunset, then divide up and come down all three trails, lighting the piles of tires dropped off on the way up. According to the corporation's historian, the men's descent is signaled from the *casa del pueblo,* where three bonfires are lit. A *capitán* on the mountaintop responds, lighting a large bonfire. Seeing this, another *capitán,* waiting with the women at the foot of the mountain, lights a third fire. This signals the men to descend. When all have gathered at the foot of the mountain, they begin the walk back to the *casa del pueblo* (Beckett and Corbett 1990: 10–11). The pilgrims arrive after dark, carrying their *quiotes* back into the center.

I only know about the descent from others' reports. I have not yet stayed on the mountain long enough to come down with the pilgrims. In 1985, when the bishop began the 11:00 mass, an hour late because of problems with the speaker-system wiring, I slipped away and descended the mountain alone. I could not put aside the sense of isolation I felt among the pilgrims. Later, at the Trujillos' home, I woke screaming from a nightmare. I did not climb again until the 1990s. Then I joined my old friend, the Las Cruces playwright Denise Chávez, along with her husband, her sister from Santa Fe, and a local botanist. In spite of the pleasure I took in their company, discussing flora, poetry, books, writing, mutual acquaintances, and in spite of the bishop's encouragement, the pilgrimage remained an ambivalent event for me.

"OK. What happens on our way up there?" the bishop asked at the Day of Recollection. "We go together with other people . . . and that's very important, we go as a community . . . we experience brotherhood and sisterhood. How do you think the bishop survives up there? They stuff him. . . . We experience community, people sharing. This is what's supposed to happen on a pilgrimage." But the pilgrimage community was different from the one shaped in the kitchen by long acquaintance. It lacked the social accountability that comes with lengthier relationships. Although pilgrimage has been viewed as a mass event in which individuality is absorbed, it may be just the opposite.[14] As Linda Lehrhaupt points out, pilgrimage is "primarily valued for the opportunity it gives pilgrims to perform personal experience" (Lehrhaupt 1990: 38). The commitment reverberates between oneself and God, rather than among a community. There were few lasting obligations to other climbers, in spite of the "spirit of sharing" acclaimed by the bishop. The largeness of the crowd enabled anonymity and secrecy. People crossed paths but didn't really travel together. For the deep communal connections tempered over time, one had to go to the *casa de la comida.*

I left the mountain just past noon and arrived in Tortugas village close to 3:00. The Chichemeca Azteca group of about forty dancers, mostly teenagers, gathered in front of the house of the group's leader, Leo Pacheco Sr. His father had brought the dance from Chihuahua, Mexico, in the 1920s, and it had been incorporated into the fiesta.[15] Leo Sr. was training his son to take over the group. On the twelfth, the Aztecas participated in the fiesta mass, danced in the plaza beside the church, and joined the corporation's final procession, but otherwise, their fiesta activities took place in the Pachecos' home. The family held a *velorio* for the dancers, gave a reception after mass on the twelfth, and hosted a dinner as well.

Theirs was a *matachín* dance, but quicker, lighter, and with more complex footwork than the Danza. There were narrative dances and masked clowns, called *payasos,* whom the corporation would not allow in the final procession. When I came upon the Aztecas in the street, they were setting out in procession to the church, carrying their own altar and image of Our Lady of Guadalupe. Accompanied by drum and violin, the procession wound through the streets to the plaza adjacent to the church courtyard. Only the Danza and Indio groups, sponsored by the corporation, danced in the main church plaza. The Chichemeca Azteca procession crossed paths with the Guadalupanos Aztecas, also on their way to the church. The Guadalupanos would practice and later perform in the plaza behind the church. The dances and outfits of the two groups were similar; the Guadalupanos, in yellow, were an offshoot of the Aztecas, in red. Both groups wore elaborate feathered headdresses (see photograph 8). I did not get to know the Azteca groups or dances as I did the corporation's; there were small clues that my presence would not have been welcomed. I watched and appreciated from a distance, and walked on to the *casa de la comida.*

For the corporation and kitchen workers who did not climb, the sunlight hours of the eleventh were a time for rest and preparation for the evening's work. At 4:00 or 5:00 in the afternoon they regathered in the *casa de la comida* to roll *albondigas,* the tiny meatballs served at the feast on December twelfth. Lorenzo's wife, Magdalena, supervised the spicing of the ground beef; there was enough to fill three large washtubs. It was Magdalena's job to powder the three washtubs with her secret proportion of spices: cumin, salt, garlic powder, and the onions we had chopped

Photograph 8.   Guadalupanos Aztecas (photo by Miguel Gandert).

the day before. Six people, two to a tub, plunged their hands elbow deep into the meat, pushing and pounding it. The rest of us would then roll out the thousands of tiny meatballs.

We sat at the long dining room tables, about thirty people. A worker set down mixing bowls full of the meat, one bowl for one or two people. On each table was a pile of cafeteria trays for holding the finished meatballs and a roll of paper towels for cleaning the sticky stuff off our hands. Pick a glob of meat from the bowl. Roll it between your palms. All around, the same meatball-rolling gesture was repeated thirtyfold, flat hands circling as if making mud pies (see photograph 9). As each tray filled, a worker snatched it up and took it to the empty row of tables, where the filled trays accumulated like the repeating steps of the Danza. In town versus mountain, aesthetic orderliness prevailed. Gradually, the trays covered the tables from one end of the dining room to the other.

To one side of me sat the cacique's sister, Isabel Cruz. Slight, but by no means fragile, she wore her long salt-and-pepper hair tied up in a bun,

Photograph 9.   Rolling meatballs, December 11, 1986.

accentuating her chiseled features. She was an engaging performer who moved easily from flirtatious charm to camaraderie to indignation. She was never bland. While she worked, Isabel chirped about the guacamole she made for the priests and how to pickle the onions that were her guacamole's secret ingredient (vinegar diluted with water). Isabel's meatballs were perfect, uniformly one inch in diameter. They slowly accumulated in perfect rows on her cafeteria tray. My own meatballs were not so neat. I could not seem to get them small enough or round enough. They lined up like unruly children.

Isabel and Magdalena were sisters-in-law: Isabel was the cacique's sister, Magdalena his wife. They were physical opposites. Magdalena was tall and ample; a walking cane accentuated her dignity. She had soft features and wore magnifying glasses and a net kerchief that held her salt-and-pepper curls in place. "Magdalena of the spices," I called her. When the last bowls were empty, she took her place in the men's kitchen, on a folding chair in front of the giant three-legged cooking pot. Her back straight, large frame elegant in a navy polka-dot dress, left hand grasping the head of her walking cane, right hand poised over the pot with a soup spoon, Magdalena directed the men where to drop the meatballs by the trayful into the pot. I have on videotape a record of Magdalena's ritual, shot by her godchild, Raul and Elena's daughter Lisa. With teasing love, Lisa questioned the older woman about her technique—"Nina, how much garlic?"—while Magdalena reached over the lip of the giant pot with the tiny kitchen spoon to stir the broth. The warming and tickling aroma, as the spices blended in cooking, anticipated the next day's feast.

Rita Sandoval led me outside several times to see if the three lines of fires on the mountain were lit yet. If so, that would tell us that the *capitanes* had reached the base of the mountain. It would then take about two hours for the returning pilgrims to progress over the desert path, under the highway, and down the highway's side road to the *casa del pueblo*. Other workers coming outside to check on the fires wondered which of the *capitanes* was coming down which mountain path. Someone insisted there were judges and an unofficial competition for the best line of fires. By 6:00 there were three complete lines of light on the mountain, only vaguely resembling the shape of a cross.

At 7:30, before the men had finished dumping the meatballs into Magdalena's stew, the corporation historian motioned that it was time to go to the *casa del pueblo* for the pilgrims' return. Time to take off the apron, sort through the coats and sweaters in the kitchen cabinet, and pile on scarves and gloves. Time to leave the kitchen for the outdoor ritual of return.

A row of four small bonfires was already lit at the edge of the empty lot across from the *casa del pueblo*. Several groups of teenage boys warmed themselves there. At the opposite end of the lot nearest the highway lay a pile of dried yucca seven feet high and just as wide. One of the men would set it ablaze as soon as the blue light of the pilgrims' police car escort was spotted. The pilgrims would arrive along the highway from the southeast. I stood with the men, who waited to light the bonfire. They joked about the day when it would be done with the push of a button. We stared at the dance of moving car lights on the nearby highway, watching for the police car escort. Someone spotted it, and a man moved quickly to light the mountain of yucca. We backed off from the sudden flare and heat.

In the light of the blaze, the returning *capitanes* shepherded the pilgrims into the lot. The only sounds were the fire popping and the pilgrims' clothing rustling as they walked, a line of men to the south, a line of women to the north. The lines joined in a circle around the fire, about fifty people in all. In hooded sweatshirts, concealing scarves or ski caps, faces illuminated by the sporadic darting of flames, the pilgrims seemed incorporeal. Their *quiotes* were outlined by the firelight, long staves crowned with the white sotol fronds. Some people had added a crosspiece to their staves so that they appeared to be giant crosses.

The *capitán de la guerra* delivered a short speech of thanks. Then the pilgrims broke the circle, separating again into men's and women's flanks. In front of them, forming a line across the flanks, were the war captains and Pueblo singers, carrying the drum (see photograph 10). Most visible among them was a wiry elder dressed in white jacket, pants, and hat, wearing dark glasses and carrying a *vara*. He was Juan Escalante, the man who had taught his daughter how to offer a guest a drink of water properly. Along with Lorenzo Serna, Juan was the most knowledgeable carrier of the Pueblo songs. And like the unofficial tradition of Magdalena spicing the *albondigas*, it had become a tradition for Juan to lead the march of the pilgrims to the doors of the *casa del pueblo*.

There was a pause. Out of the silence, a single voice chanted three even notes, then a high falsetto call descending to a single bass tone:

Ya ya ya! He-e-e ha!
Ya ya ya! He-e-e ha!
Ya ya ya! He-e-e ha!

The men took up the Pueblo song. In full and deep voices, and with sure strides, they advanced the twenty yards toward the doors of the *casa del pueblo*, the pilgrims in two flanks behind them.

Sound and movement stopped a few feet before the doors. Juan walked forward alone. Raising his *vara*, he rammed its butt against the metal door three times. Silence. He stepped back. The *capitanes* and singers took up the song again, the two lines of pilgrims filing outward to the back of the lot. Their faces were visible as they passed the fire, smeared with mountain mud and dotted with red ochre. The lines ap-

Photograph 10.   The singers advance to the doors of the *casa del pueblo,*
December 11, 1986.

proached the doors again. Again the elder rammed on it. Again silence.
Again the song, the war captains and singers leading the pilgrims to the
back of the lot for a third advance:

Ya ya ya! He-e-e ha!
Ya ya ya! He-e-e ha!
Ya ya ya! He-e-e ha!

This time the knock at the doors produced a response. A muffled voice
from within answered:

" ¿A quién buscas?" (For whom do you seek?)
"A la madre de Dios, que vive aquí." (For the mother of God, who lives here.)

One elder translated the sequence as:

"What art thou looking for?"
"My mother the Virgin. I left her here this morning."

She explained, "Before they went up A Mountain they left her there, but in the meantime the other people took her to the sanctuary. So then they let them in, and that's it for the day" (Williams n.d.).

The doors of the *casa del pueblo* opened from the inside. Electric light spilled out, showing the pilgrims to be simply tired people. Some dispersed immediately, heading for their cars. Others came inside and tossed their *quiotes* onto a pile. Onlookers gathered up the *quiotes* to take home as mementos. The pilgrimage was over.

For me, the return had an opposite effect from the going. It was the pleasure of the outdoor darkness certainly, the silent appearance of faces and *quiotes* lit by fire, the sound of drum and Pueblo vocables, the first time they were heard in the fiesta. Perhaps, too, as with the *danzantes*, I was moved by the sacrifice people had made. But the ritual of return was not like the rebounding and ribboned joyous entrance of the Danza into the Virgin's church. It evoked a different sensory world. The chant had echoes of the kiva, a more underground space. Unlike the violin's shrill bouncing sound, the Pueblo group's voices were low and throaty, the drum insistent and reverberating. The song called up another my father used to sing, a slow marching song, "The Peat-Bog Soldiers" (see Boni 1947: 212). It was a song of resistance, a declaration by the concentration camp prisoners. Where the mass of people starting the climb brought up fear, their return brought up the possibility of heroism, strength in union, strength in the service of a good cause. This was where my sentimentality resided; these were the lessons of my childhood.

In answer to my questions, no one talked about the meaning of the pilgrims' return except Bishop Ramirez, who explained the three approaches to the door as symbolic of Juan Diego's three visits to Bishop Zumaraga. But the return must also have held the memory of the cacique's council, the *abuelos*. When the *capitanes* led the people in song, it was as if the *abuelo* council had also come down from the mountain. I imagined men who knew one another well, sprinkling cornmeal in the *tuh-la*, gathering brush together in Las Uvas, the small group carrying coals up the mountain, muscles pushing, humming the Pueblo songs as Raul did now while he worked, then sitting on the top of the mountain, around the fire. All this took hours. Did the council too make the *quiotes* as pilgrims did now? What did they talk about? The past? The future? I associated their journey with the hunting trips some of the men still took together in the fall—men buddies. Feeling the stretch of climbing, in council at the top, seeing the spread of valley below, yet taking seriously the work of making sacred. Enduring the hours. Then returning to the center, bringing together the extremity of wilderness, its revivifying energy, with the security of the center.[16]

We know that during their descent, the *abuelos* proceeded from the bonfire at the foot of the mountain to another at a home in Las Cruces. They were met there by the first captain and the cacique, led to the cacique's home, and welcomed with ceremony and song. Was it the same welcome of thanks and the same song now sung before the doors of the *casa del pueblo?* They filed in the dark to St. Genevieve's nearby for a rosary. Who led it? Surely not a priest in those days of conflict with the church. Was it the cacique, like Lorenzo leading the prayers at the monthly rosary in the *capilla?* The council would return to the cacique's home for supper, prepared by the *mayordomos.* And then at one in the morning, they began the *ensayo real,* the last and "royal" practice of Los Indios, the Pueblo, or Tigua, dance group.

The ceremony of return was a ritual of reintegration, bringing those who had journeyed to the spatial wilderness back into connection with hearth, food, and the unifying rhythms of dance. It was a ritual of return and reintegration for me as well, for the pilgrimage had sent me to my own wilderness. Because I remained out of touch with the events on the mountain, my memories of it are thin. I have had to rely on other scholars' accounts to lead me back. Once the *capitanes* sang everyone back into step, I, too, could reengage.

As the pilgrims scattered, I returned to the *casa de la comida*, where the workers were cleaning up after rolling *albondigas.* They welcomed the *capitanes* with warming whiskey and jokes. Patting one captain on his bottom, a woman remarked on the lack of padding in that part of his anatomy. Someone else said they would have to raise money to get him fake buttocks. The bishop, also just down from the mountain, ate red chile stew with the cacique in the new kitchen. Watching the bishop and cacique bent over their food, eating together in silence, I thought that in spite of the bishop's more prominent public position, the two religious leaders regarded each other with mutual respect. I understood the people's love for a bishop who could at one moment don vestments and perform the high rites of Catholicism and in the next climb the mountain and sit in his ski cap at the oilcloth-covered table in the kitchen. Perhaps he, too, appreciated a return to the backstage hearth where the fiesta's spirit was fueled, the intimate space of the kitchen.

6

. . . .

Granddaughter of Mama Luz

Particularly striking in the light of the bonfires at the pilgrims' return was a dark-eyed young man with straight hair and a bandanna tied round his forehead, wearing strands of turquoise jewelry. After the singing, he joined a group of women who also wore turquoise jewelry and long-fringed dance shawls of the type worn by Pueblo women in the north. None of the other men or women dressed in this style. Among the group were a white-haired elderly woman, several of her middle-aged daughters, and two granddaughters carrying their babies. The family was familiar to me from previous years' Pueblo singing and dancing events, but since they were not corporation members and did not join the work at the *casa de la comida,* we had not met.

I was drawn to the dancing of one of the daughters, a woman of about fifty who wore a red fringed shawl. She resembled her mother, short, full-bodied, and strong, with neatly cropped curly brown hair and a dance style that was at once fluid and contained, in the style of women's dancing in the north. I was struck by her and her sisters' forthright bearing, their straight backs and open chests. The red-shawled woman had an observant gaze and a ready laugh. I slowly came to know Mireya Ruiz, her mother Maria, three of her sisters, her children and grandchildren, and many of her nieces and nephews.

As my memory of the kitchen is warmed by Elena, so my appreciation for the Indio dance is shot through with the colored threads of my times with Mireya. The day we made animals for her nativity scene. The day we drove to Isleta in the north to see Grandpa Chiwiwi. Mireya's "children's day" party, when the grandchildren played the drum and danced, demonstrating what she had taught them. The afternoon when she drummed along with my videotape of an Indio rehearsal and taught me how to dance: "Why move your head like a pigeon? Just your arms and legs." Valentine's Day, when she and her sister Sonia brought me a homemade heart-shaped pincushion. I see Mireya's daughter, with strong arms and long blond hair, dancing with the Tiguas, dancing with force, like her mother. I see Mireya's mother, Maria, the matriarch, sitting with her hands folded in her lap, watching the grandchildren dance, and Mireya's sister Sonia laughing when I wore my grandmother's mink hat to the rabbit hunt. And Mireya's gentle husband, Tony, kneeling over the plants in his garden with tender care. Too many images and hours to unravel in words that must follow one another one at a time over the page. Mireya was my turning point. She showed me a perspective on the Pueblo traditions that was different from the corporation's, and this new perspective changed the way I saw the fiesta.

After two years of watching each other at the fiesta, we agreed to meet. I drove to Mireya's house on Tortugas Drive and parked next to a small but exuberant cactus garden outside a chain-link fence. In an area of smoothed dirt within the fence, a big blue American pickup was parked. An inner adobe wall with a wooden gate separated the parking area from the courtyard. Inside the wall, the spacious courtyard was laid out in bricks in a circular pattern, the house on two sides, a tall wooden fence and the adobe wall on the two others. On both house and fence walls were ears of corn, prayer feathers, hanging plants, niches holding Pueblo pots, and several tall *quiotes,* their overlapping layers of white sotol fronds perfectly symmetrical.

Mireya greeted me at the living room door and led me through the kitchen into her sewing room. It was a denlike space with a wood-burning stove, a large sewing table, a couch, a desk, and shelves filled with both homemade and purchased Pueblo pottery, drums, and other treasured pieces. Fabric pieces were laid out on the table next to Mireya's sewing machine. She was making a dance shirt of calico trimmed with ribbon for Tony. Later, she told me that once someone from Ysleta del Sur in Texas asked her to make him a dance shirt. She put dangles made of bone, bead, and feather on the front and back of the shirt and one on each shoulder. They liked it so much at Ysleta that the next year everyone was wearing these shirts. We joked about it, how future anthropologists would write that the dangles proved the Ysletans were derived from the such-and-such tribe. They were really just part of Mireya's sewing style.

Looking at the old photographs on her walls, we plunged into talk about her family's history. According to the old-timers, Mireya said, the Isleta Puebloans were taken prisoner by the Spanish after the Pueblo Revolt and brought down the river to El Paso del Norte. The Spaniards built them an island, but it wasn't really an island, Mireya explained. The word *isleta* in Tiwa, or in the Spanish spelling, *ysleta,* means "island": an island of their own. Later, the people were freed, but they had lost their language. They missed their home and wanted to return. When the chief decided to leave for the north, Mireya's grandmother went with him, and her grandfather followed. They came to Las Cruces to work on the railroad and never got any further. This grandmother was Mama Luz, or "La Luz," and Mireya had been told she was half Tigua and half Apache. Luz married Faustino Pedraza, a Piro Indian. They came to Las Cruces with a group from Ysleta del Sur that included Juan Escalante's family.

Scholarly accounts corroborated Mireya's family history. A report submitted by anthropologist Terry R. Reynolds to the Native American Rights Commission (Reynolds 1981) affirmed that Mama Luz, or Maria Luz Duran, was born at Ysleta del Sur in 1869. She was the daughter of José Maria Duran, governor of Ysleta del Sur in 1882. Her husband, Faustino

Pedraza, was the grandson of José Pedraza of Senecú del Sur (43–46 and appendix B). When Senecú del Sur was abandoned, the Piros went to live with their Tigua neighbors at Ysleta del Sur. The dates Reynolds reports for the migration of the Ysleta del Sur group to Las Cruces coincided with the building of the railroad, completed in the late 1880s, just as Mireya had said. Mireya's awareness of her grandparents' tribal affiliation was unusual. Both local hearsay and the mass media called all the *indios* of Las Cruces "Tigua," regardless of whether their families had once lived in Ysleta del Sur, the Piro villages, or the Manso neighborhood of the Guadalupe church.

Mireya's grandmother Luz, her mother Maria, and Maria's brother, "Uncle Pete," passed on "the Indian ways" to Mireya and her sisters. There was a social dance they used to do at home with the *olla*. Mireya's mother used to get up on the roof and play this drum to call the neighbors, who would hear it and come to dance. The daughters still made *ollas*, and Mireya played them for her family, but "now when the neighbors hear it, they look out their windows and complain about the noisy Indians."

As her mother had done before her, Mireya introduced her husband to the Indian way of doing things. When Tony asked Mireya to marry him, she told him, "This is who we are and what we believe. We believe in feathers, especially eagle feathers, prayer feathers, and in corn." Tony agreed to join her in these rituals of belief. Once, when he was out throwing cornmeal to the plants, someone came along and asked him what he was doing. He told them he was fertilizing. "There are things people wouldn't understand," Mireya said.

She told this story with laughter, but she was right. Mireya's ways were enigmatic to most members of the corporation. She was criticized for not attending church regularly and for not supporting the church with donations of money. People complained about her and her sisters because they joined in the Pueblo singing and dancing but not in kitchen work. They were called "phony Indians" who only wanted to do "arts and crafts." I can hear Mireya laughing at the jibes. Laughter was her chosen way to side-step criticism. Rather than give up her ways or hide them, she chose to participate without joining the corporation. The distance made it possible for her to keep her autonomy. I see the irony in this. The cor-

Photograph 11.   Mama Luz. (Photo courtesy of Fermina Paz.)

poration, too, chose to keep its autonomy, indeed, prided itself on autonomy from the federal government.

Looking at a portrait of Mama Luz (see photograph 11), I could see
where Mireya found her resolve. "There is only one full-blooded Indian
around," Mireya said, "and that is my mother." La Luz was a large woman,

and, in the picture, she stands firmly, directly facing the camera. She wears a long embroidered skirt and a blouse with two rows of jingly metal cones sewn across the front. Perhaps this was the outfit she wore for the *olla* dance. Her belly pushes out against the buttons of the blouse, separating the fabric between the buttons. The bandanna she tied around her forehead holds her long straight hair in place. Her arms and hands are fleshy and strong, her right hand on her hip, her left relaxed and hanging down. Her chin is lifted. The picture made me want to laugh, not with derision but triumph. Hard work without sorrow shows in the muscles of her body. She resembles my grandmother in the schoolroom picture, determination in black eyes. But Mama Luz didn't smile, and her composure was surer. My grandmother's smile, and the way she leaned forward, her elbow on the desk, was a bit coy, as if she was not sure she could get by without cajoling. I could see in Mama Luz where Mireya had learned the refusal to be intimidated.

We stood before the shelf where Mireya kept her handmade drums. "The Indian ways aren't forgotten. I still have my drum, and I still know the meaning of corn," she said. I remembered the fiesta's final procession, when the people accompanied the Virgin's altar through the streets. Other people bowed their heads, and many had tears in their eyes, but Mireya's head was lifted, and she seemed to be singing toward the mountains. I mentioned this to her, and she said, yes, when she sang, it was not to the Virgin Mary but to the sky and the mountains. "The Indian people didn't know anything about God. They didn't worship anything. They only knew nature and talked with it, with the trees and the mountains."

This connection with nature was expressed in the way objects were made. Scrutinizing the costumes in a 1924 photograph of the Tigua dance, we talked about the meaning of the colored ribbons the women wore attached to their headbands. Mireya said that her mother taught her that each ribbon had a special meaning, assigned when the headband was made. The colors could signify earth, sky, sun, the seasons. One color might be assigned to stand for the personal happiness of the dancer or someone else in the family. Mireya didn't know how they got the ribbons here in Tortugas, since the women didn't wear them in the north, but I understood that the process of making them echoed Pueblo principles.

Until I talked with Mireya, I had seen the Indio dance and other Pueblo fragments as signposts of a historical past whose meanings no longer referred to Pueblo cosmology. Mireya offered a different possibility. For her and her family, the dance still referred to people's relationship with mountains, clouds, earth, corn. The making of colored ribbons forged a link between the maker, the object made, and the object or idea to which each ribbon referred. It was an act of prayer.

On Valentine's Day, when she and her sister Sonia brought the pincushion heart, I asked Mireya if she thought of herself as religious. Her immediate answer was no. Jay asked her, "Do you think of yourself as spiritual?"

"Oh, yes," she answered firmly.

Wanting to know more about what she meant, I asked, "When do you feel spiritual?"

"I feel spiritual in the morning." She went out and faced toward the sun every morning.

"Do you do the same thing every day?"

"No. I am thinking different things inside." She experienced spirituality privately, rather than in church. "If God is in church, then he's in my home. I can pray anywhere. It doesn't need to be in the church or going through the rituals."

Like many of the adults of her generation, Mireya went to a convent school, the Mesilla Park Convent. She didn't begin school until she was thirteen, when her father was threatened with imprisonment if the children didn't go. They put her in a class with the first-graders. She stayed for a while but hated it so much she finally said she wouldn't go anymore. "I got burned," she said.

By contrast with her Catholic education, Mireya talked about the education she got from Mama Luz. Her grandmother made them sleep outdoors once a week, "to get used to it." Luz would wake them up early, when the sun was rising, to watch the mountains. In one season, the rising sun would create the effect of columns in the mountains. "We used to sit, just sit there, and watch the columns appear and *jacal* houses, Indian houses.[1] When I tell people about this, they think I'm crazy." On the way to school, Mireya dawdled so she would miss the bus, walking backward and watching the *jacales* appear. One day she whispered to her teacher, "I want you to look at that place just at that time in the morning to see if you see what I see." The next day she wanted to go to school. "Yes," the teacher said, "I saw exactly what you told me I'd see." Her teacher's statement made the young girl feel very good. Mireya remembered it for forty years, a small incident, but one that spoke loudly about her sense of difference.

Perhaps Mireya and I were both outsiders. But Mireya was tough and full of humor, and I, like my grandmother, was more eager to please. I wanted to belong, to be welcomed in the warm kitchen and included in the talk. I wanted to feel the embrace of the community. I wanted my friends in the corporation to accept our differences. Perhaps the people found it easier to accept someone from far away, of a different religion and culture, than to accept one among them who did not conform. I wanted them to understand Mireya's "Indian ways." They were families I had grown to love and who called me *mi hija*. It saddened me that people spoke disparagingly about Mireya's family and their "arts and crafts." Was I that innocent? The people who had embraced me listened to my crusading and scolding, then joked with me about it later on.

The difference between Mireya's family and the others in the parish of Our Lady of Guadalupe was not entirely clear-cut. Although she stood by her Indian beliefs, Mireya was also a part of the community. She did not claim the kind of Catholic devotion others expressed, but her beliefs and actions did overlap with those of her neighbors. Rita, too, had told me she could find God everywhere. I once encouraged Mireya to talk about Our Lady of Guadalupe from her point of view. After demurring and saying that I'd better talk to someone religious like Isabel, she told me, "Our Lady of Guadalupe is the mother of God, but not just Jesus Christ; she is the mother of whichever God." When I asked if the Virgin was the same as the Pueblo Corn Mother or Aphrodite, she said she was. I once asked the bishop the same thing. His sense of humor was as playful as Mireya's: "Well, the anthropologists think so." So did Mireya. "They are all the same," she said, "just as God is all the same."

I then asked her if God might be part male and part female, as Father Elizondo from San Antonio suggested in a talk in Las Cruces (Elizondo

1987). "No," Mireya said. "God is male. The mother of God is not the same as God." Like her neighbors, Mireya recognized both Jesus and the mother of God, and she accepted a gender distinction, perhaps even inequality, in their roles. What she rejected was the exclusivity of Catholicism, its narrow application of the concepts "God" and "mother of God" to Jesus and the Virgin Mary.

I learned, too, when we sat next to each other in church, that Mireya joined in the service. She knew the sequence of sitting, kneeling, and standing. She chanted the prayers in her strong voice, unabashed. I saw her participation as an acknowledgment that she belonged to the community, even if she valued her autonomy and did not believe what others believed.[2] Perhaps the distance she kept worked better than the intimacy I cultivated. I would eventually leave, asserting my autonomy more jarringly. Mireya was able to balance engagement with distance.

Once, as we were driving south on I-25 after a visit with Grandpa Chiwiwi, a Tiwa relative of hers who lived at Isleta Pueblo in the north, Mireya asked, after a long while of driving in silence, "Do you sometimes feel very Jewish?"

"Yes," I said, "very connected to my ancestors."

"I sometimes feel very Indian," she said. "I guess that's why I have to go up into the mountains."

Mireya identified her feeling of Indianness in relation to a place, the mountains. By contrast, Elena also emphasized the importance of place to her feeling of spirituality, but Elena came closest to God through communion, in church. I tried to put Elena's experience next to Mireya's. For Elena, the bishop's mass, and maybe even her own prayers, could symbolically transform the mountaintop into a kind of church, a "house" where God could be present. For Mireya, the mountain was sacred in and of itself, simply because it was a mountain, part of an inclusive numinous presence. It didn't need a mass to sanctify it.

The difference is palpable to me, a matter of sensory apprehension and the meanings to which sensations refer. I visit my one friend in memory and find connection in an enclosing church, seeking there the vision of Christ and mother, saints and their stories, kneeling before the vision to join it, hearing the liturgy and smelling the incense, and then expanding the bounty of God-at-home to God-on-the-mountaintop, translating the mountain's mundaneness into the extraordinary. I visit my other friend in memory and watch a cloud cover the sun over a mountaintop or a tree branch moved by wind, and feel these changes as the dance of a creator spirit, its breath moving with her own. I imagine her acknowledging, celebrating, and imitating the coordination sensed everywhere, hearing it in the pulse of a drum, in whose expansion and contraction there would also be room for the vision of Christ and his mother, who is the same as Corn Mother. The different sensory truths that different people carry are the secrets of connection, some of which I could not make on the pilgrimage. Mireya's secrets were closer to the secrets my bird-watching father taught me.

Mireya's humor tempered differences and demonstrated for me the clarity with which she saw herself. On our drive south from Isleta, Mireya told me she had gotten some "coyote powder" from a mushroom. She rubbed it onto her grandsons' legs, telling them how the Indians used this powder to help the men run faster. That day seven-year-old Gregorio came home from school and boasted that he had won a race. That was a few weeks ago, Mireya said. Then, a few days ago, while they were on their way to K-Mart, he came to her all serious. "Big mother, please tell me which half of me is Indian and which half is cowboy." Mireya asked him why he wanted to know. He wanted to wear a cowboy hat, he said. "Well, you'll have to be cowboy from the waist up," she concluded. Gregorio remembered the coyote powder. "Oh, that's why I won the race," he said, putting the pieces together. Mireya laughed at the story. It was probably her grandson's innocence and seriousness that made her laugh, but beyond that, I thought Mireya could have been making a joke about herself. She, too, was half Indian and half cowboy. She was committed to the "Indian ways," and joked about the "holy rollies," but she was also a realist and part of a community that believed deeply in the religion the Spanish missionaries had brought.

She and her sister Sonia laughed at my pretensions, too. On Valentine's Day, they swept through my front door, exuberant with their gifts. Mireya presented the red pincushion heart, circled in lace and hung with beaded ribbons. Sonia brought a Valentine's card with a picture of me. Taken at the recent rabbit hunt, she had just handed me four dead rabbits that she bagged and hung from her belt. I had killed none and spent most of the day with Mireya's grandson, Jorge, avoiding the chase. In the photograph, I am wearing jeans, an orange chamois shirt, and my grandmother's warm mink cap. I am poised with one foot pointed forward and gingerly holding out Sonia's rabbits. When her daughters saw the picture, Sonia said, they imitated me, prancing around like fashion models. We all had a huge laugh over that picture. Then we talked about the *abuelos* who were omitted from the Danza. The sisters regretted the omission, for they understood that in the northern Pueblos, clowns were sacred. Alfonso Ortiz writes, "Much of what the Pueblos are and are not, as well as how they perceive alien groups, can be deduced from the dramatic performances of clowns" (1972:155).[3] Mireya and Sonia knew the clowns did not represent evil but the irrepressibility of life and the ability to laugh at oneself. There had to be laughter and a nod to the rambunctious nature of creation.

Mireya laughed to duck the biting remarks and scoldings. Calling her pottery "arts and crafts," others did not see the connections the craftings forged, did not know that the ribbons on the headbands made a bridge. They did not know that connections were made when hands shaped clay or that to sprinkle cornmeal on the plants was a way to talk with the Mother. "My good Corn Mother," I secretly called Mireya. Butterfly, eagle, bear, wolf, cloud, mountain, evergreen, corn: the filaments of connection held her. But like her neighbors, and unlike me with my antiauthoritarian bias, she also valued strictness and discipline. Mireya knew she shouldn't be singing with the men during the processions. Years ago the women did not sing with the men, she said. I asked her what she would do if they told her to get out. "Sure I'll get out," she said, "because that would mean they knew we weren't supposed to be there." She would be glad, because that was the way you were supposed to do it.

Raul and Elena regretted the new leniency of the Vatican, but Mireya missed the strictness of the old Indian ways and regretted the growing influence of the Church. Because of the Church, she said, "the animals and plants are gone." Isabel Cruz, the cacique's sister, also took pride in her Indian heritage, but she was glad the animals and plants were gone. Talking about the Spanish conquest, Isabel said, "Something good came of that, because the missionaries came and Christianized us. Before that we believed in animals and gods and things" (Williams n.d.). Isabel distinguished herself and the corporation from those she called the *paganisto* Indians. Once, in the kitchen, she pulled me aside. She was upset at having the Pueblo Indians associated with the Indians of Mexico. "Dede, you're an educated person. You know these dancers are not Aztecs. The Aztecs danced naked with just a cloth." She pointed her delicate fingers toward her female parts. The decorous distance between her pointing and what she pointed at made the gesture all the more suggestive.

It was both shocking and wonderful to me, the lewdness of her gesture, her indignation and disgust, her expressive hands that would not touch the part she found so indecorous. In Isabel's typology, dancing naked and believing in "animals and gods and things" characterized the pagan Indians, but not the Tortugas Indians, who converted, by choice, to Christianity. Isabel's mother told her, "Never be ashamed of being an Indian. Be proud that you're an Indian. . . . You're native born. You're the real Americans" (Williams n.d.). But, unlike Mireya, she also embraced Catholicism and felt at home within the church.

Differences in response to the Church went back a long way. It was as if, three hundred years after their arrival at the Pueblos, the missionaries were still present, separating out those who "thank God the missionaries came and Christianized us" from those who regret the loss of the animals and plants and "still know the meaning of corn." At the time of the Pueblo Revolt, as now, some people went with the priests by choice, and others went by force, some converted because they wanted to, some did not convert at all, and, as in the northern Pueblos, most walked a middle path, "compartmentalizing" Pueblo ways and Catholic ways.[4] When a Tewa Pueblo potter gave a lecture for the Indian students at my university, she drew a butterfly with one wing representing the Pueblo way, the other wing the mainstream American. This traditional potter went to the priests to take care of the mainstream wing, when there were problems of money, education, and law, but to spread the traditional wing and to seek answers to the deeper questions, she went to the cacique and other Pueblo religious leaders. Balance was in the center of the butterfly's body, which represented the breath of life. There were many different butterflies in Tortugas, many responses to conversion. Is a community ever monolithic?

Differences in belief were also differences in the telling of history. Isabel's family, like Mireya's, came from El Paso del Norte, but from the Manso and Piro mission of Our Lady of Guadalupe (Reynolds 1981). Disdaining the pagan religions, which she associated with Mexico, Isabel told the story of her Pueblo forebears as if they had not lived in El Paso del Norte. In an interview aired on BBC radio, she told how the Tiguas came from northern New Mexico in the early 1800s, leaving because of drought, following the Rio Grande south. In Isabel's telling, they separated into three groups, one stopping at Isleta Pueblo near Albuquerque, another arriving in Texas, and the third, "the farmers of the tribe," seeking work in Las Cruces and the Mesilla Valley. Her own ancestors, she said, were among the farmers who started the Las Cruces community in honor of Our Lady of Guadalupe (Williams n.d.).

Isabel's brother, the cacique, gave another history. Lorenzo explained that after the Pueblo Revolt, the Spanish set up the Guadalupe mission near Juarez and another mission in Mexico where the Isletans went. The Isletans, who honored Saint Anthony, "found" Our Lady of Guadalupe in Mexico. Lorenzo understood that his sister told the story differently because she did not allow that her ancestors lived in Mexico. Isabel received an award from the Doña Ana Historical Society for her contributions to local history. Since her remembrances were popularized on the radio and in print, her account spread locally. It became the accepted version, repeated even by some corporation members.[5]

For Mireya, Isabel, and Lorenzo, the Pueblo traditions were part of a family biography, but for almost everyone else, they were part of the corporation's biography. Most corporation members did not claim Indian descent at all. For them, being an *indio* was a voluntary, not a biological, association.[6] The word signified commitment to an adopted community. And membership in the corporation was inseparable from devotion to the Virgin. As Raul said when I asked him what the Tigua dance meant to him, "Religion. It's all religion."

"Is the dance the same as the rest of the fiesta?" I asked. "The singing has no special Indian significance?"

"No," he said. "It's all the same. All for religion."

For him, the Indio dance and the other Pueblo ceremonials were equivalent to attending mass, preparing food in the *casa de la comida,* or making the pilgrimage up Tortugas Mountain.

Though I did not hear it talked about directly, I understood that ethnicity, in a broader sense than particular tribal histories, was important. It was inherent in the "ancestry" of the Virgin herself. Its importance, as shared language, appeared in Rita's joke about God speaking Spanish. And Mireya told me that before we knew each other, after the day that I danced at a rehearsal of the Indio dance, she and her sisters asked one another who that *huera,* that blondie, was and why she was dancing. Still, at our first visit she said she invited me over because she wanted me to know the "truth," about *indio* history and ways, I assumed. There were objections from at least one family member, who did not think she should be talking to a non-Indian. Like her mother, Mireya was not intimidated. Like the truth she wanted me to know, Mireya was complex. She recognized that she was a contemporary American woman who talked to outsiders like me. Months later, when I was feeling overwhelmed by the number of truths there were to tell, and questioning my right to tell them, Mireya dismissed my concerns, saying I had to, that it was my work. She was sure the truth I told would be the real one.

7

. . . .

El Ensayo Real

On the evening of December 11, after the pilgrims had tossed their *quiotes* into the *casa del pueblo,* and while the kitchen workers were still dumping meatballs into the cooking pot at the *casa de la comida,* the dancers gathered for the *ensayo real,* the final practice of the Indio dance, also called the Pueblo or Tigua dance. Though sponsored by the same community, it was unlike the Danza. Referring to the corporation's origins in a Pueblo past, the Indio dance came first in the fiesta. The Indios sat in the front pews, before the other dance groups, during high mass on the twelfth; they danced first in the church courtyard after mass; and they led the day's processions. But the dance did not have the same connotations of conversion as the Danza did. There was no meditative immersion for the Indios that corresponded to the Danzantes' endurance during the all-night *velorio.* Nor did the Indios have a resting house where they could be isolated as the Danzantes were. Perhaps, like the pilgrimage, the Tigua dance pulled in two directions, Pueblo and Catholic.

For both Indio and Danza groups, dancers signed up at the November corporation meeting. Although boys weren't accepted as *danzantes* until they were ready "to make a sacrifice to the *virgen*," they could dance with the Indios as soon as they had taken first communion. Some were no older than seven. For the women, the situation was reversed. Girls who had reached their first menses were too old to be *malinches*, but they could dance with the Indios through their adulthood. A combination of grown men and young girls danced with the Danza; older women and young men and boys danced with the Tiguas, twelve men and twelve women in all. Women were a strong presence, both in the fiesta and at practices. Their influence lent Tigua rehearsals a familial ambiance.

Two corporation women, on a break from rolling meatballs, sat in the second row of benches, talking to each other. Several *malinches* and their friends whispered and giggled on the benches opposite. A few dancers came directly from the pilgrimage, and when the doors of the *casa del pueblo* opened, they collapsed onto the benches inside, disheveled from the day's march. Other dancers who did not climb, or who had returned early, arrived rested and freshened. The war captains, in charge of the Indio dance as well as the pilgrimage, met with the other singers behind the closed door of the *tuh-la* to practice the Pueblo songs. Members of the dancers' families arrived, some bringing their babies. Mireya's family was there, but we had not yet met. I greeted Isabel, there to encourage her ten-year-old grandson who was dancing. She asked me to sit with her.

As we talked, the singing in the *tuh-la* stopped. Then silence. Juan Escalante, who knocked on the doors of the *casa del pueblo* upon the pilgrims' return, came out alone. He carried the *tumbé*, a Pueblo drum painted red, with a yellow star and a border of semicircles drawn on its playing surface. The cacique, who would otherwise have led the singing with Juan, had arrived earlier and left. I learned later Lorenzo was on his way to the hospital for exploratory surgery for stomach cancer.

These two elders, Juan Escalante and Lorenzo Serna, were the unofficial keepers of the Pueblo songs. Between the two men, a continuing debate took place about the correct way to sing them. Juan Escalante's parents came from Ysleta del Sur, Lorenzo's from the neighborhood of the El Paso Guadalupe mission. In the two hundred years between the settlement of the mission communities and the migration to Las Cruces, differences among the particular villages' songs, dances, and even languages blurred. Singers and dancers from all the villages performed together at each other's feast days (Bartlett 1965:148–49; Kohlberg 1973: 29; Lange and Riley 1970: 164).[1] Whatever differences once distinguished Manso, Piro, and Tigua song traditions were insignificant enough by the beginning of the twentieth century for Lorenzo's and Juan's families to share a single repertory. But there were still disparities in the fine points of rhythm and meter, pronunciation, and melody. These were the source of friendly competition between the two elderly men.

Sitting alone on the single bench at the front of the hall, beneath a small portrait of Our Lady of Guadalupe, Juan began to drum an introduction, a long series of throbs calling the people's attention. The dancers stood in silence, men and women lined up and facing one another across the hall, men to the north, women to the south. Emilio Gamboa, *capitán de la guerra* for the year, led the other men out of the *tuh-la*. Of the same generation as Juan, Emilio was the shyest of the elders. Juan was lean and wiry in body, sharp-edged and stern in temperament. Emilio was shorter and broader, soft-spoken and absentminded. His day-old growth of white bristles matched the disarray of his close-cropped white hair. His belly pushed open the buttons of his flannel shirt. It was Emilio's son who would be shot by a neighbor for refusing to dance. This year, his son still danced with the Tiguas.

In his left hand and cradled against his chest, Emilio carried the war captain's *varas*, seven-foot branches broken off a willow bush—tradition said they must not be cut with a knife. The *varas* were thin and flexible with the drying leaves still on them. The four *capitanes* lined up without ceremony to Emilio's right, in front of the women dancers. The women were respectful, their feet politely together, hands clasped in front of them, echoing the posture of the *capitanes*. The second captain, head bowed, stepped up to Emilio. Emilio separated out one of the *varas* and without force, almost lackadaisically, whipped the man's legs.

I saw the whipping as if it were in slow motion. Lifting the *vara* high in his right hand, Emilio brought it down against the captain's left ankle, then immediately up again and down to the other side. The swish of dry willow leaves broke the silence in the hall. As he whipped, Emilio mumbled an inaudible phrase in Spanish. The captain looked straight ahead. There was a perfunctory quality to the ritual action and, aside from an easy seriousness and concentration, no show of emotion. Emilio repeated the ceremony with each of the other *capitanes.*

Afterward, Isabel whispered, "He's saying, 'So that you respect the staff and they—the dancers—respect you.'" Mireya later translated his words as, "This is the switch, so you can make order. Have respect and make respect, and God will help you."[2] The ritual whipping took only an instant and was not treated with any special attention. It was a gesture, like a priest's blessing, that was taken for granted in the flow of events. To me looking on, however, it enacted the same voluntary humility captured in the kneeling figure of Juan Diego. The whipping enacted a moment of submission to the higher authority of God, immediately followed by taking on power in the worldly community: first humble yourself before God and then receive power among men. I think now of Lorenzo's "first lesson" in local Catholicism: the angel told Mary she would bear the son of God, and Mary said, "So be it." As a result of her faith and her submission to divine will, God could not say no to her; she grew in power.

The kabbalah also includes a story about the power of a mother's love. I heard it from Rabbi David Cooper on Rosh Hashanah, the Jewish New Year. That year, Rosh Hashanah fell on the sabbath when work is not allowed, and so the ram's horn could not be blown. Instead Rabbi Cooper told this story. The patriarch Abraham was about to sacrifice his son Isaac. Sarah, Abraham's wife and Isaac's mother, saw in her mind's eye what was about to happen. She screamed with such fullness that the sound reached deep into time, back beyond the moment when the irreversible tablets of history were written. Sarah's scream came out of love, and it changed the course of history. It saved Isaac. This, the rabbi said, was the power of a prayer.

Sarah's act was different from the Virgin's. It was not an act of submission, but of resistance. She asserted herself against the will of God. Considered more deeply, her challenge was only to the God of history;

her appeal was to the nameless one beyond history. She aligned with the very principle of creation: love. In this sense, Sarah's power was like the Virgin's. The love of both mothers could penetrate the holiest of holies. It could make a difference. In moving into harmony with creation, Sarah became a creator of history. As with Mary, God could not say no to her.

I write these words knowing that the names represent for me not so much a father God and a virgin saint but the possibility of a universe in which all actions, thoughts, and intentions have effects. Like Mireya, I travel between the names for understandings that have no names. Faith depends on knowledge of the connectedness of all actions. Once this connection is felt, it brings the responsibility to act responsibly, which is to serve, whether what you serve is called God, the kabbalistic *ain sof*, or the harmonious workings of nature.

My first lesson in service came in 1984, during my introduction to the fiesta. Crowds of people stood outside the *casa de la comida* on the twelfth, waiting to be fed. I was helping out in the kitchen, then left briefly to watch the dancing at the church. When I came back, I approached the back door, but was barred by a man I did not know. He must have thought I was trying to sneak in for lunch. "But I'm here to serve," I said. Grace Serna, who led the prayers at the *velorio*, laughed behind him. "You've figured out the password," she said. "You can come in." I forgot about the incident, not registering its significance. When she later asked me, "Now what was it again?" I did not know to what she was referring. "I'm here to serve," she reminded me. Do I get it now after ten years? "So be it. I'm here to serve." The phrase represents an ideal attitude. It says in words what the statue of Juan Diego reveals in his upturned head and curled toes: giving oneself over, one receives power.

The whippers' willow branch began as a device for instilling respect and ended as a sign of the *capitanes'* spiritual authority. Submitting to the order the *varas* represented, the *capitanes* became the arm of that order. They carried their *varas* throughout the fiesta, signaling their obedience to God and their acceptance of responsibility and authority in the community.

Where did this whipping come from? What were its historical antecedents? I never heard it talked about. At Ysleta del Sur's feast day in El Paso on June 13, there was also a whipping, but it was the parishioners who were whipped, perhaps as part of the fulfillment of a *promesa*. Dressed in their Sunday best at 8:00 in the morning, they lined up before the church steps, where the cacique and war captains stood. One at a time, the people either took the steps on their knees or simply knelt down on the top step. Using similar willow *varas*, at least two of the captains whipped each kneeling person across the back.

At first I guessed that the tradition of whipping arrived with the Franciscan fathers, whose use of the whip among the Pueblos is well documented (see, for example, Sando 1992: 61; Simmons 1979: 181–84; Gutiérrez 1991: 81). The Yaquis, who invited conversion by the Franciscans, also include whipping in their Easter ceremonies. But there are Pueblo whippers who may predate the Spanish. These are the supernatural *tsave yoh* who appear at the San Juan Turtle Dance at the winter solstice, coming down from their homes in the labyrinthine caves of the sacred hills surrounding the Pueblo. Though masked, they are not kachina, nor are they sacred clowns. Rather, they are associated with the war captains, and their work is protective of the Pueblo, morally purifying and socially disciplinary. They, too, ritually whip the legs of the dancers at practice. At the public dances, they whip all who have not fulfilled their duties, including the duty to dance (Ortiz 1969).[3]

My thoughts travel to the Tortugas cacique's council and to the *abuelos*, forerunners of the war captains, and I wonder if the ritual whipping that opened the rehearsal of the Pueblo dance was a remnant of these *abuelos'* work. I think, too, of the *abuelos* who once carried whips among the Tortugas Danzantes.

Whatever the antecedents, the ritual whipping established the proper order of the universe, and the *ensayo* could begin. The second captain, in charge of the male dancers, chose the first pair by presenting two boys with their dance paraphernalia: the *guaje,* a gourd rattle painted red and hung with feathers, and the *arco,* a bow also painted red, with eagle down feathers attached at one tip. Isabel told me emphatically that this was not a warrior's bow but a hunting bow, because the Puebloans were peaceful people. She wanted me to know that the corporation's seal of bow and arrow also expressed peacefulness: the arrow lay within the bow, parallel to the bowstring rather than in shooting position. The third captain, in charge of the female dancers, chose two women in the same way, giving each feathered arrows. These were held at their midpoints, the tips blunted and facing down.

The captains took their places at the four corners of the dance space, like guardian sentinels, *varas* planted before them. Juan Escalante handed the drumstick to Raul Sandoval to lead the first round of songs. Four singers crowded around the drum. Two young men held it by its rawhide handles as Raul drummed. Any man who knew the songs well enough could drum, but that night only Raul and Juan led the singing, choosing the songs, establishing the tempo, and setting the pitch. Raul, chin lifted, his face mobile and open, gave himself to the singing. His arms hung at his sides, his shoulders riding up and down with the beat. His voice led the other men. This was no longer the shy and teasing Raul I worked with on the roof of the *casa de la comida,* nor the quietly thoughtful man with head bowed in church. He was a man immersed in work he clearly loved. Raul once told me that if he were Puebloan, he would be researching the Pueblo traditions all the time. Perhaps, coming from northern Mexico, he did not want to offend those whose ancestors came from the Pueblos by claiming their traditions as his own. But his love for the music was clear. He was transformed by it.

Pueblo music, to the ears of a stranger, sounds like an earth-rumbling chanting. A chorus of men's voices weaves thrumming vocables around a drum baseline, clearly pulsed in the accented duple meter of a heartbeat. The sung melody, moving in pyramidal steps up and down, is guided by the percussion but is more rhythmically complex and has independent patterns that veer off from the drum beat.[4] The drum announces momentary rhythmic changes in the form of pauses or triplets. To someone unfamiliar with the songs, the changes come by surprise and keep the music unpredictable. Dancers at the northern Pueblos, often one hundred or more moving together, are expected to keep time with the changes and to stop on the last note. In Tortugas, however, staying in step with the pauses and triplets wasn't essential.

Although the Tortugas songs resembled other Rio Grande Pueblo feast-day songs—some were identical in rhythm and melody to songs still sung at Isleta Pueblo—the way they were performed was different. The tempo was faster, the volume was louder, and the energy was more forceful and less contained than in the north. There was not the range of vocal dynamics, no changes in register, panted sections, or low growls. What the Tortugas men lacked in variety and subtlety they made up for in enthusiasm and intensity. The men, and Raul in particular, attacked the music with fervor.

At first, I was confused by the Indio dance, for its aesthetic did not match my experience of northern Pueblo dancing. I am looking now at a watercolor from the north, J. D. Roybal's *Rio Grande Pueblo Green Corn Dance* (Bahti 1970: 31–32). I observe faces that are all the same, *mantas,* sashes, rattles, and *tablitas* all the same. Each man has his knee lifted to the same height. The bodies are represented as being in perfect unison. The painting is both an idealized and a jocular portrait, but it makes its point: the dance depends on repetition and unity. The watercolor takes me to the Santo Domingo corn dances on August 4, the largest of the northern feast-day celebrations. The corn and harvest dances of the Rio Grande Pueblos follow a structural pattern. Two or more dance groups alternate, performing in a circuit of the Pueblo's plazas throughout the feast day. Each dance has a slow and a fast section.[5] In two long lines, each male followed by one or more females within the lines, the dancers enter the plaza in a basic foot-lifting step that the Tewa call *antegeh:* a shift of weight from one foot to the other, with bent knees, and with the accent on the fall of the right foot.

Men and women perform the step differently. The women inch forward or sideways with their feet barely lifting, brushing over the ground lightly. There is a lilt to their moves, a slight bounce that passes upward and out to the evergreen branches they carry. With their arms bent at the elbow, upper arms held close in to their sides, they alternately lift and dip the branches before them. Gliding without changing level, the women give the impression of continuity, without beginning or end.

The men are more forceful, lifting their knees higher and bringing their feet down vigorously on each step. Their footfalls have more kinetic energy and rebound. Where the women make a smooth and caressing passage over the earth, the men gain a bounding momentum from it that keeps them bobbing up and down as they advance. Leaning slightly forward, beating a light rhythm with the gourd rattles they hold, they seem to be running through the mountains.

The drum provides a reference point in the north, emerging and fading through the day, leaving an echo of its organizing pulse. As it leads, neither rushing nor losing vibrancy, it organizes my body's sense of time. Its expanding and contracting pulse focuses and steadies thought and perception. "Riding the drum," as one Pueblo friend characterizes Pueblo dancing, opens my senses so that the most panoramic and yet minutely detailed impressions are drawn together and woven around its pulse: mountain and cloud shapes, the smell of sun on the dry earth's skin, brushes of wind, the steady progression of dancers entering the plaza, the red, green, black, and white pattern of their sashes and the movement of their fringes, the sound of seeds, like rain, in gourd rattles, and the sound of bare feet or soft-bottomed moccasins shuffling over packed earth.

Robert Coles, who recorded the drawings and stories of children from different cultural communities, discovered that Pueblo children learned to "see" by metaphorically bringing themselves close to what they looked at.[6] They were taught to notice in an empathic and participatory way, to capture a sight while at the same time giving themselves to it. There was "a continuing willingness, passionate at that, to invest the mind's imagination in the world around it" and "to consider its rhythms and demands of the highest consequence" (Coles 1977: 520–21). Nothing was to be taken for granted. One girl told Coles that her parents scolded her for leaving the sun out of a drawing of the family's house, the sun to whom, her father kept repeating, "we owe our lives" (401). She was also scolded by her mother for digging up the earth and making holes in it without bothering to "fix up" what she did to the land (403). Rather than regarding the sun or earth as objects or facts, they were to be perceived as subjects.

Once, in a parking lot in Santa Fe, a Pueblo friend, an elder, showed me the step for the Eagle Dance. He bent at the knees, curved slightly forward in his spine, spreading his arms out in an echoing curve to the sides, and began stepping in a circle in the traditional *antegeh,* sinking and lifting his outstretched arms. He told me to imitate him. I could feel myself losing balance, not enough to stumble but enough to disturb my focus. He noticed and told me I had to see the eagle and let its flight fill me. I let the image of an eagle in flight ease down from my mind's eye into my back and arms, torso and legs, loosening my knees and lightening my feet. I tried the step again, focusing not on the technical imitation of his moves, which I already understood, but on the image, translated into kinesthetic sensation. Now I did not lose my balance.

I did not learn to learn this way. In public school, I was taught to distance myself from what I was trying to understand in order to see it clearly. Thinking from a Pueblo perspective, this sounds curious. But the feeling sense, proprioception, was separated from the visual, and discouraged as a way of knowing.[7] Only in extracurricular activities, the plays rehearsed after school and the Saturday dance classes, was interpenetration of seeing and feeling valued. The arts, based in bodily ways of knowing, were marginal in school. As Elizabeth Grosz (1994: 5–10) argues, from Plato onward, bodies have been regarded with suspicion in the Western polis and academy. So have artists. What a shame. How much insight we miss. Even the European stage art of dance, with its emphasis on spatial designs and spectacle, presented in a darkened proscenium theater, encourages a distanced and primarily visual attention. The stage context works against the softening of visual perception, the heightening of kinesthetic empathy, and the crossover between sensory modalities that my Pueblo friend was teaching.

These were the sensibilities and the memories of Pueblo dance I brought to the Tortugas Indio dance. Seeing only young men and boys dancing, I missed the elder men that lent the northern dancing weight. The Tortugas boys chewed gum, and many dancers wore warm jackets and sweaters over their outfits, never seen in the north. Did the Indios, unlike the Danzantes, lack seriousness? Where were the long lines of dancers filling the plaza, moving in unity? The Indio dance was performed by only two or four couples at a time, in a style that was clipped rather than liquid. It did not match my expectations. At my first *ensayo*, I overheard a woman remarking on a particularly good dancer. In my eyes, the young woman's moves were stiff and angular, far from the "continuity without beginning or end" I looked for from the women. The Tortugas men's singing emphasized force rather than the northerners' subtlety of dynamic range.

While Tortugas women wore the same *mantas,* the black sheaths attached over one shoulder, as women in the north, the colored ribbons streaming from their headbands, like the *danzantes'* ribbons, were unique to Tortugas. The males wore outfits of tan cloth decorated with red fringe, in the style of Plains' buckskins. The only plant or animal life in evidence was a single feather attached to the headbands of both men and women. The women carried arrows with blunted tips, the men bows and gourd rattles.[8] There were no evergreens, corn, or animal skins. References to the natural environment were missing. These details, in the north, had meaning. Did their absence in Tortugas suggest that new meanings were emerging there? I wanted to follow the Tortugas trajectory, understand its significance, and feel its effect.

Knowing my interest, some women prodded me to try dancing. This was soon after I moved to Las Cruces. I was ignorant of the protocols, that one had to be baptized and in good standing with the church to dance, when I approached one of the war captains at the *ensayo.*

"Do you still need dancers?" I asked.

"Do you want to dance?" he responded.

"Yes, I'd love to." They already had twelve women, he said, but some were absent, and I could fill in.

"What shall I do?" I asked him. "You'll have to tell me when to get up." I was suddenly nervous.

"I'll let you know," he said. He was smiling.

I sat with Isabel and watched carefully. There were two dance sections, as in the north. In the first and slower section, consisting of two songs, the two couples faced each other, each woman standing behind her partner (see photograph 12).[9] Keeping the distance between the couples constant, they circled in the foot-lifting step. At the same time, they zigzagged around the rim of the circle, taking a few steps sideways left, then right, as they advanced (figure 4). I asked Isabel if there was a pattern to these zigzags. She answered, "You just face the way the man faces, but when you're at the front, don't turn your back on the Virgin." This dance, too, had Our Lady of Guadalupe as its focus.

The men jogged, lifting their knees high and bouncing soundlessly on

Photograph 12.   An Indio dancer follows her male partner, December 12, 1987.

each step, covering little ground. Elbows jutting, *guajes* and *arcos* held before them, they shook their gourd rattles in time with the drum. The women inched in tiny and precise flat-footed steps or simply shuffled. They tucked their elbows in and held their arrows firmly forward, alternating them up and down sharply with the drumbeat, reminding me of

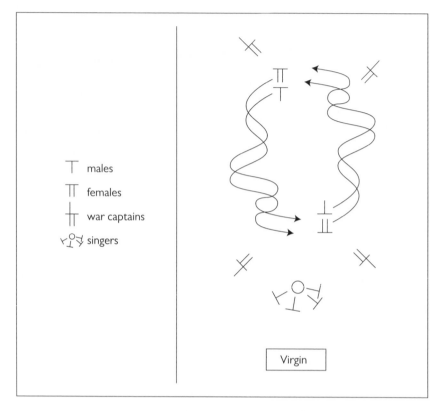

Figure 4. Choreographic pattern for the Indio dance. In this figure, front is toward the singers who stand beneath the Virgin's portrait during practice in the *casa del pueblo.* On December 12, in front of the church, the dancers face the Virgin within, and the singers stand behind rather than in front of the dancers.

the neat chopping and mincing of the kitchen. Next to me, Isabel gestured along with the women; she encouraged me to do the same. I followed her lead and alternated my imaginary arrows up and down, trying to anticipate the moments in the music when the drum interrupted the duple beat with a pause or triplet.

In the second and faster section, the women stood next to rather than behind their partners (see photograph 13). The couples faced each other

Photograph 13.   An Indio dancer stands next to her male partner,
December 12, 1987.

Photograph 14.   The men shake their rattles in the bridge section of the group dance, December 12, 1985. The *danzantes* wait for their turn to dance.

across the hall, east to west.[10] Using the double-bounce step characteristic of the north, they approached and backed up for as many times as the music allowed. In the Tortugas version of the touch-step, the men took an extra bounce before stepping down, some adding a small kick that spiced the sharpness of their dancing. Perhaps because of their youth, the Tortugas men danced with less rebound from the earth, less force than the northern men did. The women did the touch-step with a quick tap to the ground or to the other ankle before stepping down. Instead of alternating their arrows as in the first section, they moved both hands up and down together, with an extra punctuating bounce at the endpoints. Their step was small and energetic, the effect more stimulating than mesmerizing.

After the advance and retreat, a drumroll cued the dancers in a bridge section. The male dancers reached out to the right in a lunge, shaking their *guajes,* while the women waited beside them (photograph 14 shows the bridge section in the group version of the dance). The men took a few steps to the left and repeated the lunge and shake, with the women following to stand beside them. Then the couples walked counterclockwise, from their east-west positions to north-south ones. When the drummer stopped the roll and returned to the syncopated double beat, the dancers started the forward-and-back pattern again. The sequence was repeated to each of the four directions.[11]

After three sets of couples had danced, the second *capitán* motioned to me with his chin: "Do you want to dance?"

"Yes," I nodded, uncomfortable because Isabel had told me that she too wanted to dance.

The captain handed me the two arrows. I got up, squeezing out from behind the first row of benches, and took my place behind an eight-year-old boy. Raul, who was again leading the singers, began the introductory beats for the first song.

This was nothing like the lesson in the parking lot in Santa Fe. I was surrounded by the drumbeat, immersed in a dance that picked me up and carried me. As when I knelt before the Virgin, my observing and commenting mind became separated, as if it were observing the rest of me from outside a glass bubble. I became aware of my body's effort to get the step right, to coordinate my arms with my feet and both with the rule of the drum. Its beat was shockingly clear, piercing my bubble and instructing me. I heard Raul directly addressing me through the drum, leading me, and I felt blessed by his kindness. I was aware of the overall decorum of my body and its containment, revisiting the humility to which I was unaccustomed. Was this what the disciplined boundaries of religious ritual produced? Here, as when kneeling before the Virgin, I was enacting prescribed movements, and both times a sense of lucid doubling occurred, and the feeling of humbleness. I was especially aware of the downward glance of my eyes.

I saw the feet of the woman in the other couple, and I followed them. In the first circling section, I passed by the captains in their four corners, the sweet support of one, the judgmental gaze of another. His glance penetrated my weakly constituted decorum. Though I followed after the feet of the other woman, I have no memory of who she was. Looking down, I sensed, rather than saw, my small partner's presence and was grateful for it. During the bridge section's long drumroll, I followed him side to side and waited when he lunged to shake his rattle. At that moment of waiting, I crossed my arrows over my chest as the other woman did and suddenly saw myself in that position, as an *indio* woman, a still image of a self-contained woman. I shook off the sight, the fantasy discomfiting me: I was wary of projection.

Then it was over. My face was hot, probably red, less from exertion than from the conviction that I had made a terrible botch of the dance. I berated myself for having missed the subtle changes in rhythm and, most embarrassing, for not having been able, in the touch-step, to coordinate hands and feet. I slunk back into the second row next to Isabel. Her comment was unexpected. "You shouldn't dance like a man. Keep your feet firmly on the ground." My feet were coming off the ground? I had not intended them to, having seen that the women didn't lift their feet. In my nervousness, they must have taken off on their own.

"But you got the rhythm very well," Isabel assured me with cheerfulness. "You'll get it!"

After one more round of dancing, the second *capitán* again gestured to me to get up. Now we would all dance together, the twelve men in a line on the south side facing the twelve women on the north. This final group dance followed the same pattern as the couple dances. For the slow section, we circled counterclockwise, zigzagging in the basic foot-lifting step. For the fast section, we reformed into separate men's and women's lines and danced toward and away from each other, using the touch-step. Here was the kind of solidarity I had seen in the north, but so engrossed was I in doing the step correctly that I hardly noticed the group carrying me through.

Immediately, the dance lines disintegrated, and people seemed to be leaving. I turned to the woman next to me, one of Mireya's sisters. "Is that all?" I asked. "Is it over?" She laughed at my astonishment. "Yes," she said simply, moving away to get her coat. Raul approached and, standing at my side, showed me the step, imitating the small precise moves of the women, keeping his feet close to the ground. "You were dancing too much," he said, echoing Isabel's criticism. I thanked him. Then he too left me to assess my own dancing. I felt least successful about rhythmically

synchronizing with the drum, but Isabel thought I had done well with
that. Instead, she and Raul criticized my dancing on a point of form: I had
danced too enthusiastically, like a man.

"Let's pretend," Mireya later said, after the fiesta was over and we
were getting to know each other. We sat in my living room, watching a
videotape of a Tigua rehearsal. She got up to dance. "Follow your dancer
and face the way your dancer does," she instructed, taking the man's role
and indicating for me to get behind her. I followed her in a circle around
my living room, both of us zigzagging to the music of the videotape. She
watched what I was doing and corrected my style. The arrows shouldn't
cross in front, but move straight up and down. "Get your hands out." I
held them too close in to my chest. One woman we watched on videotape
moved her head back and forth, "like a pigeon." There should be no large
movement in the body, but a slight bounce. And my step was "too big,"
a confirmation of Raul and Isabel's criticism. I was stepping out to the
side, like the men. The women's feet should stay close together.

In the north, the distinction between men's and women's dancing was
aesthetically significant. "[Women] should dance with more restraint
than men, never lifting their knees as high as a man. In dance categories
they follow a style one notch more subdued than the men" (Kurath and
Garcia 1970: 35). Gender aesthetics, the references to nature, and the struc-
tured formality of dancing all served the same end: the renewal of life
or, as the Puebloans put it, "to seek, to find, and to regain life" (Sweet
1985: 1; Laski 1959). Gender difference, sexuality, and the generation of
life formed a progression. The difference between men's and women's
dancing was aesthetically basic because it was cosmologically basic.[12]

Though the Tortugas Indio dance echoed the Pueblo emphasis on gender difference, for most people it no longer sustained the references to
corn and rain or renewing life. The cosmological web that unified dancers
in the north had been transformed here by Catholicism. Isabel once told
me, "The tom-tom is the voice of the Pueblo. It is almost as important as
the Virgin." *Almost.* What a large word, meaning "not quite," meaning
"the Virgin is more important than the drum." I saw this in Isabel's dancing when she was at last called on at a practice. In her high-heeled boots

and a neatly ironed blouse worn outside sweat pants, she clipped her way around the dance circle in neat zigzags. Her chin tilted up, she wore the small confident smile of one who knew how well she was dancing. As Isabel approached the Virgin's portrait, she turned first one way, then the other, before deliberately facing the Virgin head on, as if with a final, utter giving of herself. "Never turn your back on the Virgin," she had said. She did not.

There was ambiguity about whether the Tigua dancers faced the Catholic Virgin or the Pueblo four directions. The New Mexico anthropologist Sylvia Rodríguez suggests looking at the dancers' shoes. Though the subject of her discussion is New Mexican *matachines,* perhaps Rodríguez's idea is relevant. In Pueblo *matachines,* the dancers wear soft-soled moccasins, in Hispano *matachines,* shoes with heels. Shoes are the dancers' connection to the ground, both as earth and as *begründen,* ideological ground. In Tortugas, Isabel, an elder, wore high-heeled boots. Photos from the 1920s show all the women wearing heeled shoes. Was it because, at that time, the *indio* community faced discrimination, and so people sought conformity? But many of the younger women were now wearing Pueblo moccasins. Were they more concerned with resisting assimilation and asserting *indio* identity? There were also young women who still preferred heeled shoes. What would Rodríguez have to say about a dance involving both kinds of shoes? The dance veered two ways. The signs were exuberantly and uncooperatively messy.[13]

The problem of reference was epitomized in the Indio songs. Isabel whispered to me during one *ensayo* that the words "heya, heya" really meant *ella, ella,* "for her, for her," the Virgin. Most people assumed the language of the songs was Tiwa, but Tiwa people at Isleta in the north could not understand the Tortugas words. They joked that the words must be Apache. No one in Tortugas spoke any Native American language, and no one could translate the song texts. Mireya told me that Juan Escalante once knew the meaning of the songs, and that they were of the war-dance type, appealing for peace between the Pueblos. One song, she said, mentioned the Laguna and Jemez Pueblos and had words like, "Let's all surrender our weapons and be one family." Only one song, sung at the New Year, had Spanish words. It was "Santa María" and referred to the Virgin.[14]

No one has formulated a hermeneutics connecting the Indio dance to the Virgin's narrative, as Rico had done for the Danza. Nor did the Indio dancers talk about dancing in the same way as the *danzantes* did. Instead, they debated the fine points of technique. Should the men hold their *guajes* above or below their *arcos*? Should they be in a lunge or a squat when shaking their rattles in the bridge section? Did the men's touch-step have a small kick emphasizing the doubled pulse of the drum? "That may be the way they do it up north," one woman, a Pueblo descendant, argued, "but it's not the way we do it here." On a visit to Ysleta del Sur's feast day in El Paso, a Tortugas man commented that the dancing was "too sloppy." The Ysleta music, steps, choreography, and dance outfits were almost identical to their Tortugas counterparts, but the dancing was more fluid in style.

At that moment I understood that the neat Tortugas aesthetic was intentional, a matter of pride, and not an uninspired version of the northern dances, as I had at first imagined. The dancers had to be controlled, neither too stiff nor too loose. When one new woman dancer allowed her hips to undulate with each step, and her shoulders to shift back and forth, Isabel remarked that her dancing was "too sexy." Mireya criticized women for being jerky when they moved like automated wind-up dolls. It was more difficult than it looked to keep up with the drum and still attain the Tortugas ideal. The most experienced dancers achieved a punctuated exactness softened by an imperceptible cushioning bounce from the knees. This was the way "we" danced *indio,* and it was like no other Pueblo's dancing.

The insistence on a unique Tortugas aesthetic and the debates about the fine points of technique substituted for discussions of meaning. Meaning hinged on the question of identity, in particular, what it meant to be *indio.* Being *indio* was a unifying concept that was not itself unified, calling up the community's contested history and its unique tensions and reconciliations. Depending on the construction of personal descent, on religious belief, and on the conjunction or disjunction with the corporation's history and current direction, the word held different references for different people.

Both Mireya and Isabel made a point of their Pueblo ancestry. But their understandings of what it was to be Indian differed. For Isabel, the missionary's arrival was a blessing: "Before that, we believed in animals and gods and things" (Williams n.d.). Belief in "animals and gods and things" might characterize the *paganisto* Indians, to use Isabel's term, but not us, the Tiguas. Mireya regretted the influence of the church on the fiesta, because the animals and plants were gone. For both women, being *indio* concerned personal biography, but it implied different choices of belief and practice. Mireya's Indianness referred to the continuities from pre-Spanish times, Isabel's to the conversion introduced by the Spanish. In Werner Sollors's words, "Given a grandparent or two, one chooses to shape one's consciousness by one history rather than another" (Sollors 1986: 33).[15] It was partly by descent, but largely by the specific choices made, that each woman identified herself as *indio*.

While Isabel and Mireya understood *indio* identity in terms of personal biography, Raul did not. Nor did most corporation members. *Los indios* was a shortened reference to the name of the corporation, "Los Indigenes de Nuestra Señora de Guadalupe." And loyalty to the corporation was inseparable from loyalty to the Catholic religion. As Raul had insisted, for him the Tigua dance was no different from the rest of the fiesta: it was all for religion. Participation in the *indio* dance was equivalent to attending mass, serving as a corporation officer or *mayordomo*, preparing food in the *casa de la comida*, or making the pilgrimage up Tortugas Mountain.

For Raul and most other members, the Catholic religion and the *indio* practices were neither mutually exclusive nor contradictory. "Religion" meant Catholicism, but not Catholicism in general. Catholicism had its own biography, one that included the Pueblo conversions and migration, the Virgen de Guadalupe and the history of contact encoded in her story, incorporation in Las Cruces, and the twentieth-century local history of struggle and reconciliation between the *indios* and the church. Being *indio* signified commitment to an adopted community.[16] Whether his forebears were Puebloans or not was irrelevant to Raul's loyalty. It was the corporation's ancestry, not his personal biography, that mattered. When Raul said the Indio dance was "the same" as the rest of the fiesta, and "all for religion," it was the entire historical complex of the corporation's identity to which he referred.

Constructions of identity, Sollors writes, can be based upon "real or imagined descent, on old or newly adopted religions, on geographic area of origin, socialization, or residence, on external categorization, on voluntary association, or on defiance" (1986: 175). Being *indio* covered several of these possibilities: both real and imagined descent, old and newly adopted religions, both intentional and coincidental coming together in Las Cruces, voluntary association, especially voluntary religious association, and insistence on self-determination. Within its malleable parameters, diverse symbolic constructions of identity rubbed shoulders.

The question of Indian descent and the nature of the corporation's "*indio*-ness" became issues in the late 1940s when the split occurred. Citing the corporation's president (brother of the man who was then cacique) for incompetence and financial mismanagement, the membership elected another man to the presidency. They sued the brothers for the corporation's records and ritual paraphernalia. The cacique and former president formed an opposition group, calling themselves the San Juan de Guadalupe Tigua. They sent out a call to all those in the Las Cruces area who could claim Indian descent and began their campaign for federal recognition as an Indian tribe. A few who left the corporation argued that the changes planned by the new officers went against their Indian traditions. These changes included banning a carnival that took place in conjunction with the fiesta and cementing over the earthen floor of the *casa del pueblo.*

For the most part, those corporation members who endorsed the newly elected president saw themselves as having acted in accordance with the injunctions of the founding fathers: to support members, make physical improvements in the community, found and maintain a church, and keep the old customs. According to one member, the carnival was terminated for the same reason that the *abuelo* had been eliminated from the Danza: it impinged upon the religious seriousness of the fiesta. Cementing the dirt floor of the *casa del pueblo,* like installing water and sewage lines in the village or switching from wood fuel to gas for cooking in the *casa de la comida,* was seen as a positive modernization, fulfilling the injunction to secure improvements in the Pueblo. Ironically, and sadly for the Pueblo descendants in its membership, this opposition group was not able to maintain continuity of the Pueblo traditions on the scale of the fiesta. It was the corporation, most of whose members did not claim Pueblo descent, that kept alive the performance tradition that the *indio* families had brought from El Paso del Norte.

The Tigua dance embodied this montage of history and possibilities inherent in the term *indio*. Montage implies an interweaving and layering of history and memory out of which, at any moment, individual pieces may flash out as meaningful (Taussig 1987: 435–46). Within the shared performance of the Tigua dance, fragments of alternative histories and significations did indeed flash out, depending upon who was weaving the story. Perhaps the ambiguity of meaning was temporary, and someday the songs and dances would refer to the Virgin's appearance on Tepeyac Hill, and the signs of a Pueblo past would be merely that, signs without cosmological referent. But for now, the old Pueblo meanings pulled. Mireya and her sisters, who were not corporation members but were nevertheless a strong presence in the Tigua dance, cultivated their connections to the north, sewing them into dance outfits and sculpting them into clay pots. They knew it was inappropriate to interfere or to tell the corporation what to do, but their presence tugged against the Catholicization of the Pueblo traditions. The Pueblo heartbeat still sounded in the drum, still showed in the choreography that honored the four directions, and could still be felt in the soft-soled moccasins worn by Lorenzo's granddaughter.

8

. . . .

The Twelfth of December

Mireya often talked about her childhood memories of the twelfth, Guadalupe Day. When she and her sisters and brothers were young, Mireya said, it was the biggest event of the year, bigger than Christmas. All year her mother saved scraps of cloth, saying, "This would make a nice piece for your dress for Guadalupe Day." Mireya also spoke of how wonderful the carnival in the lot across from the church was for a child from a poor family. The children would rather be at the carnival than the dances. There were booths where pottery and trinkets from Mexico were sold, and food they'd never tasted at home. Though the carnival was gone, the sense of expectancy remained, and many people still sewed or bought something new for Guadalupe Day. More than Christmas, the twelfth was the climax and turning point of the year, lacking in commercialism and thoroughly familiar from childhood.

The overall movement of this third and final day of the fiesta was choreographed in peaks and troughs of intensity. There were different kinds of intensities in the fiesta: the endurance of the *velorio*, the persistent repetition of behind-the-scenes kitchen work, the concentration of people packed together in church for the fiesta high mass, the synaesthesia of four dance groups dancing at once on the twelfth, and the climactic, emotionally charged procession when the Virgin's image was passed from the current to the next year's *mayordomos*. More like the overlapping of waves than a linear stream of activities, the events of the twelfth interpenetrated one another.

On the official calendar the corporation printed for the public, the day began at 9:00 A.M. with the fiesta high mass. However, an informal and unpublicized procession, too small to be named, preceded it. Meeting at the *casa del pueblo* at about 8:00 A.M. to have their faces painted with *almagre*, the *mayordomos*, with the Indios and Danzantes, walked to the church two and a half blocks away. Their march was driven forward by a Pueblo walking song. Indeed, for the remainder of the day, each time the focus of activities switched from one place to another, the change was marked by a small procession. Through the processions, the events of the day were linked into one continuous stream.

Elena told me that the mass was the high point of the fiesta for her, and this was true for many others as well. At 9:00, the church was packed with visitors squeezing into the side aisles, vestry, and main entrance. Outside, the two *polvederos*, shotgun guards, kept a relaxed vigil at the door. They were dressed in the same red-fringed tan outfits that the Indios and *capitanes* wore. Today, for the feast day proper, everyone dressed up. Visitors who could not squeeze into the church listened via a sound system that piped the mass out into the church plaza. A fragile covering of snow had left patches that by morning were melting and muddied under a cloudless sky. No wind moved the branches of the groomed conifers lining the long dirt plaza.

The procession of *mayordomos* and dancers, newly arrived from the *casa del pueblo*, filed into the church. I slipped in by a side door and found a standing place next to a bulletin board covered with *milagros*, the tiny replicas that supplicants pinned up to represent their hopes and their troubles. The poet Sandra Cisneros names them:

So many *milagritos* safety-pinned here, so many little miracles dangling
from red thread—a gold Sacred Heart, a tiny copper arm, a kneeling
man in silver, a bottle, a brass truck, a foot, a house, a hand, a baby,
a cat, a breast, a tooth, a belly button, an evil eye. So many petitions,
so many promises made and kept. (Cisneros 1991: 125)

People posted them as an appeal to the Virgin and as a promise to
serve her.

The entire right side of the church was reserved for *mayordomos*, Tigua
dancers and their *capitanes*, Los Danzantes, and the two neighborhood
matachín groups. The high mass and, later, the afternoon procession
would be the only times in the fiesta when all the groups were together,
and the right side of the church was a patchwork of their colors. The *capitanes' varas* jutted above the white cotton shawls of the women Tigua
dancers and the tan and red of the men. There was a red block of Aztecas
Chichimecas, a yellow of Guadalupanos Aztecas. The *danzantes'* high
headpieces flashed multicolored ribbons, bits of mirror, and shiny costume jewels.

When the dancers were seated, the clergy entered: Father Giles, five or
more visiting priests, deacons, and lay clergy. Bishop Ramirez filed down
the aisle last in a white robe and tall white miter, carrying the hooked staff
of his office. One of the women had embroidered the edges of his starched
white robe with a string of joined half-rectangles imitating an Aztec ar-
chitectural motif. She sewed a portrait of Our Lady of Guadalupe onto
the front. Bishop Ramirez grew up in the Southwest and considered himself a "people's priest." He called himself *indio* like his parishioners and
identified the religion here as "folk" or "Indian Catholicism." As did Father Giles, he encouraged the people to value the symbols of their Indianness while also translating those symbols into Catholic meanings. The
Pueblo tradition of smoking corn-husk cigarettes, the bishop explained,
had the same meaning as the priest's incensing of the church altar: in both
cases, the smoke sent prayers to heaven. When I asked Father Giles what
effect he thought he or the bishop would have on the community, the
priest said that they were both interested in retaining the old Indian customs. The bishop's "specialty," he continued, was taking the people's previous cultures and traditions and putting them into the liturgy. The bishop
had taken a similar approach in old Mexico and the Philippines. Finally,

Father Giles said, "I'm not doing much more than the old missionaries did," finding ways to incorporate "what the people do" into the liturgy. "God does the work," he said, "letting what's natural work its way."

In one sense, religious devotion in the Guadalupe community could be looked at as the result of continuous missionizing activities begun by the Franciscan friars who first "settled" the *indios* in the missions of El Paso del Norte. Seen by some outsiders in negative terms, the work of Father Giles and Bishop Ramirez was a continuation of the early prose-lytizing that undermined indigenous religions while incorporating some of their practices into local Catholicism. Accordingly, the Aztec motif on the bishop's robe, or the altar cloth Father Giles wanted to commission from a weaver at Isleta Pueblo, was simply a sign of once viable, but now usurped, spiritual practices. But this was not the way the people of Tor-tugas saw it. They saw their religion as a single whole, including both Catholic and Indian elements.

Whatever charges of colonialism and extermination of indigenous re-ligion might be leveled against the missionaries who helped to conquer Mexico and the southwestern United States, the relationship between clergy and people in Tortugas cannot be discussed now as if it were the sixteenth century and a coercive clergy were trying to convert a reluctant population. Indeed, some corporation members were more conservative about retaining traditional Catholic concepts and practices than some clergy. One woman objected to the idea expressed by Father Elizondo (1987) of San Antonio, Texas, that there was "a feminine face of God." It was inconceivable to her that God could be both masculine and feminine. Likewise, she could not accept the idea of women priests. Bishop Ramirez was active in the refuge movement that offered sanctuary to people escaping political oppression in Central America, while the son of one Tortugas family worked on the border patrol keeping illegal Mexican im-migrants out. The bishop and other clergy in the liberation movement rep-resented a hierarchical church, but they were a vanguard force against the very institutions of political, economic, and social privilege that the original Catholic church in the Americas was instrumental in establishing.

Here, in the Tortugas church on the morning of the twelfth, there was a shared savoring of the unfolding Catholic mass. The bishop performed his opening circumambulation of the altar table, swinging the censer to penetrate the altar with sacred smoke. The high mass evolved in short sections, chanted prayers alternating with homily and the choir's singing. The bishop addressed the people in Spanish as well as in the local vernacular. He moved from the teasing, lyrical voice of home and streets, accompanied by small pats and points, to an expansive and formal chanting when he spoke of Jesus, the Mother, Juan Diego, or the church. He performed the most ritualized sections of the mass, incensing the altar or preparing the chalice and wafer for communion, in smooth rounded gestures and in lullaby time. There was a sensual quality to his ministrations. His chanting was full-bodied, lyrical, and clear; he, too, evidently savored the celebratory subtext of the performance. As combination native son and religious authority, the bishop elicited both fellowship and respect. A baby cried, but otherwise the feeling of the congregation was one of easy, unforced attention.

There was no hurry or impatience with the ritual ceremoniousness. Each event was given its due time, for this high mass was where the fiesta itself was consecrated. It established an experiential connection among the people, the Catholic religion, and the fiesta. When the people came together at a normal weekly mass, their performance re-created the link that joined them together as Catholics. They also gave witness to the truth of what anthropologist Roy A. Rappaport called "ultimate sacred postulates," religious statements of belief like the Catholic Credo, that could neither be proven nor disproven because they referred to transcendent beings or experiences beyond reference (Rappaport 1979a: 129). When the ultimate sacred postulates of liturgy merged with the subjective feeling of divine presence, as they certainly did for many during the mass, there would be, Rappaport claimed, a resultant feeling of religious wholeness, or "unison" (1979b: 213). This unison was declared, performed, experienced, and shared at the mass.

The fiesta itself was brought into that unison in a brief ceremony called "the investiture of new *mayordomos*." It occurred just after the Credo. The four outgoing and two incoming *mayordomos* who were seated in the front pew stood. A priest handed each outgoing *mayordomo* a lit candle and each incoming *mayordomo* an unlit one. After the bishop introduced next year's *mayordomos* to the congregation, he talked to them, with jokes and in seriousness, about their upcoming responsibilities. The outgoing *mayordomos* then turned to the incoming and lit their candles. The congregation applauded, and the ceremony was done. The bishop's spatial position above the *mayordomos,* and the fact that the investiture occurred during high mass, clarified the source from which the *mayordomos* drew their authority. They and, through them, the fiesta were ritually joined with the liturgy, the church, and God. The fiesta had been consecrated.

The sanctification of wine and wafer followed in a particularly exultant, drawn-out moment. The bishop made another circumambulation of the altar table with smoking censer. The choir sang the Sanctus. Surrounded in an arc by priests, deacons, and altar boys, the bishop lifted high first the goblet and then the wafer. A bell rang. The bishop sang out the sacrament. The moment of transubstantiation was electric; the miracle of transforming the mundane into the spiritual sent a palpable wave of elation through the congregation. While the whole fiesta was an opening to the Virgin's immanence, it contained within it the high mass, and that contained within it the sanctification, an opening to God's immanence. The Virgin's fiesta was the womb holding God's presence.

Here, more than on the pilgrimage, was the opportunity for conversion. Anywhere in the world, through the ritual words and actions of the transubstantiation, an opening occurs, joining Catholics in the passage from durative to eternal time.[1] People could put behind the jokes, conflicts, worries, and pleasures of everyday life in Tortugas, New Mexico, and enter the liminal space where the angel spoke to Mary, where Jesus suffered, and where God reigns forever and ever, amen. Just as the investiture incorporated the *mayordomos* into the mass, the transubstantiation, and the communion that followed, incorporated individuals into the larger communitas of Catholicism. But while local particulars were blurred, they were also illuminated. "God" may define the state of undifferentiated union, but people define the path to it, its windings through times and places, the color of its ribbons, the texture of its fabrics, the choreography of its symbolic actions.

For the erasure of difference to be meaningful, it must first be detailed. One must go back to the Pueblos, that first journey down the river, the years in El Paso del Norte. And one must join that thread with another from the south: the encounter between Spaniards and Nahuatls in Mexico City, the spread of religion and politics northward. One must carry to Las Cruces the meeting among Puebloans, Europeans, and Mexicans. The conversion occurring in the church was a convergence not only between Europe and America, but also between north and south, Indios and Danzantes, then thickened and complicated with the influx from northern Mexico, Chichimecas, and Guadalupanos. The specifics of local, temporal histories collapse into a single story of conversion: the first moment the first indigenous *mexicano* said yes to the first priest, the moment of Juan Diego's conversion, memorialized in his vision, embodied on the fiesta altar, and echoed in the moment each child took first communion at the church of Our Lady of Guadalupe in Tortugas.

Communion followed the transubstantiation at a slower pace, the bishop personally offering wine and wafer to the *mayordomos* and dancers one by one. I watched Elena and remembered our conversation and how she came closest to God in church during communion. I watched the parade of ribboned *cupiles*, white communion veils, feathers, and *mantas*, each individual carrying the signs of a history, each history witnessed, accepted, then left behind in the ritual of communion that the Spanish conquerors introduced. The people had found a place in that world where a native son now held power, a bishop. Whatever atrocities the Spaniards committed, they did not, as the Protestants did in New England, choose land over people, killing off whole populations. Spanish clergy traveled with, sometimes in advance of, Spanish soldiers; theirs was a conquest of souls as much as a conquest for wealth.

I could not take communion or join the others lined up to receive the host on their tongues. I could only imagine it, the lightening of flesh, the transformation of body into spiritual substance. The day before, Jay and I had visited the empty church. We looked at the *milagros*. Jay was disturbed by them; he could find no path from the objects on the bulletin board to the hopes of the people who pinned them there. Though not a believer, he preferred the abstractions of a Protestant tradition. I had no trouble with the acts of imagination that invested the material world with transcendent meaning. It was precisely the sensory and symbolic richness of Catholicism that I admired. But to enter its metaphors, I had to *make* belief, and I could do so only temporarily; mine was a "transportation" rather than a "transformation" of being (Schechner 1985). I could be moved by the church ceremony, but I could not make the consequential change to conversion that those ceremonies were intended to propel.

The choir discharged the intensity of communion with celebratory guitars and voices, the people with hugs, handshakes, and laughter. The *mayordomos* led the way up the center aisle and out into the open air of the plaza. Two by two, one hundred or more dancers followed, trailed by the congregation. Once the people who were packed together in the enclosing intimacy of the interior stepped outdoors, their enthusiasm swirled outward and around the church. There were more greetings as everyone waited for the dancing to start. In time, the Indios gathered into two lines before the church portal, men to the north, women to the south. The Danzantes lined up behind them, the two groups forming a corridor of colored ribbons and fringes from the church to the wire fence at the street. The two neighborhood *matachín* groups left, the Chichimecas Aztecas moving to the adjacent plaza, the Guadalupanos Aztecas to the plaza behind the church. Each group pulled with it a stream of spectators. Throughout the morning, the movement of spectators from one dance space to another strung the plazas together.

Overlapping sounds of drums and violins from the three different plazas, and the continuous hubbub of conversation, obscured the details of the dancing. My attention chose broad outlines and patterns rather than the fine strokes that were audible and visible at the *ensayos* and the *velorio*. It was difficult to stay focused on how many zigzags the Indios made in their circling or even which *figuras* the Danzantes were performing. The synaesthesia of the dancing, each group's rhythms and flash brushing against the others', carried us.

The dancing continued, but corporation members moved on to the *casa de la comida*. Days of dicing onions, sorting beans, vacuuming and washing floors, cleaning out cabinets, arranging for donations of meat and cheese from the town merchants and cakes from corporation women would culminate here in the feeding of two to three hundred people. By 11:30, the workers had finished setting the tables, filling salt and pepper shakers and napkin holders, cutting bread, preparing coffee, and rounding up serving bowls and spoons. We once again sat around the oilcloth-covered table in the women's kitchen, continuing the news, the stories, and the jokes begun two days before. By now, workers were beyond fatigue, synchronized in the concurrent rhythm that comes after personal edges are smoothed by long immersion in a shared labor.[2]

The approaching sounds of drums, rattles, and violins announced that the morning's dancing was over and that the dancers were on their way to the *casa de la comida* to eat. Some of us stepped out the back door to watch them approach, a slow-moving procession of *mayordomos*, clergy, Pueblo singers and dancers, Danzantes, and guests. The Pueblo marching song was punctuated with celebratory shouts of "Eeee-ha! Eeee-ha!" With a blast from the shotgun guard's rifle, the people stopped in the empty lot behind the dining hall, the same place where Lorenzo stirred tar ten weeks before.[3] They formed a circle around the drum and singers to a diameter of about fifty feet. Some of us, still in our aprons, joined in. Some people linked arms. Facing inward toward the drum, we shuffled and bounced counterclockwise in small side steps in the Friendship Dance.

When the circle broke, the Indios performed one dance and the Danzantes two, like thanksgiving prayers before a meal. They then lined up single file to enter the dining room. The dancers filled two of the three rows of tables. Clergy and honored guests filled the third. The bishop, followed by the cacique, offered blessings. It was time to eat. There were serving bowls filled with the bright red broth of chile stew dotted with hunks of beef, little *albondigas* in their soup, beans, baked macaroni, and aluminum roasting pans piled with slices of the spongy white bread. We servers squeezed through the rows of benches to pour coffee and hot chocolate, pick up the emptied serving bowls, and deliver filled ones. We lined up in the doorway between the dining hall and the men's kitchen to have the bowls refilled, the men over the huge cooking pots ladling out saucepans of beans, chili, *albondigas*.

Dancers and clergy finished eating and left, replaced at the tables, row after row, by the 250 visitors who had lined up outside. For three hours, the serving was continuous. About twelve servers, family and friends of corporation members, worked in a rotation system. We cleared the tables as people finished eating, while someone posted at the door ushered in a new group. We passed dirty dishes through the small window that opened to the sink in the men's kitchen where a rotating crew did dishwashing duty. Some of us reset the tables, while others lined up at the cooking pots to fill emptied serving bowls. The work continued without stop until there was no line outside the dining room door. The system was so efficient that at almost the same time the last meal was eaten, the last dish was washed.

In the women's kitchen, the fatigue was palpable. Elena, Graciella, Rita, Lena, and the others sat around the worktable drinking coffee and hot chocolate. In the dining room, their daughters stood at the dishwasher's window, joking with the men. Some of the kitchen workers ate their meals, spread out at the long tables. I joined the older women, talking with Graciella about how we planned to keep warm during the afternoon procession: we showed each other the long underwear we wore under our slacks.

The talk was light. How many people came to eat this year? How much red chile stew was left over? The women would not serve themselves lunch until the men had eaten. The major work of the day was done. In an hour or so the *mayordomos* would turn over their responsibilities, and the Virgin's image, to next year's *mayordomos*. In anticipation, I returned to the church plaza, where the afternoon dancing continued. The morning's excitement calmed, and the mesmerizing repetition of drums and violins smoothed the rough seams of the diversified crowd. It was possible to look carefully at the dancing. I began to notice the differences in the way each male Indio dancer did the lunge step. I saw that the *danzantes* tilted sideways as they rounded the corners during the *son de la malinche*. I enjoyed the December afternoon sun and let myself follow the slow braiding and unbraiding of the *figuras*. I compared individual *danzantes'* movement styles and tried to remember which dancer was under which *cupil*. And I drifted in and out of the drum's pulse, the violin's path, the view of the Organ Mountains. Through sustained immersion, the spectators, too, had become participants.

The afternoon of the twelfth was the only time the Indios performed the *baile grande*. When Lorenzo told me the elders instructed him to "keep changing things," it was the *baile grande* he was speaking about. This

Pueblo dance was unique to Tortugas, and the cacique himself had invented one of its *figuras*. Performed by all the dancers at once rather than in couples, and done to the same music, with the same basic step as the Indio dance, its innovation lay in the choreography. Out of the group formation, a men's line to the north, women to the south, various place exchanges and directional facings resulted in the formation of an X and a Christian cross.[4] The cross formation was Lorenzo's. By adding a cross, he had effectively choreographed the historical event of conversion into the four-directional orientation of the Pueblos.

Shortly before four, after the dancers took a break, they returned to the church plaza one last time. Spread out across its width, just inside the chain-link fence and gate, lines of dancers faced the church. In the wide front line were the five *capitanes*, carrying their *varas*. Behind them came a long single line of Tigua dancers, men and women alternating. The Danzantes formed the third flank. Last, in a small knot, followed the Pueblo singers and drum. They took up the introductory call for the same song used in the circle dance, "Heya hey! Heya heya heya," followed by the entire group advancing toward and away from the church. They repeated the advance and retreat three times, the *capitanes* turning after the first two advances to face the dancers. It was a slow but upbeat reentry into the plaza, heralding the last round of dances before the moment when the Virgin would be brought from the church.

The church bells pealed, the *polvederos* delivered a round of shotgun blasts, and the *mayordomos* emerged from the church with the Virgin's palanquin. Anyone could carry her palanquin later, during the procession, but the *mayordomos* had the honor of taking the Virgin from the church. The men carried the forward handles of the palanquin, their wives beside them (see photograph 15). The hundred and more people still there for the procession fell in behind.

The people spread out to fill the wide earthen trough of the churchyard, thinned to pass through the chain-link fence gateway, turned right onto Paroquia Street, and left onto Church Street, pressing east toward the ceremonial buildings and the mountains. It was two blocks to the *capilla* at the corner of Espina, another to the *casa de descanso* on Juan Diego, then left a half block to the *casa del pueblo*. There the Virgin would be

Photograph 15.   Mayordomos carry the Virgin's altar from the church while the Indio dancers approach her, December 12, 1986.

turned over to the incoming *mayordomos,* who would carry her back to the church, continuing the second arc of the circle. The procession moved slowly; it would take an hour to complete the short circuit.

I moved ahead and up the embankment, poised with my camera to "catch" the approach. On the side, too, near his house, was the young man who had worn turquoise jewelry two years before, watching but not joining in, never joining in with the "religious" parts. It was the Pueblo Corn Mother who still spoke to him. Rifle blasts from the shotgun guard sounded, and I jumped, making some teenage boys laugh. They slid down the embankment of loose dirt at the side of the road and ran further ahead. I followed.

Two blocks ahead of the procession, where Church Street met Juan Diego, it was quiet. The setting sun turned the Organ Mountains pink and purple, with the metallic light of that hour transforming the valley and the street. A police car with its rotating blue light blocked a side road. Separated from the procession's mass, Emilio Gamboa, the *capitán de la guerra,* carried his *vara* down the center of the dirt road. Two boys followed behind him, one carrying a pennant with the Virgin's portrait and the other a standard, the *custodia*.[5] These three people made up the vanguard. Emilio was headed for the *casa del pueblo*, where he would draw a line across the dirt road, marking the spot where the turnover would take place.

Following Emilio and the boys, three *malinches* also ran ahead of the main procession, chattering, throwing pebbles, and scuffing their shoes to raise dust. One began to turn, making her white veil spin out. A lone photographer rushed from one side of the road to the other, turning toward the oncoming procession to see which spot was best for a good shot. Vanguard, photographer, and I were the only spectators at this forward point. The sudden appearance of a large group of Aztecas straggling toward us from the center announced that their group had just finished a round of bowing and dancing before the Virgin. They reformed into lines for their next advance. The drum and violin for the Guadalupano group was now audible, and soon they too were running forward of the procession, puffing from their exertion, getting ready to advance into the heart again.

Looked at from above, that heart could appear as a steadily advancing huddle of more than a hundred people, with two mirror-image wheels spinning before it. From closer in you could see the Virgin's palanquin, carried by the *mayordomos*, flanked by the singers and musicians, and, behind them, the crowd. The double wheel was the dancers in double file, hurrying to pay homage to the Virgin, one group at a time and one right after the other, each pair of dancers rushing up to her in a nonstop, bowing choreography, then filing outward to be replaced by the next pair (photograph 15 shows the dancers of the Indio group beginning this pattern). Musicians for Tiguas, Danzantes, Chichimecas, and Guadalupanos played together now, switching from Indio to Danzante music, Danzante to Chichimeca, Chichimeca to Guadalupano. As each twosome came within a few feet of the palanquin, they bowed, quickly, without a break in their dancing or in the forward movement of the procession. Each couple came face-to-face with the Virgin at the still point of the turning wheels. These meetings were proclaimed with gunshot blasts, drums, violins, and, intermittently, the pealing of church bells.

In the center, close in, where the Virgin was carried, a quieter song was sung:

La Guad-a-lu-pa-a-ana, La Gua-da-lu-pa-a-na,
La Gua-da-lu-pana bajo al Tepeyac.

The "Alabanza Guadalupana," its rhythm organizing everything.

What is at the crossroads of a song?

Behind the *mayordomos* carrying the Virgin's palanquin was the place
of the grandmothers, their round warm bellies just an hour ago leaning
up against the oilcloth-covered table in the *casa de la comida,* their hands
patting tortillas into place, working the news into the dough. This one's
son is now working at Safeway and that one's husband at White Sands.
"Did you see Lorenzo's grandson, dancing again?" The women walked
steadily, slowly, creating the center. Their voices carried the crowd, the
news, the day, working them together now with their footfalls into the
clay dirt of the street, kneading them into the Virgin's presence.

La Gua-da-lu-pa-na, our mother who art in heaven. She has been with
them for three days, filling the spaces between thought, sifting memories
like flour. From inside the song and the slowed rhythms of lucidity, I gazed
out at the passing movement of houses, trees, mountains, then dropped
back in to the steadying song: *La Guadalupana bajo al Tepeyac.* Its waves
spread out under the pound of the Azteca tom-tom, drumming up to
the Virgin in pum pum pum, and under the violin that entered with the
Danzantes as a tickling screech, lifting heels off the ground, smooth
and bouncing, bringing back Rico's words, "She's coming! She's coming,
the bishop has said yes, and the crowds are coming into the Virgin's
temple."

The song continued under the men's Pueblo chant, a rumblous echo
of rain in the mountains, always referring me to the mountains, and to
Mireya in my living room singing heya hey. But the "Alabanza" reined in
such thoughts, too much pagan attention to the mountains, and brought
them back to the joy of longing, the call to the Virgin, *La Gua-da-lu-pa-na,
La Gua-da-lu-pa-na . . .*

What is at the crossroads of a song?

Here the current of fleeting experience meets the current of memory.
The memories lived as the sinew of our bodies, accumulating and slough-
ing meanings over time. I should not be surprised that Mireya, on the

phone, still asks after Jay, though Jay and I have lived in different cities for five years now. People remember the time he rolled meatballs and helped fix the broken water pipe outside the *casa de la comida*. The memories reconfigure my body as well. I let them work, recuperating fragments: the year the *danzantes* wore plastic over their headpieces; the sensation of entering the warm kitchen at 2:00 A.M. after a walk from the *casa del pueblo*.

Putting one foot in front of the other along the procession route in 1988, we marked the memory of Moises, who made a *promesa* standing up to his knees in the mud of the Rhine River, German bombs making swells of water around him. "If you take me through this I will dance for you forever." He did, his arms hanging stiff with arthritis, teaching the younger men what it was to dance with the Virgin. His presence washed over and through the notes. The people sang him into her, and she gave him back as memory, folded into the footfalls.

The song brings back Magdalena in her navy dress with the white polka dots, her apron removed now, thickened ankles—Magdalena had "bad legs"—stuffed into stockings and shoes with stack heels. The net scarf held her hair in place, and her voice, raspy and strong, held the song in place at the center. She and Lorenzo lived in the old section of Las Cruces, where the cacique's Pueblo ancestors first settled when they moved upriver from the mission communities of El Paso del Norte. The houses here were made of *jacal*, painted soft pink or green. In front of their house, the garden was overgrown, and a plank, probably for Magdalena's wheelchair, led onto the porch. Someone built a pyramid of Coke cans in the front picture window, probably the grandchildren, Junior and Marcía. When I went to their house, cartoons were on the TV. Marcía came out of the back room to announce that her grandparents were "crashed out." The next time I went there, it was to pay respects to Magdalena after Lorenzo's death. She was waiting for him to come back and get her. And he did, within a year. Did they join those familiar presences, Christ and the saints, whose portraits hung on the walls above where we sat, the Christ whom Lorenzo saw "going up"?

"You can only see the real Virgin at times of crisis," Father Angeli once said. He had been the priest of the Guadalupe parish for nine years, before the Franciscans provided the church with priests in two-year rotations. I had asked Father Angeli and Elena if it was possible for anyone to see the Virgin, following my sense that people had the same kind of experience during the fiesta that Juan Diego had had on Tepeyac.

"The great apparitions," Father Angeli said, "have come at times of historical crisis. Anyone could have the vision, but there had to be a reason, a sickness to be healed, or trouble in the country."

I asked if the people could feel the Virgin's presence. Yes, they agreed. Yes, you could feel it on the mountain; yes, the *danzantes* could feel it when they danced; yes, the three days of fiesta were a time when she was present and when that presence could be felt; but these things were different from seeing the Virgin. The critical distinction was between seeing and feeling. The ability to see the Virgin was not under a person's control. We could not see her at will; we could only have the feeling of her presence.

What did it feel like? Her story answers. "Am I not here who am your mother?" There is a play, a bedtime story written by the Las Cruces novelist Denise Chávez, who brought her father, in a wheelchair, to see the dances every year and who still climbs the mountain. Her story tells how the Virgin looked at Juan Diego:

> Juan Diego is breathless. He can hardly catch his breath. For the Lady is looking at him! Yes, at him! She is calling his name! Juanito, Juan Diegito! She's looking down at Juan, that's you . . . She loves you! Just the way that I love you and all mothers love their children! (Chávez 1987)

Juan Diego heard the Virgin, then he saw her, then he felt her touch. The Virgin arranged the roses in his *tilma,* in Juan Diego's farming apron. Like an everyday mother, the Virgin fixed his clothing. She touched him. She fiddled with the folds in his apron. She fussed over the roses. Perhaps she stepped back to check the effects of her work, like the women who came together to dress the Virgin, to place the rhinestone tiara over her portrait and pin the folds of satin cloth, fussing with the details of the arrangement. Her presence was intimate and sensory, it seeped through the quotidian chores of pinning and folding. And it was reciprocated; it called forth caretaking from both women and men. Though the ideal of caretak-

ing was represented as maternal, it was inclusive. Community survival
depended on it.

"What is religion?" I asked the men standing in the narrow corridor
next to the back door of the *casa de la comida*. It was 1989, on December 10,
during a late-night lull. The people had passed that irritable high point
of frayed nerves and exhaustion that they told me happened every year.
Beyond some boundary of resistance was a palpable sense of well-being.
Even Ruben Baca in his cowboy hat and boots, on foot or in his pickup,
dashing from one spot to another with his walkie-talkie radio at his ear,
keeping track of time and flow, his high-wires making all the connections, even he came to rest. Religion is a matter of obligation, he said. "I
get a feeling of fulfillment from it, a satisfaction in fulfilling the obligation." Another answer came from a son, the most gentle of men, who had
gone to live in San Antonio in a picket-fenced house and was welcomed
home at fiesta: "Fulfilling your obligation is also a way of helping other
people with their obligations." Raul passed by and overheard our conversation. "Faith," he said. "It's all a matter of faith."

Holding the line of obligation, strictness in the holding. The soft center of faith needs to be protected. This is what the people taught me. This
is what I had come to learn. George Cruz, Isabel's son, who later became
the cacique, told me before I left that I didn't yet know how much the
people had taught me. He was right. Ten years later, the messages continue to unfold. Strictness and authority, the hard edge of discipline I
struggled with, protected the vulnerable space of connection. Faith, which
is choosing to imagine that the experience of connection will happen
again, depended on trust that the authority holding the boundaries together was good. Strictness and holding.

The mothers held the line, walking in step with the song, making perfectly round tortillas, vacuuming the rug, and making sure the children
did not cross their legs in church. Magdalena's granddaughter, Marcía,
dyed her hair purple. Someone said she joined a satanic cult. I didn't believe it; she only dyed her hair purple. After all, she had made a *promesa*.
"I will go to church every Sunday for—forever. I will go to Mexico City
and see the Virgin. Grandpa Lorenzo wanted me to."

"Have patience, you all," I imagine her saying. "Have patience. I am young. I am working. I am getting my certificate to be a hairdresser. My grandpa is here with me, leading me with the drum. They tell me I am a beautiful dancer." Still, some of the children slipped out, preferring wienies and pizza.

It was not very far from mastering the roundness of tortillas and keeping your legs uncrossed in church to Lorenzo's lesson in faith, when the angel told Mary she would bear the son of God. "So be it," Mary said. Not very far to "Have respect and make respect, and God will help you." If you cannot keep your legs together in church, how will you learn how to pray? With crossed legs, the children will be too busy with other thoughts to make room for the saints. If you can't make round tortillas, how will you pass on to the next generation how it feels to know the Virgin in the kitchen?

Perhaps obligation, that hard edge of discipline, was the presence of God the Father behind the Virgin. "He is always there," Elena said, "but the Virgin is more available." Serving the Virgin, one is obedient to the will of God the Father. So be it. I'm here to serve. You have the password, you can come in, into the Virgin's temple with the Danzantes. There is no polarization between the hard edge of discipline and the soft center of devotion, no polarization between God's law and the Virgin's availability. To serve the Virgin was to know both. It has taken me years to make sense of these lessons. Faith and obedience were the same.

La Gua-da-lu-pa-na, La Gua-dal-u-pa-na. Magdalena sang, claiming it, and from there giving it out in the keen, sustained and sliding between the notes, winding down among the bass tones to a final wail: *precip-y-sa-a-a-vi-dad!* It was sung at the Virgin's wake, but it was not about death, this song, only sorrows and choices, gossip and joy. The song pushed up the topsoil from below, and we walked spongy on it, continuing, continuing around the corner to a view of the Organ Mountains, turning gold because the sun was beginning to set.

The sliding melody penetrated my distance and stopped the frenetic rush of my feet until I was part of the bundle, carried in its wave, letting my thoughts smooth out from the inside, watching the boys on the embankment, smiling at the shotgun guard, recognizing Ruben Baca with his oversized cowboy hat and walkie-talkie. Not even a smile was necessary: we'd been through too much fiesta together. We barely spoke, guardians of the Virgin's motherhood. We were dressed up; we looked each other in the eye. We laughed because she was so carried here, in Magdalena's voice, and Ramona's, and Kuka's. There were some mothers whose histories of trouble I didn't know, pinned up in *milagros* on the bulletin board, and other mothers whose families' illnesses I did know, told in the kitchen yesterday and last year and the year before.

I came to know her, too, this Virgin. She invited me to get down on my knees and smell the hair spray and candle wax in the *casa del pueblo* all night. Once held in its hollow, I too became a fiesta memory, baked into its *biscochos,* ironed into its satins, and plastered into its red adobe performance. From a café in California, again I rest with the women inside the *capilla* and the community kitchen, dicing images, sensations, and words like onions, lettuce, and tomatoes, holding memories in the bowl of my body and savoring their mix. I see their hands, fluid and fluttering, tucking folds into satin, pecking at recalcitrant places in the fabric, dusting the benches. And I hear Elena joking, as I snapped a picture, "Tell them this is how we clean."

The images recede and stretch out to a more distanced memory of a professor, looking for symbolic meanings in the cow horns under the Virgin's feet. Can you hear the women singing, professor? Those cow horns are their voices pinning up the Virgin's skirts on the back of an angel. Can you hear the farmers' voices at the Lantern Cafe, where they sat early in the morning to trade on the day's farm news and talk about the weather? Can you feel Magdalena's feet stuffed into her stack-heeled shoes? These are the things you have to know, because we are talking about Guadalupe, *la morenita,* who isn't afraid to embrace the aches and pains, even the varicose veins, of the people who pin them up as *milagros* in the church. This is theory.

The lowdown undertones of theory begin at the place where ideas bubble up in the body as sensations, taking shape, sometimes as a dance, sometimes as an image, sometimes as words. Sounds at play as meanings, they grope through experience. Stay close to the pen and meditate on the way stillness generates memory: I am pounding nails on the roof of the *casa de la comida,* inching along the chicken wire in one-foot increments, reaching for nails in the pocket of the carpenter's apron Raul has tied around my waist. The learning is conceptual surely, but his hands tying the apron are not beside the point. One learns grace this way, yielding, embarrassed, joking, helping out and fitting in, putting in one's two cents, a small wave in response to the one offered, holding the line with the grandmothers and asking for humility to cover the distance. The song works its way down and up, over the years, recuperating sensory fragments.

The procession arrived at the changeover line Emilio had drawn in front of the *casa del pueblo.* The sun, setting behind the church, turned the line of clouds in the western sky yellow. The air was cold, and as the sun began to sink, the sky slowly grayed. Sound and movement stopped. Father Giles stepped out into the open space between the *mayordomos* and the dance groups, with some of the people who were huddled close to the Virgin easing out to form a large circle around him. He delivered a short speech thanking the *mayordomos* and encouraging everyone to continue the fiesta tradition. People packed tight around the Virgin and *mayordomos,* in goodwill and solidarity, and perhaps to keep warm in the chilly late afternoon. The church bells two blocks away chimed faintly in this silent pause.

The changeover itself was short and simple. One of the *capitanes* moved quickly to take the wooden arms of the palanquin from the *mayordomos.* The new *mayordomos* squeezed forward from behind the outgoing ones. Old and new exchanged embraces all around. A few others from the crowd offered hugs or handshakes (see photograph 16). The two new male *mayordomos* took up the arms of the palanquin, their wives stepped beside them, and the old *mayordomos* slipped back into the crowd. The musicians started up again, the dancing recommenced, and the procession moved on, continuing the circuit back to the church. In 1987, the last year the cacique participated in the fiesta, it was he who spoke rather than the priest. Lorenzo died the following February. That year, after the changeover, the Indios performed the *baile grande* in his honor.

The changeover took fifteen seconds. But in the videotape I have of

Photograph 16.   The changeover of *mayordomos,* December 12, 1985.

that 1987 changeover, I can watch the seconds expand. Raul, no longer a *mayordomo,* reached out to take the arms of the palanquin from one of the outgoing *mayordomos.* Lorenzo, fragile and leaning on his cane, made his way through the crowd. Rita, now an outgoing *mayordoma,* watched Lorenzo from her place behind the new *mayordomos.* The tilt of her head, a barely discernible smile, and her appreciative gaze, unselfconscious, echoed the Virgin's. The young man about to become a *mayordomo* for the first time hugged the other outgoing *mayordoma,* gently and fully, cheek against cheek and firmly holding her around the back. He tried to suppress a grin, and then tears, as he stepped into his new place next to the Virgin. Others did not hold back their tears. In the midst of the hugging, Raul came face-to-face with the Virgin, and in a private moment that perhaps only my camera caught, his eyes moved over the portrait, as if absorbing a beloved face. He then bowed his head and no longer seemed to attend to the activity around him.

9

. . . .

The Movement Does Not Stop

Surrendering oneself
like the Virgin,
like Juan Diego,
that's part one.
Like when the angel
appeared to Mary
saying, "You will bear
the son of God,"
and she just did it.
(Easy to do in innocence,
  like the time I was barred
  from the back door
  of the kitchen.
"But I'm here to serve," I said,

and Grace Serna laughed.
"You know the password.
    You can come in.")
    Do you get it
    now after ten years?
"So be it. I'm here to serve."

    Part two is clenching
    the teeth and toeing
    the line
    of service,
    like the *capitanes*
    whipped on the ankles,
    and a daughter
    taught to fold
    her arms and wait
    while a guest
    drinks a glass of water.
    Oh there are many
    stories. And stories
    of my many failures.
("You must sometimes do
    what you don't want to do,"
    the old man whispered.
  "When a dog wants a bone,
    he can't just sit there. He has to
    get up and get it."
    His accusing finger
    pinned my thoughts.)

    Here is
    where

> you come
> face to face
> with your God
> and do battle
> with monsters,
> keeping counsel
> keeping silence
> and taking action,
> doing when you
> don't want to do.
> In faith.

Faith. I came to learn. I became part of a community, felt its rhythms, repeated its cycle, incorporated memories, and became part of others' memories. For a time, I walked with the people of Tortugas. Then I left the rhythms and the daily news, the easy phone calls and the circle around the table. My presence was not worked into the memories of 1990 or 1991 the way it had been worked into 1986 and 1987. My relationship with the people changed when I became a writer, an outsider, and I felt the loss. Something that had been was no longer.

It was more than loss. There were loose ends. Differences that in person could be accommodated in the forgiving arms of the fiesta had a sharper sting at a distance. The assertiveness that was a good joke around the kitchen table looked like a transgression of solidarity when it appeared on the page. My book would be a ceremony of ending. I put off its completion for five years, waiting to find connection in Tortugas in new terms.

Still, I returned in 1994. Raul and Elena had given their house to the children and moved to a new subdivision south of Tortugas. Moises, who danced for life after his promise to the Virgin from the mud of the Rhine River, had passed away. So had Rico's wife, Graciella: complications from diabetes. The women who formed the circle in the *casa de la comida* were getting sick, dying. Isabel, neatly tapping her arrows up and down in 1986, was in a nursing home, suffering with Alzheimer's disease. Her son, George Cruz, was *capitán de la guerra* and about to become cacique.

Rico had stepped down from his position as *monarca*. Elena's two youngest girls had married, which completed her raising of children but not of grandchildren. Though she was not old, she was the oldest active woman in the kitchen.

But most of all, I think of Emilio Gamboa's boy, killed that year. When a boy is shot in his front yard, it is no longer possible to think of Tortugas in the old way. The world had knocked. Tortugas was no longer separate from it. One of the men who helped out in the kitchen told me that drug dealers were dropping cocaine from airplanes in the hills north of the city. They moved into houses on the man's block, and "expensive L.A." cars and trucks would arrive to pick up drugs. The man organized a neighborhood vigilante group to confront them. It worked and they moved out, but it didn't stop the airplane drops.

Perhaps the intrusive world was the reason for a new carved wooden sign that appeared on the door of the *tuh-la* in 1995. It proclaimed, "Corporation members only," in English. Would only the insensitive English speakers barge in? The new cacique announced there would be no photographing inside the *casa del pueblo*. It was a new phase of fiesta history. Mireya told me the cacique had been "doing a lot of things." He had the old schoolhouse painted and the old bathrooms and trough kitchen sink in the *casa del pueblo* refurbished. The ceiling had a fresh coat of adobe red paint and new ceiling fans. "Keep changing things," the elders told Lorenzo. The movement does not stop. Nothing remains fixed, though the outline seems to be stable. What was the outline? The timetable of fiesta events? The fixed geographical points of A Mountain to the east, the Rio Grande to the west? The symbolic markers, like the fires on the mountain or the Virgin's altar? The fires were gone; the tires created an environmental hazard. The altar was changed, A Mountain replacing Tepeyac Hill.

Edges of the picture crumble. A new picture is taking shape, but I am not there to see it. The current *monarca,* Rico told me, wants to bring back the old ways. What does that mean? Will he bring back the narrative dances? The *abuelo* with his whip and mask? George Cruz had learned the Indio songs in just a few years, so that, as cacique, he could lead them. His uncle Lorenzo taught him. I watched George lead the singing at an Indio practice. Bent over the drum, his face sweating and contorted with effort, he pounded with hard, precise, punching gestures, ferocious even, the attack so intense it slowed the pace. With the dancers, he was gentle and insistent, making sure the couples paired up properly with no spaces between them. More members of Mireya's family were dancing, and, long familiar with the songs, they brought an orderliness that matched George's discipline. The dance patterns took shape, slow-moving snakes coiling and uncoiling, a river moving, rain breaking up still surfaces, and a neat cross formation, the one Lorenzo introduced. The dance was reemerging, no weaker sister to the Danza, but the dance of the Pueblo, a center pole that could hold the history intact. The *tumbé* talking with the Virgin:

> A deaf boy dances
> beautifully
> hearing the drum
> through his feet
> better than the others.
> He jumps to it
> as if he himself
> were the drumstick.

Lorenzo's grandson, Junior, was dancing again. He had not danced since 1986. This time, he said, he was here to stay. Junior danced like Lorenzo, compactly, with his back hunched. On the foot-lifting step, his knees came up high, almost meeting his chest. I saw Lorenzo dance just once, in 1984, the first year I visited the fiesta. It was at the last informal dance. After the changeover procession and an afternoon rosary in the church, a reception with whiskey and cookies is hosted by next year's *mayordomos* in the *casa de la comida*. Though the reception officially marks the end of the fiesta, it is followed by one last informal dance in the *casa del pueblo*, what Richard Schechner would call a "cool-down" (Schechner 1985: 18–19). Here, Danzantes and Indios, corporation members and workers let go their obligations and danced.

Anyone could join the dancers. Elders, like Isabel, could dance as a *ma-*

linche, reliving their girlhoods. Women could dance as *danzantes.* Danny Amador's brother could borrow his older brother's *guaje* and *palma* and pretend to be old enough to dance. The *danzantes* could dance as Indios. Kitchen workers could take off their aprons for the group version of the Indio dance. After the whiskey of the *mayordomos'* reception, it was a time for muddled efforts, giddy jokes, and laughter. People said the dancing used to continue into the night, but 1984 was the only year I saw it extend beyond one round of Danza and one of Indio. That year Lorenzo Serna and Juan Escalante, the elders in friendly competition over the correct way to drum the rhythms and do the knee-lifting step, were invited to perform together in the couple version of the Indio dance. Mireya danced with Juan, her sister Sonia with Lorenzo.

Though the two men were in perfect rhythmic synchrony, their postures and steps were distinctive. Both bent from the waist, but Juan's back was straight, strict. His steps were sharp, with a tiny and precise punctuation at the top of the knee lift. Lorenzo was the opposite. With deeply rounded back, his feet wide apart, he danced smoothly, softly, looking down. His was a posture of humility; he reminded me of a small, shy boy. His emphasis was not on the knee lift but on the stamp, where he pressed down strongly but with a soundless touch. It was the rounded back, the gentle touch, and the humility that reappeared ten years later in his grandson. Coming back for good, would Junior, like his uncle, some day inherit the position of cacique?

I, too, joined in the last informal dancing, the first years with the Indios, and then, in 1987, with the Danzantes. Before that I was certain I would not be able to coordinate the different rhythms of *guaje, palma,* and feet. But I watched Mireya's sister resolve the difficulty by simply shaking the *guaje* and not moving the *palma* at all. In 1987, with the encouragement of the dancers who joked that it was time to reverse our roles, I volunteered to dance. Frankie Valdez, who had taught me about Danzante strictness, handed me his *guaje* and *palma* and insisted I also wear the *cupil.* He fastened its leather band tight, pinching my forehead. To keep my head from wobbling under the weight, I had to tighten the muscles of my neck. It was hot under the layers of leather, fabric, and decoration. It was also dark and private. Looking out over the bandanna and through the fringes,

I could see a world of dappled light, distinct from the one within my headcovering. I knew, too, that my face could not be seen. Distanced and enclosed, I felt both disoriented and safe.

The violin started up with the *son de la malinche,* a long dance of processions. I quickly gave up trying to do the arm gestures and simply tried to keep up with the step and with the line of dancers. Laughter and calls from the outside of "Go Dede!" tickled me. I enjoyed the reversal as much as the men did. By the end of the dance, my left arm was numb with the weight of the *palma.* But I understood better the stamina and attention the men needed to perform the many rounds of dancing. And I had a small sampling of their somatic experience, the sensation of being enclosed in the hot, hidden space provided by the mask, driven to continue by the repetitive tune of the violin, and falling into unison with the other anonymous dancers.

Though I would return for the fiesta in 1989 and other years, that year I knew would be my last living in Las Cruces; the farewells that came after the speeches of thanks at the end of the dancing were particularly poignant. Raul had switched from calling me "my Jewish friend" to calling me "*mi hija.*" Elena and I tried to imagine stepping into each other's lives. Mireya gave me a small dish she made with a turtle, a *tortuga,* molded into its bowl. When Jay and I took Raul and Elena out for a final celebratory dinner, Elena handed me a plain brown box the size of a shoe box, tied with pink ribbon. "So that you don't forget us," she said. In it was a statue of the Virgin. Her cloak was bright turquoise and dotted with gold stars, her dress pink. She tilted her head, looking down with the familiar compassion and perhaps a little melancholy.

My fieldnotes for that year were meager, focusing on the death of Emilio Gamboa's son and my discomfort, after Jay and I separated, at being a single middle-aged woman at the fiesta alone. I was an anomaly. The very independence that enabled me to be in Tortugas, leaving home, traveling as a single woman, also estranged me. Though the youngest daughters were becoming engineers, teachers, and businesswomen, they were also marrying and raising families. I was not. There came a time, after that visit, when I thought it was time to step away for good. So much had changed. Still, I was drawn to Tortugas and returned, again and again.

On December 10 in 1995, at midday, I walked into the *casa del pueblo*, held back and anxious. Just inside the door, on the next-to-top rung of a ten-foot ladder, Linda, Elena's daughter-in-law, stretched, dusting the *vigas*. Donna's daughter Doreen held the ladder. They were joking and working, in the way I remembered. It was not the hurried and efficient way any one of us might dust in our homes. Rather, their actions had a sense of no-time, moments suspended like stories in the fiesta's arms. "Hello! How are you?" Doreen asked. "We didn't know if you'd be coming this year. How's Jay?"

Linda paused to listen. Perhaps she was responding to the discomfort beneath my offer to help when she said, "Why don't you just check it out? There are times to regroup." She returned to dusting with a careful brush of the cloth in the crack between *viga* and ceiling. Then she came down the ladder. The two women shoved it, bulky and unyielding, a few inches. Then Linda went up the ladder again. She readjusted the rag over the broom and poked it into the next section of crack. They continued while I watched and talked. I saw the ladder teeter and reached out to steady it, without thinking. In that gesture, I slipped once again into the familiar rhythms of fiesta work. My body adjusted. In the time it took for that single gesture, I stepped from outside to inside.

What had I learned? I do yoga. I meditate. But nowhere else have I entered into communal sacred time, for that is what the Tortugas fiesta was. Abraham Joshua Heschel (1966) captures the sense of sacred time for the Jewish sabbath, but we had not observed sabbath in my family. Our actions in the fiesta—dusting, chopping onions, walking in the procession—created not just the synchronized rhythms of people habituated to working together but a transformation of attention. Attention was both diffuse and focused. Time was roomy, allowing impressions, ideas, and memories to slow and sharpen. The space of awareness expanded, becoming a cave of generosity. In it, our thoughts were held by a shared pulse, sending impressions and memories jumping the synapses between us. Over time, I had learned to recognize and step into this space.

"Tell them this is how we clean," Elena once said, joking about my writing. But the joke named a truth: the fiesta's transformative capacity lay in the details of work. If I could indeed tell how my friends in Tortugas cleaned, I would be showing how the fiesta achieved its effect. This was what I had set out to understand starting from that first visit when Elena and I drank iced tea. In the years since, I learned that spiritual experience in Tortugas came as a doing, a transformation enacted upon oneself through the details of work.

This statement hinges on a slippery understanding. The potential for transformation lies in a property of *doing:* one does and feels oneself doing at the same time. Movement is unique among the media of expression. In other media, the mode of production is different from the mode of reception. We produce sound kinesthetically, via muscular movement, but we hear it aurally; we paint kinesthetically but review it visually. While the results of movement can be seen and heard, they are primarily received by the person doing it as felt experience, as kinesthesia.[1]

The doubled act of moving and feeling oneself moving can have an uncanny effect. Dancer and anthropologist Sally Ann Ness describes the experience of "becoming" her arm. She repeated an arm movement until she lost awareness of the "I" of everyday life and became "an exotic mind composed by a limb's neuromusculature intelligence, a mind exploring its environment through something other than its eyes and ears" (Ness 1992: 5). Awareness of experiencing what one is ex-pressing is the kind of somatic transformation emphasized by disciplines like yoga or breathing meditation. It is an ultimate intimacy, a doing while being with oneself.

I call this way of apprehending, "dropping down into the body" or, redirecting a phrase from anthropologist Thomas Csordas (1993), "a somatic mode of attention."[2] I use these phrases to refer to a research method: one attends to doing with proprioceptive awareness. Proprioception: the reception of stimuli produced within one's own body, especially as movement. It is a dancer's impulse. In the world of dance studios and rehearsal halls, we learn to translate visual and verbal information into movement sensation. A teacher demonstrates a position; we see it and "try it on" in kinesthetic imagination. We learn to hear the somatic references in words. My mime teacher's metaphor, "the antennae of a snail," pinpointed the subtle dynamics of a snail's antenna touching an object, vibrating, and retracting in a slow and sustained recoil. We learned to achieve this in movement. We became accustomed to distinguishing nuances between dynamics, feeling them, seeing them in others' moves, and recognizing their reverberations in words.

There is nothing mysterious here. The capacity for translating between sensory modalities is innate, though developed differently.[3] Child psychologist Daniel Stern reports on experiments demonstrating that infants can recognize by sight something they had previously known only by touch, extrapolating from the feel of a ball in their hands to its sight before their eyes. From such "amodal perception," they abstract global structural patterns like sphericity and rhythms (Stern 1985: 47–51). More relevant, infants can also abstract the feelingful dimensions of events. Feelings here are not the complex emotional states of happiness, sadness, and anger as Darwin proposed. Rather, they are kinetic qualities, the dynamics of energy inherent in all activity, dynamics like rushing, smoothing, jabbing, or squeezing. Stern calls these "vitality effects" and reports that infants can recognize them before they can recognize the activities or objects that carry them (54–57). Just as they order structural features like shape, so, too, infants "yoke" together vitality effects to arrive at global patterns of "feelings," the "activation contours" of events (57–58).

Stern admits that vitality effects can best be perceived in expressions that have no narrative content, like dance and music (56); symbols and narratives too easily distract from sustained focus on kinetic dynamics. Indeed, before discovering Stern's work, I saw, in a flash of insight, the difference in vitality between two dance forms. I watched a Balinese *kebyar* dancer and apprehended, as if it were my own felt experience, the taut vibrating intensity passing through his arms and chest from finger tips to finger tips, like electricity passing along a high-voltage wire. Next to this, I saw and felt, in imagination, the weighted and drawn-out footfalls of a Kwakiutl bear dancer, like the spreading echoes of a deep underground reverberation.[4] In the moment of seeing/feeling the qualitative difference between the Balinese and Kwakiutl movements, I recognized that all movement could be comprehended and described in terms of the way it manipulated kinetic energy. Stern's work offers a vocabulary for discussing these kinetic understandings.[5]

When I described the effect of the Danza as the swing of the cacique's pickax, I was attempting to capture a particular vitality effect: the accelerating momentum and intensified force that come with swinging a heavy object and letting it be carried down by gravity. Words encouraged *seeing* the swing of the pickax in order to *feel* its kinetic vitality, then to subtract the activity of pickaxing and transpose the vitality alone to the Danza. The swing of the pickax "feels" different in kinetic quality than the women's gestures of smoothing folds of satin into place on the Virgin's altar. Such descriptions urge extrapolations across sensory modalities, attending to changing dynamic contours.

Extrapolating between sensory modalities, discerning similarities and differences in structures and vitalities, and abstracting global patterns are not merely perceptual operations. They are also conceptual: they organize experience. The philosopher Mark Johnson argues that all abstract conceptualizations are built on these sensorial orderings, which he calls "embodied schemata" or "image schemata."[6] "The bodily works its way up into the 'conceptual' by means of imagination," Johnson writes (1987: xxi). Rejecting the idea that meaning is objectively inherent in a Cartesian world, to be uncovered through rational thought, Johnson sees meaning making as a human activity, grounded in embodiment and built via the metaphors of embodied schemata. For example, "balancing an equation" would be an abstraction from the embodied schema of equilibrium. The political concept of "power" would ride on bodily knowledge of vitality, force, and effectiveness. The process is universal, but the particulars of embodied schemata are shaped and reshaped in social worlds, in flux and continuous. They are works of imagination: dynamic, permeable, overlapping, and indeterminate. They are the more and more complex elaborations of the cross-modal extrapolating and ordering process Stern described for infants.

While we experience and express embodied schemata across all sensory modalities, as images, sounds, gestures, and qualities of touch, we manipulate them predominantly as words. Words not only symbolize experiences, they also participate in the embodied schemata to which they refer. When infants learn to speak, the cross-modal orderings they have already mastered incorporate a verbal dimension, a name, like "ball" or "rushing." The name is associated to the schema so that it both evokes and works upon the somatic pattern.

In mathematics, scientific reasoning, and propositional thinking, names and symbolic representations are split off from embodied schemata and worked as abstractions in relation to each other. It is easy enough to add two and three without counting on one's fingers and common enough to discuss abstract theories without feeling the kinetic reverberations of words. But it is also possible to bid words to continue to participate in the pool of somatic understandings that constitute them as embodied schemata. Then the process of thinking with words becomes a process of evoking their somatic reverberations. If I say to myself "ball," I recognize that the letters refer to the word *ball,* but I can also summon what I saw or felt or remembered when I said the word: the dirtied pink Spalding (pronounced spal-*deen*) we threw against apartment building walls in Brooklyn, its chalky texture, the exciting rebound of a "good" ball, the thud of a "dead" one, the friend I played with whose grandfather owned the grocery where we stuck our hands into the brine of a barrel of sour pickles.

Like Rico's mnemonics in the Danza, my fragments of memory are thought-forms, the stuff of sensual thinking. In a somatic mode, one's body becomes a laboratory of proprioceptive details, and thinking itself an aesthetic embrace. Aesthesis is gnosis, hermeneutics made of doings, hermeneutics that change the doer. Here the verbal process imitates the doubling I described for kinesthesia. Just as moving while feeling oneself moving creates the uncanny experience of doing while being with one-self, so, too, does "wording" that reverberates with somatic memory create a sense of uncanny intimacy, as if the world is made numinous. One *feels* the meaning of words, as movement and rhythm, texture, shape, and vitality. The object is made subject. And words become *the* word, creating what they name. The word made flesh. Words as sacred.

What I have described, I believe, is the process and experience of spiritual knowing. Whereas propositional understandings depend on excluding somatic effects from what counts as meaningful, both aesthetic and spiritual understandings depend on them. Anthropologist Roy Rappaport writes, "In the union of the sacred [proposition] and the numinous [somatic effect] the most abstract and distant of conceptions are bound to the most immediate and substantial of experiences" (1979b: 217).[7] Statements like the Credo, "I believe in the Lord Jesus Christ," or the

Shema, "Hear, Oh Israel, the Lord our God is One," contain no information in a technical linguistic sense, because their referents are immaterial.
They are "ultimate sacred postulates." Meaning here depends on identity,
"the radical identification of self with other" (1979a: 127). As in the Danza,
where story and dancing merge in the person of the dancer, in an experience of ultimate sacred postulates, the person participates with what
the statement signifies.

The process is not merely symbolic. It is somatic. The "states of being"
to which statements of belief refer, Rappaport writes, are "actual physical and psychic states" (1979b: 217).[8] But there is a missing piece in Rappaport's argument: the process binding sacred word and numinous effect.
It is the process I described as dropping down into the body, the doubling
of doing and feeling oneself doing, or wording and feeling the somatic reverberations of words. This is aesthesis. The difference between aesthetic
knowing and spiritual knowing is that in spiritual knowing, otherness,
the divinity, provides the doubling. In the fiesta, the Virgin's presence enabled one to be aware of oneself. Thus, when I stepped into the *casa del
pueblo* and found the two women dusting, then reached out to steady the
ladder, I stepped not just into a choreography with known gestures and
rhythms, but also into a state of being. Its name was the Virgin of Guadalupe. This was "the cave of generosity" in which we swam.

There is inherent reason to treat the fiesta of Our Lady of Guadalupe as
a somatic and feelingful spiritual space. The nature of the Virgin herself,
described in her narrative and image, and experienced as her presence,
points to her appreciation for the sensory details and felt experiences of
everyday life. Unlike God the Father, distant and abstract, the Virgin is
available through the most quotidian of actions. She arranges the roses in
Juan Diego's *tilma*, touching him, adjusting his clothing, fussing. Her close
attention, full of care, animated the details of work. When the women
dressed her altar or the men nailed chicken wire, they invited the Virgin's
presence by entering the somatic space that was her way of doing.

While the experience alternately called presence, or unity, or numinos-
ity may be the same across spiritual traditions, the "ways of doing" are
different. Presence comes in a multitude of flavors. "Our Lady of Guadalupe," as words, is an embodied schema different from "Buddha" or "God

the Father." The story of the Virgin who appears in a rainbow on a hill-top is different from the story of the Buddha who travels the world until he comes to meditate under a Bodhi tree. Kneeling in prayer before the Virgin is a different bodily experience from sitting cross-legged in medi-tation. Both the natures of the divinities and the ritual practices performed in their names are elaborated in distinct communities to do different work upon soma.[9] Sacred names have no material referents, but they do have content. That content is the details of *doings:* the actions, words, postures, rhythms, stories, objects, dynamics, melodies, images, liturgies, instruc-tions, news, sicknesses, changes, and memories that make up "Our Lady of Guadalupe" or "Buddha" as embodied schemata.

In the northern Rio Grande Pueblos, people use the word *doings* for the preparatory and cloistered (or "kiva-ed") sacred work done in the days before a public dance. I use the word to mean bodily actions, but I also intend the undertones of spiritual transformation. Chopping onions in the women's kitchen was not like chopping onions at home. In the doubled awareness that was the Virgin's presence, meaning was worked into the rhythms, postures, sounds, and dynamics of doings. Presence and doings worked in contradistinction and also in tandem. The state of being that was the Virgin's presence transformed the details of doings. In turn, the details of work done in her honor called up the Virgin's presence. While presence was invoked as otherness, it was also evoked as subjective so-matic experience.

When I stated at the beginning of this chapter that spiritual experience in Tortugas came as a transformation enacted upon oneself through the details of performance, this was where I was headed: sacred time and space were created by attending to the details of doings, both functional and somatic. Spiritual knowledge is as much a somatic state as a content. As a mode of attention, it can be entered and engaged. Holding the lad-der and dusting the *vigas,* we incorporated that state into us and were also incorporated by it. That state was the Virgin's (spiritual) body. It was also the body of the fiesta, its memories and its unfolding.

The relationship between the divinity's presence and the details of do-ings was like the design on the *danzantes' cupiles:* the tiny portrait of the Virgin at the center as the feelingful awareness of presence, the shiny bits of jewel and lace surrounding her portrait as the sensory details of her honoring. In this metaphor, it is appropriate that the Virgin's portrait was imported from elsewhere, given as "ready-made" otherness, that the decorations were crafted differently according to each dancer's relation with the Virgin, and that the overall pattern of Virgin surrounded by decoration was a convention given and shared by the community.

The results are not necessarily ineffable. If, as I have suggested, somatic knowledge is shot through with words that remain permeable to their somatic reverberations, then it should be possible to work words to evoke those reverberations. Dipping into memory from a space of somatic attention, one can allow the permutations of thought-forms to *take* form as words (or pictures or choreography). But it demands a revised relationship with language.

I set out to write so that my words would embody what I had learned. After working with a poet and succeeding only in writing what she called "mouse tracks," empty traces of the living organism that once passed by, I stumbled, by coincidence, into a method for bringing up words that worked both as symbols and as somatic reverberations. Writing in a restaurant, I stopped to listen to the piped-in jazz. My notes report:

> The sound comes
> as a throbbing
> in my foot, the vibrations
> of the bass spreading
> through the bar stool and
> up my leg, engaging
> heartbeat, organizing
> it into sympathetic pulse,
> and conniving my body
> into the production of words.
> They emerge in sync
> with the wavy throbs
> of the baseline and
> swishing skirts of melody.

The waves are generative.
They pass upward,
the rhythm engaging
pools of memory —
images, other moves,
word-sounds,
flashes of insight.
My words ride the music.

"My words ride the music" was a reference to information shared with me by a Pueblo friend. Pueblo dancers "ride the drum," she said, letting themselves be carried out and in on its pulse, the strong beat sending awareness out to the land, the echo beat bringing it back into the body. Out and in, other and self. The drum becomes a backup, a reinforcement of the heartbeat and a substitution for the scattered focus of everyday thought. It provides a center of concentration and attention that is diffuse, but deep and total. All thoughts ride the pulse of the drum, out and in like a sound wave dispersing and regathering, all senses attending. Thus attached to a beat, sensations and thoughts proceed, no longer fragmented.

Eventually I was able to induce this somatically synchronized state, simply by giving full attention to my breathing, as in Vipassana meditation or yoga. Focusing on the out and in of breath shifted awareness away from my everyday stream of verbal thoughts, so I could bring attention to the stream of sensation in all modes. Consciousness shifted, slowing down, until thinking became a territory without boundaries, unfolding not as a quick firing of words but as a watery dance of sensory particulars: images, sounds (including word-sounds), qualities of touch, smells.

In this state of somatic attention, I would give myself a memory or idea from Tortugas to contemplate, envisioning the line of *danzantes* leaning inward as they rounded a corner in the *son de la malinche* or recalling the sound of the women's voices in the "Alabanza Guadalupana." I allowed the image or sound to call up further fragments of sense memory. I could then watch, listen, feel, and register the progression of associations. I became a researcher at the site of my own body. If I distanced reflective attention away from the unfolding of sense memory to analyze the process verbally, the flow stopped. But if I attended to the words that arose in the dance of sensory particulars, the words called up further memory:

> Hold.
> The mothers hold the line,
> walking in step with the song,
> vacuuming the rug
> and making tortillas
> that are round.
> It is the test. Are you holding?
> Marcía, the granddaughter, dyed her hair purple.
> Someone said she had joined a satanic cult.
> I don't believe it,
> she has only dyed her hair purple.

Sometimes theoretical insights arose in the rhythms of my somatic contemplations, and I wrote these down, too, in poetic form:

> The lowdown undertones of theory
> begin at the place where
> ideas bubble up in the body
> as sensations
> taking shape,
> sometimes as a dance,
> sometimes as words:
> Sounds at play as meanings,
> words grope through experience.

This rhythmically rich associative thinking is the voice of my dancing body. Writing as metadancing.[10]

While she was putting together the panel called "Alternate Sensibilities" for the 1996 American Anthropological Association meetings, my colleague Katherine Young suggested a title for my paper: "Sensory Trajectories of Writing and Witnessing." Does writing, she wondered, extend the experience of fieldwork, through the body, onto the page? Or do we shape the contours of writing to those of experience, "as an aesthetic gesture to create sensuous access to experience through its representation"? "Both," I answered. But rather than "aesthetic gesture," I would say that writing is "an aesthetic embrace that invites sensuous opening," almost as if words need to be irresistible, to partner bodily experience at all its levels of intensity, intimacy, and multiplicity.

I realized then that I was pulling out the point of relation between language and bodily experience, and doing it through my own body. I also saw that, in writing, I was imitating the transformative process enacted yearly in the fiesta, evoking presence. Considered this way, there is no conflict between experience and words because they are mutually generative, part of the same epistemological process. The process constitutes meaning making and also body making. The body is itself a process, one that organizes as it apprehends and becomes what it organizes. One of the problems in talking about the "body" is that the concept is already so nailed to the schemata of "container" and "vehicle" that it is difficult to unhinge. The body does not hold experience; rather, it *is* experience, a process rather than an object. Somatic understandings emerge as a process of incorporating and configuring information into the body one is always in process of becoming.

The critical difference, then, is not between experience and words, or body and thought, but between conventions of knowing or modes of apprehending. In spiritual knowing, words are not asked to stand apart from and explain but to participate in and evoke, one stream in a larger and deeper cognitive process.

I immersed myself in a community different from the one in which I grew up to understand faith from an embodied standing place. I synchronized my rhythms to others', molded my posture to the benches and stools, and engraved in bodily memory the fiesta's unfolding. What did I learn? Spiritual knowledge in Tortugas was a way of knowing as well as the contents known. Indeed, it was a way of *producing* knowledge. That way was a participation with symbols.[11] As imaginative abstractions from embodied schemata, symbols are like pressure points that can be touched to evoke larger and deeper territories of knowing. It is the toucher and the touching that produce lasting affects and motivations. Symbol cannot be separated from soma without robbing religion of its power.

Rico choreographed the Virgin's narrative into the Danza, and dancing gave him back the Virgin's presence. Mireya sewed clouds, mountains, and happiness into the Tigua ribbon headbands, and the ribbons gave her back clouds, mountains, and happiness. The women around the kitchen table worked the news into the dough, and the *biscochos* gave them back the unfolding story of their shared lives. I sing the "Alabanza Guadalu-pana," and the sound puts me in the procession. Symbols reverberate back to doings, reviving somatic engagement. In the cyclical process, the connection between doings and presence, symbol and soma, is real-ized as a way of knowing.

> I live in limbo
> revising a book,
> immersed again
> in the watery places.

I am looking for the otter space, the curling sensual undulations. I feel myself to be part of the watery world and also articulate within it. I share its substance but discern the differences that create form. I drop down into the watery places to feel the reverberations of movement through my body, adjusting muscles, in degrees of tension and release, to the rhythms of life. Each moment has a dynamism that can be felt and passed on in words. Swimming in a desert, I shape myself to, and am shaped by, its structures: falling into line in the procession, taking a place in the circle with the women, shying from the edges. I learn about bones, the hard sub-stances that enable form.

What does it feel like in my body, this apprehension of the hard edge of discipline that holds the watery place of connection? What did I learn? Too much hardness of bone, without water, and there is no dance, only rigidity. Too much water with no bones, and there is no shape, no differ-entiation. Without bones, watery words are mushy sentimentality. With-out water, bony words are brittle barricades.

What does it feel like in my body, this exchange of water and bone, movement and words? The conversion of sensation to "backbone." A balance between lower and upper body. I bring attention to my solar plexus, where the butterfly breathes and furls her wings from sternum through rib cage and shoulder blades. The small muscles adjust in little waves, reverberating through larger muscles, each otterlike. I breathe, dive down, and emerge, leaving traces in words.

Notes

   1.   Unlike method acting, Decroux's work shunned sensory memory as an avenue to veracity, emphasizing instead technical precision in creating bodily attitudes and gestures. A technical method, Paul Ekman (1983) writes, is as effective in eliciting emotion as sense memory. Working with actors from the American Conservatory Theatre in San Francisco, Ekman compared two means of eliciting emotion: mechanical manipulation of facial gesture and mental recall of past emotional experience. In one experiment, he told the actors to contract specific muscles of the face, one by one, so that the end result would depict a specific emotion; during this process the actors did not know what emotion they were simulating. In a second experiment, Ekman asked the actors to remember and internally relive a past emotional experience for thirty seconds, an approach known in American theater training as emotional recall or affective memory. He discovered that both methods worked to produce emotion-specific activity in the autonomic

197

nervous system for six emotions—surprise, disgust, sadness, anger, fear, and happiness. He also found that the mechanical approach was more effective than the emotional-recall approach. As Richard Schechner wrote about this research,

> What is truly surprising about Ekman's (1983: 1210) experiment is not that affective memory or emotional recall work but that "producing the emotion-prototype patterns of facial muscle action resulted in autonomic changes of large magnitude that were more clear-cut than those produced by reliving emotions." That is, mechanical acting worked better in getting the actor to feel. (Schechner 1986: 347)

2. Qualitative movement analysis draws on the work of Rudolf Laban, who devised both a quantitative system for notating the shapes, choreographic patterns, and timing of movement and a qualitative system for discerning combinations of "effort qualities." These include the qualities of weight (light or strong), time (quick or sustained), space (direct or indirect), and flow (bound or free). For an explanation of the efforts, see Laban 1971; Lomax, Bartenieff, and Paulay 1968 and 1974; Bartenieff 1974; and Dell 1977. Several dance anthropologists worked qualitative movement analysis into ethnographic report. See, for example, the exemplary work of Cynthia Bull, a.k.a. Novack (Novack 1990; Bull 1997). Dance critic Marcia Siegel distilled the effort qualities into a method for writing movement description; it was from Siegel that I learned qualitative analysis. Teaching in the department of performance studies at N.Y.U. in 1984–85, she paired studio exercises on the range of efforts with descriptive writing from field observation. Siegel's teaching and writing demonstrated the power of words to evoke kinetic knowledge. The most salient expression of her approach is given in Siegel 1991. For her application of Laban's principles to dance criticism, see, among other works, Siegel 1977 and 1979. I am also indebted to Elsie Dunin's courses in movement analysis taught at U.C.L.A. in 1980–82, Joann Kealiinohomoku's "Field Guides" (Kealiinohomoku 1974), Richard Schechner's "whole performance sequence" (Schechner 1985), and Allegra Fuller Snyder's "levels of event patterns" (Snyder 1978). Lavender and Oliver (1993) provide a helpful introduction to dance observation. For the "movement analysis guidelines" that I developed for fieldwork in Tortugas, see Sklar 1991b and Sklar, forthcoming.

3. I discuss this process fully in chapter 9. Elsewhere (1991a and 1994), I have called the process of translating from visual to kinesthetic modes "kinesthetic empathy":

> Empathy here does not imply the first definition given by *Webster's New Collegiate Dictionary,* "an imaginative projection of a subjective state into an object so that the object appears to be infused with it," but the second, "the capacity for participation in another's feelings or ideas." Webster's defines *kinesthesia,* from the Greek, *kinein,* "to move," plus *aisthesis,* "perception," as "a sense mediated by end organs located in muscles, tendons, and joints and stimulated by bodily movement and tensions. Also sensory experience derived from this sense." Putting the two terms together, kines-

thetic empathy would mean the capacity to participate with another's movement or another's sensory experience of movement. (Sklar 1994: 15)

As far as I know, the first use of the term *kinesthetic empathy* in dance writing occurs in Martin (1978 [1939]), though it is discussed earlier in anthropology. See, for example, Dilthey (1976 [1914]). The concept was criticized by David Best (1975 and 1978), who argues that empathy refers to emotional responses and therefore denies a place to reason in the apprehension of dance. I use the term in reference not to emotional responses but to kinetic ones. Kinesthetic empathy, for me, is a mode of apprehending kinetic qualities, no more or less reasonable than the mode of apprehending words.

4.   Participant observation, James Clifford wrote, "serves as shorthand for a continuous tacking between the 'inside' and 'outside' of events: on the one hand grasping the sense of specific occurrences and gestures empathetically, on the other stepping back to situate these meanings in wider contexts"(1988: 34). Participant observation, he concluded, is a "dialectic of experience and interpretation." The problem, he acknowledged, was in trying to pin down techniques for arriving at the "inside" of events, getting "a 'feel' for the foreign context" and "a sense of the style of a people or place" (35).

5.   Bull continued, "When I dance, I experience kinesthetic, visual, tactile, and auditory sensations, and my sensible dance experience includes and implies intelligible choreographic and social meanings" (Bull 1997: 269). She warned against the dangers of either evoking sensual experience and "slighting the cultural content inherently implied" or of abstracting and interpreting to such an extent that the sensual experience is overwhelmed (270). Elsewhere, Bull (a.k.a. Novack) admonished anthropologists: "Translations of movement into cognitive systems can be illuminating, but sometimes they subsume the reality of the body, as if people's experience of themselves moving in the world were not an essential part of their consciousness and of the ways in which they understand and carry out their lives" (Novack 1988: 103).

CHAPTER 1. TRAVELS

1.   The Tiwas belong to a larger linguistic family of Tanoan speakers who also include the Tewa and Towa. The Tewa Pueblos are San Juan, Santa Clara, San Ildefonso, Pojoaque, and Tesuque along the Rio Grande, and Tewa Village on Hopi First Mesa. Jemez is the only remaining Towa village. Keresan speakers reside at Zia, Santa Ana, San Felipe, Santo Domingo, Cochiti, Acoma, and Laguna. The Hopi and Zuni languages are unrelated to each other and to the languages of the other Pueblos (see Eggan 1979).

2.   Until 1848, El Paso del Norte included the current cities of El Paso, Texas, and Juarez, Chihuahua. In 1848 the Treaty of Guadalupe Hidalgo drew the current boundaries that divide Mexico from the United States.

3.   Following popular and academic spelling, I will refer to the people of Ysleta del Sur as "Tigua" and to the people of Isleta in the north as "Tiwa."

4.   See Hackett 1942 for a European-American account of the Pueblo Revolt, Sando 1992 for a Puebloan. For information in particular on the process of Pueblo settlement in El Paso del Norte, see also Hughes 1914; Jenkins 1974; Walz 1951; Beckett and Corbett 1990. For information about the Tiguas of Ysleta del Sur, see Houser 1970 and 1979; Gerald 1974.

5.   On the Piro and Tompiro Pueblos, see Schroeder 1979 and Bandelier 1890 and 1892.

6.   Detailed information on the dates, populations, and establishment of the El Paso del Norte congregations is given in Walz 1951; Hughes 1914; Jenkins 1974; and Bloom 1938.

7.   For information on the Mansos, see Bandelier 1976: 165; Gerald 1974: 117–23; Hughes 1914: 334–42; Walz 1951: 5–8, 135–54; Jenkins 1974: 257–58; Lange and Riley 1970: 156–64; Bandelier 1976: 246–49; and Beckett and Corbett 1990.

8.   For information on this period in El Paso del Norte, in addition to Bowden 1974 and Reynolds 1981, see Gerald 1974; Bloom 1903; and Lange and Riley 1970: 156–67.

9.   See Oppenheimer (1957) for an analysis of the sociological effects of the railroad and Elephant Butte Reservoir on the Las Cruces *indio* community.

10.   There is still a disparity between the earnings of Spanish speakers and non-Spanish speakers in Doña Ana County. In 1980, for example, in every age group, the median income of Hispanics was lower than that of non-Hispanics. Income was least divergent at the youngest age: median salaries for Hispanic earners from the ages of fifteen to twenty-four were $7,067 versus $8,503 for non-Hispanics. Earnings were most divergent at the ages of forty-five to fifty-four, when career advancement would normally be at its peak. At this age, Hispanics earned an average of $15,184, while non-Hispanics earned $21,217. The total population of the county in 1980 was 96,340, of whom 52.1 percent declared themselves to be of Spanish origin (U.S. Bureau of Census 1980).

11.   For information on early settlements in the Mesilla Valley, see Bloom 1903; Baldwin 1938; and Curry and Nichols 1974.

12.   For a review of the history of the church and parish of Our Lady of Guadalupe in Tortugas, including these causative incidents at St. Genevieve's, see Carie 1989. Reference to additional St. Genevieve's clergy is given in Nichols and Curry 1974: 83–84.

13.   Tortugas appears on an 1854 United States exploration and survey map

drawn in anticipation of the railroad (Parke 1857 VII: Map #2). Although the map labels the village San Juan, in the text of the report, Tortugas is also named. "Las Cruces, Las Tortugas, and the military post of Fort Fillmore are the only settlements between Doña Ana and El Paso" (II: 6). Parke estimated the combined population of these three villages as less than fifteen hundred.

14.   I have changed the names of participants to protect their privacy.

CHAPTER 2. FROM THE *CAPILLA* TO
THE *CASA DEL PUEBLO*

1.   A rabbit hunt could be called at any time during January or February. Traditionally, only the men hunted the rabbits, trading them for *empanaditas*, pastries filled with sweetmeats or fruit, prepared by the women. Recently, both men and women went after the animals. The women still brought the *empanaditas* and other food. For a description of the rabbit hunt, see Beckett 1974.

2.   It was the people of Tortugas who advised me to go to books for the story. My retelling relies most heavily on the story's earliest written version as published by Demarest and Taylor (1956) and on a variation by the Guadalupe scholar Father Virgil Elizondo (1976), on a children's story by Tommie de Paola (1980), and on the manuscript of a play for voices by the Las Cruces novelist Denise Chávez (1987). For an illuminating study of the history and symbolism of Guadalupe in Mexico, see Lafaye (1974). The narrative given by Demarest and Taylor is derived from the "Lazo de la Vega narrative," the earliest available Nahuatl text of the Guadalupe story, published in 1649. Demarest and Taylor's English translation was made from an 1895 publication of the Guadalupe Basilica in Mexico City, the *Album de la Coronación de la Santíssima Virgen de Guadalupe*. This text is Lorenzo Boturini's eighteenth-century Spanish translation of the Nahuatl original (Demarest and Taylor 1956: 52-53). Elizondo's text is his translation from the *Album del IV Centario Guadalupano*, published by the Mexico City Guadalupe Basilica in 1938. Denise Chávez offers a local Las Cruces version. De Paola's children's story is a contemporary popular treatment. I have drawn on my own experience of the stylistic and emotional tenor of participation in the fiesta to render the story in a way that evokes its qualitative "feel" as well as its narrative content and structure.

3.   Unless otherwise indicated, all translations are by the author.

4.   The song was sung unaccompanied and did not precisely follow a chromatic scale. My notation is therefore an approximation.

5.   This and all quotes from Rico Bernal (pseudonym), unless otherwise noted, were transcribed from taped interviews conducted with him on October 21, 1986, and March 12, 1987, in Las Cruces, New Mexico.

CHAPTER 3. DANCING WITH THE VIRGIN

1.   A version of this chapter has appeared in *Dance Research Journal* (Sklar 1999).

2.   J. D. Robb (1954 and 1961) has notated a more extensive collection of *sones* for the Tortugas *matachines*. His early notation of *la ese* (1954: 761) lacks the second phrase. His later version (1961: 99) includes it but differs from the one given here. The tune changes over time, as the violinists change.

3.   Descriptions and diagrams, as well as video clips, of all the dances are available on the author's website (www.arts.uci.edu/dsklar); the diagrams can also be found in Sklar 1991b.

4.   Left and right here are from the perspective of the Virgin or of someone sitting before the dancers at the front of the hall.

5.   A discussion of the origins and relatives of *matachín* dances is beyond the scope of this book. Briefly, although some scholars have emphasized the dances' European ancestry (Hawley 1948; Robb 1961; Forrest 1984), most agree that European concepts and elements were grafted onto dances of indigenous origin (Kurath 1949, 1956, 1957; Lea 1963; Champe 1980–81; Rodríguez 1996). There seem to have been similarities between Old World *matachines* and some New World dances. Bernal Diaz de Castillo, observing Montezuma's dancers in 1568, remarked that "some danced like those in Italy called by us Matachines" (Castillo 1800: 43). See also Marie (1948) for excerpts of other early missionary reports on the dance. The battle between Spaniards and Moors is depicted in the Americas more literally in *moros y cristianos* performances, which often involve spoken texts and maneuvers on horseback, than in *matachines* (see, for example, Kurath 1956; Lea 1963; Champe 1980–81; and Marie 1948).

6.   In New Mexico, people referring to themselves prefer the term *mexicano* when speaking Spanish; Hispano or Hispanic, when speaking English (see Rodríguez 1996: 159).

7.   There is a large literature on *matachines*. Among other sources, Bennett and Zingg (1976) describe a Tarahumara version, Spicer (1980) a Yaqui version. For New Mexico, Rodríguez (1996) gives the most complete and recent comparison of Pueblo and Hispano versions along the Rio Grande. Champe (1983) provides a thorough scenario for San Ildefonso, and Kurath and Garcia (1970) discuss the San Juan version. Parsons (1939) also describes an early San Juan performance and compares Pueblo, Yaqui, Tarahumara, and Mayo versions. There is video footage of the dances of Bernalillo (*Matachines* 1980) and San Juan (*Matasina* 1980), as well as a comparative treatment of New Mexico *matachines* (*Los Matachines,* 1988). My own unpublished fieldnotes touch on Bernalillo, Santa Clara, Tucson Yaqui, and Mayo *matachines* and an Alcalde *moros y cristianos* performance. In addition to video of the Tortugas dances, I have footage of more

than twenty Mexican *matachín* groups performing at the San Lorenzo feast day in Juarez on August 10, 1987.

8.   There may once have been a connection to the narrative. According to the *Rio Grande Republican* of December 15, 1888:

> There were two dancing parties, one consist[ed] of about twenty young Indians and represented the court of Montezuma. They were gaily dressed, and had a huge head gear trimmed with jewels. One represented Montezuma, and his daughter was personated by a little girl of twelve, called Malinche, who joined in the dance.

But the "court of Montezuma" may not be a reference to the story of Malintzin, Cortés, and Montezuma. In a 1904 account, Alice Lute Foster also calls the *danzantes* "Montezuma and his followers." However, in her account of the Danza story, Montezuma's two little daughters were captured by the Spaniards and hidden. They prayed to Our Lady of Guadalupe to find them and promised that in return for her aid they would dance once a year (Foster 1904: 9).

We know that the Danza was performed as part of the annual celebration at the Guadalupe mission in El Paso del Norte, for as John C. Reid reports for December 12 of 1858, after the church mass, "a dozen or more young men, and a single woman" danced.

> The men were dressed fantastically, the young women very neatly. These now emerged from the church, and took their positions facing the door, when with toys, that make a tinkling noise, in their hands, they kept time to the music of two fiddles. They danced to and from the door of the church, till the movements lost their charm; the crowd dispersed and left them alone. (Reid 1858: 162)

Bandelier also noted the performance of "a Matachina" in El Paso in 1888 (Lange and Riley 1970: 164). The Danza was probably brought from El Paso and performed in Las Cruces from the fiesta's beginning. According to a Tortugas elder whose father was the *monarca* in Las Cruces at the turn of the century, the Pueblo had at first invited a "maestro" from a town south of El Paso to lead the Danza. But the maestro soon "urged the pueblo men to master the dances and tunes because he foresaw the day when he would not be able to visit the valley because of his advanced age and difficulties of crossing the border" (*Las Cruces Sun-News*, December 10, 1971). The first *monarca* in Las Cruces was Mariano Madrid. He was replaced in 1904 by Francisco Dominguez (Isabel Cruz, personal communication).

9.   Reports from earlier in the century describe similar themes. Foster (1904) writes that as "the bogeyman" the *abuelo* wore an animal mask and cracked a whip. A 1922 report says that the "abuelo or scarecrow, a grotesque figure wearing a horrible mask" represented "the Evil Spirit, who is trying to seduce Purity" (McCollum 1922). An account in the *Las Cruces Citizen* of December 12, 1926, states that "a man in a buffalo skin," representing evil, is beaten away from a little girl "dressed as a bride" who represents good.

10.   An *olla* is a clay pot. The drum used for the *baile de olla* ("clay pot dance") is a small red clay pot with a skin stretched over the opening. Unlike the dances during the Virgin's fiesta, the *baile de olla* was considered a secular dance with no religious obligation attached. It was performed on February 13 of 1988 in the *casa del pueblo,* after a lapse of three years. Oppenheimer (1957: 97–98) reports that the dance was performed on San Juan day, June 24, in 1951, and on the Saturday following the Guadalupe fiesta in 1950. Fewkes (1902: 67–68) describes a Nakü-püra, or House Dance, for Ysleta del Sur, whose features resemble the Tortugas *baile de olla.* Oppenheimer's Isleta informant identified the Tortugas dance as being Isleta's Hanch or Comanche Dance (98n7).

The following is a description of the *baile de olla* performed in the *casa del pueblo* on February 13, 1988. The idea was to have a good time. People brought eggshells stuffed with confetti and sealed with paper towels. They cracked these over the heads of unsuspecting victims who then danced with confetti-covered hair. The war captains tried to cajole people into dancing—the more people the better. Men and women formed separate lines, about six feet apart. The dance step resembled a sailor's hornpipe, a small jump and kick from one foot to the other, but done in a shuffle, with feet barely leaving the ground. Posture was erect, with arms hanging loose, even flopping from the momentum of the dancing.

As Juan Escalante began the drumming and singing, the two lines danced in place, facing the drummer. Upon a change in the drum pattern, the two lines filed outward and back, walking, to face the rear of the hall. There the lines faced each other again and resumed the jump-and-kick step.

There was disagreement on the order of patterns that should follow. On this particular evening, the dancers filed forward together into a single line, men and women alternating, and marched up to the drummer. There they separated out into men's and women's lines and again filed out and back. In the next round, each man stepped in front of his female counterpart, faced her, and put a hand on her shoulder. He then shuffled backward, leading her to the front of the hall. This first moment of physical contact was charged with hilarity.

Men and women separated out again and filed to the back. Now, the women stepped in front of the men and faced them with a hand on their shoulders, leading the men to the front. In the next round, each man reached out to the woman opposite, and man and woman held each other around the waist as they walked down the center together—once again, the touch a cause for serious joking. This time, instead of men peeling off one way, women the other, the first couple peeled right, the second left, and so on, so that when the two lines faced each other at the back of the hall, each line had men and women alternating. For the final round, two couples, one from each line, walked down the center four abreast, arms around one another's waists. Here the joking seemed to turn to solidarity.

Raul Sandoval later told me that there should have been a sequence before the hands-on-shoulders pattern in which women and men alternate in the two lines, women before men, then once again in alternation, men before women. He also said that the section of women leading men should have come before men leading women. This should be followed, he said, by a single file, men and women alternating where, as they reach the front of the hall, men file right, women left, back into separate lines. This is where the fun is, he said, because if someone goes the wrong way, they end up being the only man in the woman's line or the only woman in the man's line.

Diagrams and photographs of the 1988 *baile de olla* can be found on my website (www.arts.uci.edu/dsklar). Oppenheimer's diagrams for 1951 show both similarities and differences in choreographic patterns (98). His description of the levity of the event is consistent with the 1988 dance.

11.   For a summary of Ysleta del Sur's successful bid for federal recognition, see Houser 1979: 340–41. For newspaper coverage of corporation actions in the matter of tribal recognition, see Tessneer 1973 and 1974.

12.   Bishop Henry Granjon, after passing through the Mesilla Valley in 1902, wrote on *compadrazgo*. His description is similar to Vélez-Ibáñez's:

> To be invited to serve as a godfather is considered a great honor and a sign of deep friendship. It establishes, from that moment, between the godparents and parents of the child tight, strong bonds which cause the godfather to be considered as a member of the family and treated as such until death. The institution of *compadres* and *comadres* is universal among Mexicans; it fills their lives with an important role, and they value it like the pupils of their eyes. You can ask any service of your *compadre*; it will not be denied. Your house is his; your belongings are at his disposition. These multiple attachments, mostly between families, maintain the unity of the Mexican population and permit them to resist, to a certain extent, the invasions of the Anglo-Saxon race. (Granjon 1986: 38)

CHAPTER 4. CHOREOGRAPHY OF THE KITCHEN

1.   M. T. Velez finds that the major difference between Mexican-American and European-American childraising is that Mexican-American infants are raised in "thick contexts," with infants having longer and more frequent contact with other people besides their mothers. Indeed, the children she studied were rarely alone (Velez 1983, cited in Vélez-Ibáñez 1993: 138n14). "Thickness" in Tortugas meant that relatives were always available to help raise the children. Most young mothers worked, partly out of choice in a time of changed expectations of women and partly out of economic necessity. See also Kelly (1990), who finds that for Chicanos in Los Angeles there is a tension between women's intentions to fulfill notions of family, in which men act as providers and women as caretakers of children, and the necessity, because of underemployment, for women to work. In most of the families I came to know, the grandmothers baby-sat their daughters' children.

2.   The folklorist Américo Paredes, writing about ethnographers' tendency to mistake wordplay for gossip in Mexican-American communities, writes: "If aggression or resentment against the absent victim is quite on the surface, the joke may fall into the category of gossip-like banter. But even in such cases, the audience understands the whole thing as artistic license rather than as statement of alleged fact, as gossip would be" (Paredes 1977: 13).

3.   My comments about the Yaqui Easter ceremonies in Tucson are drawn from three visits (1981, 1982, 1987) to Barrio Libre and New Pascua. See Painter 1950 for an overview of the ceremonies.

CHAPTER 5. PILGRIMAGE

1.   This "compartmentalization" (Dozier 1957; Spicer 1962: 508) was similar to that of the northern Pueblos, where organization followed a tripartite structure: traditional religion, including the various sacred societies, under the cacique(s); Catholicism under the priests and church; and outside government-oriented relations under the governor and his council. For the members of the corporation, the separation between church and cacique had narrowed and for many disappeared. Nonetheless, traces of the compartmentalization remained in the division of duties between *mayordomos,* cacique and *capitanes,* and corporation officers.

2.   Beckett and Corbett (1990) write that the women climb up a center trail, while the men separate into two groups and climb on a north and south trail (10). I climbed up the center trail, where there were also men climbing.

3.   The same materials, yucca fronds and juniper branches, were also used at Easter time to make *ramos,* the "palms" of Palm Sunday. These were shorter versions of the *quiotes,* built upon a pair of twigs tied together in the shape of a cross. Every day for the week before Palm Sunday, volunteers gathered at the *casa del pueblo* to make *ramos.* The *ramos* were then distributed in the church on Palm Sunday.

4.   For an overview of Pueblo cosmology, see Ortiz 1969. Though Ortiz writes from the perspective of the Tewa Pueblos, the general pattern of center and four directional points applies throughout the Rio Grande Pueblos.

5.   The Puebloans also fought in El Paso del Norte. Men from Ysleta del Sur engaged with Apache raiding parties. Their last strike was in 1881, followed by their last "scalp dance" (Gerald 1974: 40-41). Kohlberg comments on the Indians of El Paso del Norte that they "are not savages; they are Pueblo Indians. They live with the Mexicans. Their principal occupation is to trail the Comanches and Apaches, wild Indians, after they have made a raid and stolen cattle" (Kohlberg 1973: 29). An 1888 news article, describing the fiesta mass at St. Genevieve's, suggests that the muskets fired during the procession were "said to be a relic of days past when savage Apaches would swoop down upon the worshippers, and hence

this defense" (*Rio Grande Republican*, December 15, 1888). Fewkes (1902: 67) reports on a Küfüra, or Scalp Dance, at Ysleta del Sur that was no longer performed in 1902. However, there were elders in Tortugas in 1986 who still knew the songs and dances and could describe the formations. Its name had been changed to the Comanche Dance.

6.   The *humero* was required to fast starting at midnight the previous day. His mountain lunch was prepared for him by the *mayordomas* and included handmade tortillas. Needless to say, they were elegantly round.

7.   Here the term *abuelo* means "respected elder" rather than, as Oppenheimer suggests, "clown." Oppenheimer may have conflated the *abuelos* of the cacique's council with the *abuelos* of the Danza (Oppenheimer 1957: 55). He is correct, however, that in the northern Pueblos, *principales* are not religious offices or part of the cacique's council but secular officers, assistants to the governor (57). When I asked Raul about this group, he said that all the people who climb are called *abuelos* when they come back. In English, they are pilgrims, but in Spanish, *abuelos*. The three members of the cacique's council are called *el consejo*.

8.   Tessneer writes that the "last-known" cacique's council "was made up of Francisco Dominguez, first; Miguel B. Fierro, second; and Faustino Pedraza, third" (Tessneer 1973). Francisco Dominguez passed away October 29, 1939 (*Las Cruces Sun-News*, November 1, 1939). Faustino Pedraza passed away in 1941, and Miguel Fierro in 1951. Either the cacique's council was reestablished after an interlude or Tessneer was mistaken in its disappearance, for there is at present a cacique's council of three men (personal communication, Mireya Ruiz). Raul reported that the corporation has recently reinstituted the practice and that the three oldest members have now been chosen to serve.

9.   In 1939, for example, "five hundred souls" climbed (Stoes 1939) and "hundreds of cars from the city, country and many neighboring towns of the state" parked on the sides of the road to watch the pilgrims return (*Las Cruces Sun-News*, December 12, 1939).

10.   Reynolds mentions Hood 1938 and 1946, and Cunningham 1938. See also Bouldin 1937 and Stoes 1937 and 1939. The sociological study is Loomis and Leonard 1938.

11.   As the corporation modernized, a schism split it. The breach revolved in part on the strengthened connection between corporation and church and on the loss of traditional *indio* practices that came with modernization. My understanding of the split draws on Reynolds (1981) and Oppenheimer (1957) as well as on discussions with individuals in the corporation and with Luke Lyon (see also Hurt 1952; Tessneer 1973 and 1974). It began in the 1930s when the cacique rented out his land across from the church to a carnival, sponsored by the church and held during the fiesta. The corporation protested that the levity of the carnival interfered with the religious nature of the fiesta, while the cacique's group argued that the carnival was a traditional part of the fiesta celebration. In 1946, a group of

corporation members, including Raul's and Lorenzo's fathers, accused the corporation president, brother of the cacique, of incompetence and financial mismanagement. Further, the president had moved to California in 1943, and many members didn't think he could satisfactorily carry out his presidential responsibilities at long distance. The membership elected a new president and, in 1948, successfully sued the cacique and his brother for the corporation's records and ritual paraphernalia. They also sued over the carnival and won this case as well.

The cacique's group then formed an organization based on the same corporate structure as Los Indigenes de Nuestra Señora de Guadalupe. Beginning in 1965, the new group sent out a call to all those in the Las Cruces area who could show Indian ancestry and began a campaign for federal recognition as an Indian tribe. They called themselves the "San Juan de Guadalupe Tiwa." In 1971, they drew up a constitution that was signed by 136 people (Reynolds 1981: 95), many of them descendants of *indio* immigrants from the missions of El Paso del Norte. But they did not continue the fiesta tradition or the round of ritual activities brought from El Paso. By 1981, membership and participation had greatly declined. According to Reynolds, the anthropologist hired to assist them in their bid for recognition, this was due to continued internal dissension and the gradual decline of the older generation (Reynolds 1981: 99). As of 1998, the San Juan de Guadalupe Tiwa had not been granted federal recognition.

12.   The Tortugas pilgrimage also refers to the annual pilgrimage to Tepeyac Hill near Mexico City. Some corporation members have been on this pilgrimage.

13.   Taken in 1987, photograph 1 shows the new Tepeyac.

14.   See, for example, Victor Turner's thoughts on pilgrimage and communitas (Turner 1973; Turner and Turner 1978) and Sallnow's response (1981).

15.   According to Hurt (1952: 118), the father of Leo Pacheco brought the dance from Mexico in 1921. According to Oppenheimer (1957: 111), he brought it in 1925.

16.   The historical information is from Oppenheimer 1957: 105-6 and Williams n.d. The corporation continued the tradition of serving supper to the pilgrims, but in the *casa de la comida*. This lasted until 1969 when it was abandoned because, as the pilgrimage grew, the task of feeding hundreds of people twice in two days was beyond the corporation's resources (*Las Cruces Sun-News*, November 30, 1969).

CHAPTER 6. GRANDDAUGHTER
OF MAMA LUZ

1.   A *jacal* house is an adobe hut. The word also has connotations of "the old Indian ways." It is of Nahuatl origin and implies a "thatched roof and walls made

of upright poles or sticks covered and chinked with mud or clay" (*Webster's New Collegiate Dictionary*).

2.   The idea that to perform a religious ritual signals acceptance but not necessarily belief is inspired by Rappaport (1979b: 193–94).

3.   For a discussion of Pueblo clowning, see also Beck and Walters 1977; Sweet 1989; Babcock 1984; Hieb 1972.

4.   See note 1, chapter 5.

5.   This is now changing, especially since the local publication of an overview of the Guadalupe community's early history. See Beckett and Corbett 1990 for a general history, Carie 1989 for Guadalupe church history.

6.   My discussion of ethnicity by consent as opposed to descent draws on Sollors 1986.

CHAPTER 7. *EL ENSAYO REAL*

1.   The collaboration among villages continued in Las Cruces. The *Mesilla Valley Democrat* of December 17, 1889, reported that "Chiefs and representatives of the Manzas [*sic*], Tiguas and Piras [*sic*] were here from Ysleta, Texas, El Paso and Senecú, Mexico to help observe the feast."

2.   As far as I could determine from people's reports, the words in Spanish were "Aquí está la vara, para que la respectes, y la hagas respectar. Y así, Dios y la virgen te van a ayudar."

3.   Gutiérrez claims that flagellation was an aspect of preconquest rituals among the Pueblos. He cites Benavides, who noted in his diaries that flogging of the war chief legitimated his use of force as son of Father Sun. Gutiérrez writes that the Spaniards outdid the Puebloans in their ability to withstand ritual whipping, thus asserting political authority (Gutiérrez 1991: 87–88).

4.   For an analysis of the melodies and rhythmic structures of Pueblo dance music, see Kurath and Garcia 1970; Humphreys 1989.

5.   Though "corn" and "harvest" dances differ from Pueblo to Pueblo, their format can be generalized. See Kurath and Garcia (1970) for a detailed description of the steps, floor patterns, and music in Tewa versions of the *xoxeye,* or corn dances. See also Sweet (1985) on Tewa Pueblo dances. Earlier anthropologists treated Pueblo dances at less descriptive length. Parsons (1929) gives an overview and calendar of Isleta Pueblo dances.

6.   Coles does not specify which Pueblo the children were from, beyond saying that it was a Rio Grande Pueblo between Santa Fe and Albuquerque.

7.   The feeling sense refers to what anthropologist Maxine Sheets-Johnstone calls kinesthetic-tactile, the combined sense of movement and touch that enables us to be aware of such actions as breathing (Sheets-Johnstone 1990: 5). I discuss the difference between feeling and emotion in chapter 9.

8. Because of the arrows, one Isleta friend connected the Tortugas dance to the old Isleta Scalp Dance. However, as previously mentioned, Tortugas has another dance called a Scalp Dance, not performed at the fiesta. Still, the Tigua dance of Tortugas is probably what Kurath calls a "semi-sacred" type (Kurath and Garcia 1970: 12).

9. There were three songs to each dance set, two slow songs accompanying the first dance section (the first varying between 170 and 190 metronome beats per minute and the second between 130 and 140) and a faster, duple-beat song in the second dance section (about 160 beats per minute). The third song is easily distinguishable from the other two because of its syncopated rhythm and because it marks a new choreographic section. Whoever does the drumming makes the choice of which songs to play within the repertory of these three song types.

10. The entrances of both the *casa del pueblo* and the church faced slightly to the north of east. The Virgin's altar was placed opposite the doors, slightly to the south of west. Therefore, to say the couples faced each other east to west is the closest approximation to the actual layout.

11. In the northern Pueblos, this faster double-bounce section would have more complex floor patterns, such as opposite partners circling around each other, reversing positions across the lines, or reforming into a single line. See Kurath and Garcia 1970.

12. This does not imply that there was no room for homosexuality in everyday life, and no androgyny in ritual performance, but rather that thinking of gender only in human social terms is too limited here. The complementarity of male and female was a cosmological principle. That is why, when a missionary protested the overt sexuality of a sacred clown's performance, a Hopi elder could say,

> Well, white man, you want to see what goes on, don't you? You have spoiled our prayers and it may not rain. You think this business is vulgar, but it means something sacred to us. This old *katchina* is impersonating the Corn Maiden: therefore we must have intercourse with her so that our corn will increase and our people will live in plenty. If this were evil we would not be doing it. You are supposed to be an educated man, but you had better go back to school and learn something more about Hopi life. (Simmons 1963: 190)

13. When I suggested this idea to Mireya, she said that the reason the women used to wear high heels was that there were no moccasins available in Las Cruces. Moccasins were made in the Pueblos up north, and there was neither time nor money to go and buy them.

14. A colleague at Isleta Pueblo remarked that the Isleta dance closest to the Tortugas dancing was the Santa Maria Christmas dance. Parsons (1929: 303) describes a Christmas Eve dance at Isleta with a "quadrillelike" figure that seems to resemble the Tortugas dance. She also mentions a "Santa Maria" song for Christmas (305).

15. Sollors suggests replacing the category of ethnicity with the concept of "cultural constructions of the codes of consent and descent" (Sollors 1986: 39).

16. I am grateful to Barbara Kirshenblatt-Gimblett for suggesting the idea of adoption.

CHAPTER 8. THE TWELFTH OF DECEMBER

1. My thinking on durative and eternal time has been influenced by the writings of Eliade (1959) and Turner (1967, 1969, and 1974).

2. Edward Hall (1977) explains the synchronizing of rhythms as a form of communication and the rhythms of nonverbal communication as an overlooked and critical aspect of cultural identification.

3. Shotgun guards accompanied all the processions on the twelfth. The *Rio Grande Republican* of December 15, 1888, declares them to have been "a relic of days past when savage Apaches would swoop down upon the worshippers, and hence this defense." More recently, an elder wrote protesting the popular misconception that they drive evil spirits away. Rather, she said, "Pueblo members fire blank shots . . . to express their joy at being able to pay homage in their own way to the Virgin of Guadalupe, their mother in heaven" (Narvaez 1968).

4. A detailed description of the choreographic patterns of the *baile grande*, as well as photographs and a video of the Tigua dance, can be found on my website (www.arts.uci.edu/dsklar).

5. The *custodia* was recently introduced into the fiesta by the bishop. It is a combination staff and cross, made from yucca stalks. Where the arms of the cross meet, overlapping fleshy white sotol fronds form a circle, and thin rays of green sotol blades radiate out from its center. Below the circle, eagle feathers are tied onto the staff with red wool. Tony Ruiz, Mireya's husband, made it.

CHAPTER 9. THE MOVEMENT DOES NOT STOP

1. The anthropologist Maxine Sheets-Johnstone recognizes the inseparability of the kinesthetic sense from the tactile. It is only through touch, the relationship between parts, that movement can be felt. She writes, eloquently, "[The living body] is first and foremost the center of a tactile-kinesthetic world that, unlike the visual world, rubs up directly against things outside it and reverberates directly with their sense. The tactile-kinesthetic body is a body that is always in touch, always resounding with an intimate and immediate knowledge of the world about it" (Sheets-Johnstone 1990: 16).

2.   Csordas intended the phrase differently. Positioning himself at the dialectical juncture between Maurice Merleau-Ponty's subjective perception and Pierre Bourdieu's collective practice, Csordas explores collective ideas about embodiment. For him, "somatic modes of attention" refers to the "culturally elaborated ways of attending to and with one's body in surroundings that include the embodied presence of others" (Csordas 1993: 138). Among appropriate subjects of research, Csordas lists erotic attraction, the concept of fatness, attention to body position and movement, meditation, pregnancy, and hypochondria (139).

3.   Howes and Classen (1991) provide guidelines for discerning the "sensory orders" of different cultural groups.

4.   The image of "a Kwakiutl bear dancer's footfall" comes from *Shadow Catcher* (1993), a video of the film about photographer Edward Curtis. Curtis "staged" the bear dance on the prow of a Kwakiutl boat.

5.   Stern's work also clarifies Suzanne Langer's philosophy of dance. Langer writes that dance embodies "virtual powers" or the "play of powers made visible" (Langer 1953). She recognized the action of virtual powers as present in all the vital processes of life and singled them out as the critical and elusive content of gesture in dance. Langer's "play of powers made visible" becomes comprehensible if one understands them to be Stern's vitality effects.

6.   I prefer the term "embodied schemata," because the visual emphasis of "image schemata" too easily reinforces the visualist bias of European and American history, erasing kinesthetic, auditory, and other somatic modes. See Howes 1991 on the visual bias of Western cultures and Howes and Classen 1991 on cultural differences in sensory profiles. Gardner (1983) discusses multiple intelligences as differences in the way people organize experience. Bandler and Grinder (1979), students of anthropologist Gregory Bateson and originators of neuro-linguistic programming, found that different people think via different sensory modalities, especially seeing, hearing, and feeling (kinesthesia).

7.   Rappaport distinguishes three levels of linguistic meaning. At the lowest, everyday semantic level, "b-a-l-l" is equivalent to what we recognize as a ball. This level is closely related to the technical definition of information as that which reduces uncertainty by making distinctions. At the second level, higher-order-meaning statements decrease distinctions and try to establish similarities, as in the metaphors " the Danza is like a steam engine working at full boil" or "kneading the news into the dough." They connect what we already understand with what we are trying to understand. At the highest level of "ultimate sacred postulates," meaning lies in bringing self and other into unity (1979a: 127).

8.   For a discussion of the physiological dimensions of the transformative effects of religious ritual, see especially Barbara Lex (1979).

9.   Victor Turner's discussion of the multivocality of ritual symbols is relevant. He found that the multiple references of symbols worked along a contin-

uum from visceral-physiological to normative-ideological poles. (Among his many treatments of this topic, see, for example, Turner 1974: 55.) Turner's continuum suggests Johnson's embodied schemata, grounded in bodily experience and working its way up to abstract ideas. It also reverberates with Rappaport's understanding of spiritual experience as joining ideas that have "no content" with bodily states of being. At the end of his life, seeking to reconcile biological and cultural approaches to human behavior, Turner went further. He hypothesized that the kinds of knowledge and function belonging to each brain layer are "laminated" in ritual symbols (Turner 1983). For example, Ndembu visceral-physiological referents, including mother's milk, breasts, nubility, and the "milk tree" would have a connection to the older so-called reptilian brain layers, while ideological-normative referents, like matrilineage, the place where "our" tribe began, the place where the ancestors slept, and the Ndembu nation itself would arise from neocortical layers. These referents were associated within the same symbol complex, leading Turner to conjecture that ritual symbols may "accrete" semantic references from all the brain layers.

10.   I thank Norma Cantú for this phrase.

11.   Clifford Geertz writes that religion is a "system of symbols." I am suggesting that it is not the symbols that produce "powerful, pervasive, long-lasting moods and motivations" (Geertz 1973: 90), but rather people's participation with symbols.

References

Amador, Danny (pseudonym). 1987. Interview with the author (taped), Las Cruces, NM, December 16. (For copies of the taped interview, contact the author, c/o Department of Dance at the University of California, Irvine.)

Armstrong, Robert Plant. 1971. *The Affecting Presence: An Essay in Humanistic Anthropology*. Urbana: University of Illinois Press.

Babcock, Barbara A. 1984. "Arrange Me into Disorder: Fragments and Reflections on Ritual Clowning." In *Rite, Drama, Festival, Spectacle: Rehearsals Toward a Theory of Cultural Performance*, edited by John J. MacAloon, 102–28. Philadelphia: Institute for the Study of Human Issues.

Bahti, Tom. 1970. *Southwestern Indian Ceremonials*. Las Vegas: KC Publications.

Baldwin, P. M. 1938. "A Short History of the Mesilla Valley." *New Mexico Historical Review* 13, no. 3: 314–24.

Bandelier, A. F. 1890. *Final Report of Investigations Among the Indians of the Southwestern United States Carried on Mainly in the Years from 1880 to 1885*. Part 1. Papers of the Archaeological Society of America. American Series 3. Reprint, Cambridge: Cambridge University Press, 1976.

————. 1892. *Investigations Among the Indians of the Southwestern United States Carried on Mainly in the Years from 1880 to 1885.* Part 2. Papers of the Archaeological Society of America. American Series 3. Reprint, Cambridge: Cambridge University Press, 1976.

Bandler, Richard, and John Grinder. 1979. *Frogs into Princes.* Moab, UT: Real People Press.

Bartenieff, Irmgard. 1974. "Effort/Shape in Teaching Ethnic Dance." In *New Dimensions in Dance Research: Anthropology and Dance—The American Indian,* edited by Tamara Comstock, 175–92. Committee on Research in Dance Annual 6. New York: Committee on Research in Dance.

Bartlett, John Russell. 1965. *Personal Narrative of Explorations and Incidents in Texas, New Mexico, California, Sonora, and Chihuahua, connected with the United States and Mexican Boundary Commission, during the years 1850, '51, '52, and '58.* Vol. 1. Chicago: Rio Grande Press.

Beck, Peggy V., and Anna L. Walters. 1977. "Sacred Fools and Clowns." In *The Sacred: Ways of Knowledge, Sources of Life,* 291–316. Tsaile, AZ: Navajo Community College Press.

Beckett, Patrick H. 1974. "A Tiwa Rabbit Hunt as Held by the Tortugas Indians." *Awanyu* 2, no. 1: 40–46.

————. 1979. "The Major Ceremonies of 'Los Indigenes de Nuestra Señora de Guadalupe.'" In *Collected Papers in Honor of Bertha Pauline Dutton.* Papers of the Archaeological Society of New Mexico 4. Albuquerque: Archaeological Society Press.

————. 1982. "Tortugas." *The Las Cruces Historic Buildings Survey,* text by Mary M. Steeb, Michael Romero Taylor, Anthony C. Pennock, et al. 1st ed. Las Cruces, NM: Doña Ana County Historical Society.

Beckett, Patrick H., and Terry L. Corbett. 1990. *Tortugas.* COAS Monograph no. 8. Las Cruces, NM: COAS Publishing and Research.

Bennett, Wendell C., and Robert M. Zingg. 1976. *The Tarahumara: An Indian Tribe of Northern Mexico.* Glorieta, NM: Rio Grande Press.

Bernal, Rico (pseudonym). 1986. Interview with the author (taped), Las Cruces, NM, October 21.

————. 1987. Interview with the author (taped), Las Cruces, NM, March 12. (For copies of the taped interviews, contact the author, c/o Department of Dance at the University of California, Irvine.)

Bernstein, Basil. 1965. *A Sociolinguistic Approach to Social Learning,* edited by J. Gould. Penguin Survey of the Social Sciences. London: Penguin.

Best, David. 1975. "The Aesthetics of Dance." *Dance Research Journal* 7, no. 2 (spring/summer): 12–15.

————. 1978. *Expression in Movement and the Arts: A Philosophical Enquiry.* London: Lepus Books.

Bloom, Lansing B., ed. 1938. "Bourke on the Southwest." *New Mexico Historical Review* 13: 190–209.

Bloom, Maude McFie. 1903. "A History of the Mesilla Valley." Thesis, New Mexico College of Agriculture and Mechanical Arts. Courtesy of Rio Grande Historical Collections, New Mexico State University Library, Las Cruces.

Boni, Margaret Bradford. 1947. *Fireside Book of Folk Songs.* Arranged for the piano by Norman Lloyd. New York: Simon & Schuster.

Bouldin, Edna. 1937. "Flames Across the Hills." *New Mexico Magazine,* December: 14–15.

Bowden, Jocelyn J. 1974. "The Ascarate Grant." *Apache Indians.* Vol. 2. New York: Garland Publishing.

Bull, Cynthia Jean Cohen. 1997. "Sense, Meaning, and Perception in Three Dance Cultures." In *Meaning in Motion: New Cultural Studies of Dance,* edited by Jane Desmond, 269–88. Durham, NC: Duke University Press.

Carie, Giles. 1986. *The Guadalupe Triduum in Tortugas.* Mesilla Park, NM: Parish of Our Lady of Guadalupe.

[Carie, Giles]. 1989. *Tortugas, New Mexico: Our Lady of Guadalupe 75th Jubilee. 1989. Directory of Our Lady of Guadalupe.* Mesilla Park, NM.

Castillo, Bernal Diaz de. 1800. *The True History of the Conquest of Mexico by Captain Bernal Diaz de Castillo Written in the Year 1568.* Translated by Maurice Keating. London: J. Wright Piccadilly.

Champe, Flavia. 1980–81. "Origins of the Magical Matachines Dance." *El Palacio* 86, no. 4 (winter): 35–39.

———. 1983. *The Matachines Dance of the Upper Rio Grande: History, Music, and Choreography.* Lincoln: University of Nebraska Press.

Chávez, Denise. 1986. *The Last of the Menu Girls.* Houston: Arte Publico Press.

———. 1987. Manuscript of a play for voices, presented at Guadalupe 87 Conference, Las Cruces, NM, October 31.

Cisneros, Sandra. 1991. *Woman Hollering Creek and Other Stories.* New York: Random House.

Clifford, James. 1988. "On Ethnographic Authority." In *The Predicament of Culture: Twentieth-Century Ethnography, Literature, and Art,* 21–54. Cambridge: Harvard University Press.

Coles, Robert. 1977. *Eskimos, Chicanos, Indians.* Volume 4 of *Children of Crisis.* Boston: Little, Brown.

Commissioners of the Town of Guadalupe. 1914a. Deed of Indenture no. 35360, September 14. Doña Ana County Clerk's Office, Las Cruces, NM.

———. 1914b. Warranty Deed no. 21447, October 26. Doña Ana County Clerk's Office, Las Cruces, NM.

Csordas, Thomas J. 1993. "Somatic Modes of Attention." *Cultural Anthropology* 8, no. 2 (May): 135–56.

Cunningham, Anna Blanche. 1938. "Rhythms of the Tom-toms in Tortugas." *Desert Magazine* 2, no. 2: 21–22, 29.

Curry, Ella Banegas, and Shan Nichols. 1974. *Our Heritage, Our People: Selections of the Mesilla Valley.* Las Cruces, NM: Curry.

Dell, Cecily. 1977. *A Primer for Movement Description Using Effort-Shape and Supplementary Concepts.* New York: Dance Notation Bureau.

Demarest, Donald, and Coley Taylor, eds. 1956. *The Dark Virgin: A Documentary Anthology.* Freeport, ME: Coley Taylor.

Dilthey, Wilhelm. 1976 [1914]. *Selected Writings.* Edited by H. P. Rickman. Cambridge: Cambridge University Press.

Douglas, Mary. 1970. *Natural Symbols: Explorations in Cosmology.* New York: Random House. Reprint, New York: Pantheon Books. 1982.

Dozier, Edward P. 1957. "Rio Grande Ceremonial Patterns." *New Mexico Quarterly* 27, nos. 1–2 (spring/summer): 27–34.

Efron, David. 1941. *Gesture, Race and Culture: A Tentative Study of Some of the Spatio-Temporal and "Linguistic" Aspects of the Gestural Behavior of Eastern Jews and Southern Italians in New York City, Living Under Similar as Well as Different Environmental Conditions.* Reprint, The Hague: Mouton, 1972.

Eggan, Fred. 1979. "Pueblos: Introduction." In *Handbook of North American Indians,* William Sturtevant, gen. ed. Vol. 9, *Southwest,* edited by Alfonso Ortiz, 224–35. Washington, DC: Smithsonian.

Ekman, Paul, Robert W. Levenson, and Wallace V. Friesen. 1983. "Autonomic Nervous System Activity Distinguishes Among Emotions." *Science* 221 (September 16): 1208–10.

Eliade, Mircea. 1959. *The Sacred and the Profane.* New York: Harcourt Brace.

Elizondo, Father Virgil. 1976. *La Morenita, Evangelizer of the Americas.* San Antonio, TX: Mexican American Cultural Center.

———. 1987. Talk presented at Guadalupe 87 Conference, Las Cruces, NM, October 31.

Fewkes, J. Walter. 1902. "The Pueblo Settlements near El Paso, Texas." *American Anthropologist* 4, no. 1: 57–75.

Forrest, John. 1984. *Morris and Matachin: A Study in Comparative Choreography.* London: English Folk Dance and Song Society.

Foster, Susan Leigh. 1995. "Choreographing History." In *Choreographing History,* edited by Susan Leigh Foster, 3–24. Bloomington: Indiana University Press.

Foster, Thora Alice Lute. 1904. "The Folklore of the Mesilla Valley: A Contribution to the Folk-lore of New Mexico." Thesis submitted to the New Mexico College of Agriculture and Mechanical Arts. Courtesy of Rio Grande Historical Collections, New Mexico State University Library, Las Cruces.

Gardner, Howard. 1983. *Frames of Mind: The Theory of Multiple Intelligences.* New York: Basic Books.

Geertz, Clifford. 1973. *The Interpretation of Cultures: Selected Essays.* New York: Basic Books.

Gerald, Rex E. 1974. "Aboriginal Use and Occupation by Tigua, Manso, and Suma Indians." In *Apache Indians.* Vol. 3. New York: Garland Publishing.

Goffman, Erving. 1959. *The Presentation of Self in Everyday Life.* Garden City, NY: Doubleday.

Granjon, Monsignor Henry. 1986. *Along the Rio Grande: A Pastoral Visit in Southwest New Mexico in 1902.* Edited and annotated by Michael Romero Taylor. Translated by Mary W. de López. Albuquerque: University of New Mexico Press.

Griffin, Susan. 1992. *A Chorus of Stones: The Private Life of War.* New York: Anchor Doubleday.

Grosz, Elizabeth. 1994. *Volatile Bodies: Toward a Corporeal Feminism.* Bloomington: Indiana University Press.

Gutiérrez, Ramón A. 1991. *When Jesus Came the Corn Mothers Went Away: Marriage, Sexuality, and Power in New Mexico, 1500–1846.* Stanford: Stanford University Press.

Hackett, Charles W. 1942. *Revolt of the Pueblo Indians of New Mexico and Otermin's Attempted Reconquest, 1680–1682.* 2 vols. Albuquerque: University of New Mexico Press.

Hall, Edward T. 1977. "Rhythm and Body Movement." In *Beyond Culture,* 71–84. New York: Anchor.

Hawley, Florence. 1948. "Dance of the Devil-Chasers." *New Mexico Magazine,* September: 16, 35, 37, 39.

Heschel, Abraham Joshua. 1962. *The Earth Is the Lord's* and *The Sabbath.* Philadelphia: Jewish Publication Society. Reprint, New York: Harper & Row, 1966.

Hieb, Louis. 1972. "Meaning and Mismeaning: Toward an Understanding of the Ritual Clown." In *New Perspectives on the Pueblos,* edited by Alfonso Ortiz, 163–95. A School of American Research Book. Albuquerque: University of New Mexico Press. .

History of New Mexico: Its Resources and People. 1907. Vol. 1. Los Angeles: Pacific States Publishing.

Hood, Margaret Page. 1938. "Faustino." *New Mexico Sentinel,* December 18.

———. 1946. "The Day of the Virgin." *New Mexico* 24 (December): 21, 43, 45.

Horgan, Paul. 1954. *Great River: The Rio Grande in North American History.* New York: Rinehart. Reprint, Austin, TX: Texas Monthly Press, 1984.

Houser, Nicholas P. 1970. "The Tigua Settlements of Ysleta del Sur." *The Kiva* 36, no. 2: 23–39.

———. 1979. "Tigua Pueblo." In *Handbook of North American Indians,* William Sturtevant, gen. ed. Vol. 9, *Southwest,* edited by Alfonso Ortiz, 336–50. Washington, DC: Smithsonian.

Howes, David. 1991. "Sensorial Anthropology." In *The Variety of Sensory Experience: A Sourcebook in the Anthropology of the Senses*, edited by David Howes, 167–91. Toronto: University of Toronto Press.

Howes, David, and Constance Classen. 1991. "Sounding Sensory Profiles." In *The Variety of Sensory Experience: A Sourcebook in the Anthropology of the Senses*, edited by David Howes, 257–88. Toronto: University of Toronto Press.

Hughes, Anne E. 1914. "The Beginnings of Spanish Settlement in the El Paso District." *University of California Publications in History* 1, no. 3. Berkeley: University of California Press.

Humphreys, Paul. 1989. "Form as Cosmology: An Interpretation of Structure in the Ceremonial Songs of the Pueblo Indians." *Pacific Review of Ethnomusicology* 5: 62–88.

Hurt, Wesley R., Jr. 1952. "Tortugas, an Indian Village in Southern New Mexico." *El Palacio* 59, no. 4 (April): 104–22.

Jenkins, Myra Ellen. 1974. "The Tigua Indians of Ysleta del Sur during the Spanish Colonial Period." In *Apache Indians*. Vol. 3. New York: Garland Publishing.

Johnson, Mark. 1987. *The Body in the Mind: The Bodily Basis of Meaning, Imagination, and Reason*. Chicago: University of Chicago Press.

Kealiinohomoku, Joann. 1974. "Field Guides." In *New Dimensions in Dance Research: Anthropology and Dance—The American Indian*, edited by Tamara Comstock, 245–60. Committee on Research in Dance Research Annual 6. New York: Committee on Research in Dance.

Kelly, M. Patricia Fernández. 1990. "Delicate Transactions: Gender, Home, and Employment among Hispanic Women." In *Uncertain Terms: Negotiating Gender in American Culture*, edited by Faye Ginsburg and Anna Lowenhaupt Tsing, 183–195. Boston: Beacon Press.

Kohlberg, Walter L., trans. 1973. *Letters of Ernst Kohlberg 1875–1877*. Southwestern Studies Monograph no. 38. El Paso, TX: University of Texas.

Kurath, Gertrude Prokosch. 1949. "Mexican Moriscas: A Problem in Dance Acculturation." *Journal of American Folklore* 62: 87–103

———. 1956. "Dance Relatives of Mid-Europe and Middle America: A Venture in Comparative Choreology." *Journal of American Folklore* 69, no. 273 (July–September): 286–98.

———. 1957. "The Origin of the Pueblo Indian Matachines." *El Palacio* 64, nos. 9–10 (September–October): 259–64.

Kurath, Gertrude Prokosch, with Antonio Garcia. 1970. *Music and Dance of the Tewa Pueblos*. Museum of New Mexico Research Records 8. Santa Fe: Museum of New Mexico Press.

Laban, Rudolf. 1971. *The Mastery of Movement*. 3d edition, revised and enlarged by Lisa Ullman. Boston: Plays.

Lafaye, Jacques. 1974. *Quetzalcóatl and Guadalupe: The Formation of Mexican National Consciousness 1531–1813*. Translated by Benjamin Keen. Chicago: University of Chicago Press.

Lange, Charles H., and Carroll L. Riley, eds. 1970. *The Southwestern Journals of Adolf F. Bandelier 1883–1884*. Albuquerque: University of New Mexico Press.

Laski, Vera. 1959. *Seeking Life*. Memoirs of the American Folklore Society. Vol. 50. Philadelphia: American Folklore Society.

Lavender, Larry, and Wendy Oliver. 1993. "Learning to 'See' Dance: The Role of Critical Writing in Developing Students' Aesthetic Awareness." *Impulse* 1, no. 1 (July): 10–20.

Lea, Aurora White. 1963. "More About the Matchines." *New Mexico Folklore* 11: 7–10.

Lehrhaupt, Linda E. 1990. "Pilgrimage in Modern Ireland: Case Studies of Lough Derg, Croagh Patrick, and Knock Shrine." Ph.D. dissertation, New York University, New York.

Lévi-Strauss, Claude. 1969. *The Raw and the Cooked*. Translated by John and Doreen Weightman. New York: Harper & Row.

Lex, Barbara. 1979. "The Neurobiology of Ritual Trance." In *The Spectrum of Ritual: A Biogenetic Structural Analysis*, ed. Eugene G. D'Aquili, Charles D. Laughlin Jr., John McManus, et al., 117–51. New York: Columbia University Press.

Lomax, Alan, Irmgard Bartenieff, and Forrestine Paulay. 1968. *Folk Song Style and Culture*. American Association for the Advancement of Science, Publication 88. Washington, DC: American Association for the Advancement of Science.

———. 1974. "Choreometrics: A Method for the Study of Cross-Cultural Pattern in Film." In *New Dimensions in Dance Research: Anthropology and Dance— The American Indian*, edited by Tamara Comstock, 193–212. Committee on Research in Dance Research Annual 6. New York: Committee on Research in Dance.

Loomis, C. P., and O. E. Leonard. 1938. "Standards of Living in an Indian-Mexican Village and on a Reclamation Project." United States Department of Agriculture, *Social Research Report* no. 14. Washington, DC.

Los Indigenes de Nuestra Señora de Guadalupe. 1914. Articles of Incorporation, April 13. Doña Ana County Clerk, New Mexico.

Los Matachines. 1988. Produced by KGGM-TV. Albuquerque, NM. Video program, January 23.

Lyon, Luke L. n.d.. Papers. Rio Grande Historical Collections, New Mexico State University Library, Las Cruces.

Marie, Sister Joseph. 1948. "The Role of the Church and the Folk in the Development of the Early Drama in New Mexico." Ph.D. dissertation, University of Pennsylvania, Philadelphia.

Martin, John. 1939. "The Nature of Movement." In *Introduction to the Dance*, 31–55. Reprint, Brooklyn, NY: Dance Horizons, 1978.

Matachines. 1980. Bernalillo, NM. Produced by Ken Marthey. Funded by New Mexico Arts Commission. 16 mm, 28 minutes.

Matasina. 1980. San Juan Pueblo. Funded by New Mexico Arts Commission. Commentary by Herman Agoya. 16 mm, 16 minutes.

McBride, Dr. R. E. 1908. "Doña Ana County in New Mexico." New Mexico Bureau of Immigration. Courtesy of Special Collections, New Mexico State University Library, Las Cruces.

McCollum, Pansy P. 1922. "The Fiesta Guadalupe." Thesis submitted to the New Mexico College of Agriculture and Mechanical Arts. Courtesy of Rio Grande Historical Collections, New Mexico State University Library, Las Cruces.

Miranda, Isidro. 1988. Interview with the author (taped), Las Cruces, NM, March 10. (For copies of the taped interview, contact the author, c/o Department of Dance at the University of California, Irvine.)

Narvaez, Emma. 1959. "Tortugas History Given By Indian." *Las Cruces Sun-News*, December 9.

———. 1968. "Annual Celebration to Honor Lady of Guadalupe Starts Today." *Las Cruces Sun-News*, December 10.

Ness, Sally Ann. 1992. *Body, Movement, and Culture: Kinesthetic and Visual Symbolism in a Philippine Community.* Philadelphia: University of Pennsylvania Press.

Novack, Cynthia J. 1988. "Looking at Movement as Culture." *Drama Review* 32, no. 4 (T120): 102–19.

———. 1990. *Sharing the Dance: Contact Improvisation and American Culture.* Madison: University of Wisconsin Press.

Oppenheimer, Alan James. 1957. *An Ethnological Study of Tortugas, New Mexico.* M.A. thesis, University of New Mexico, Albuquerque.

Ortiz, Alfonso. 1969. *The Tewa World: Space, Time, Being, and Becoming in a Pueblo Society.* Chicago: University of Chicago Press.

———. 1972. "Ritual Drama and the Pueblo World View." In *New Perspectives on the Pueblos,* edited by Alfonso Ortiz, 135–61. A School of American Research Book. Albuquerque: University of New Mexico Press.

Painter, Muriel Thayer. 1950. *A Yaqui Easter.* Tucson: University of Arizona Press.

Paola, Tommie de. 1980. *The Lady of Guadalupe.* New York: Holiday House.

Paredes, Américo. 1977. "On Ethnographic Work among Minority Groups: A Folklorist's Perspective." In *New Directions in Chicano Scholarship,* edited by Ricardo Romo and Raymund Paredes, 2–28. Santa Barbara: Center for

Chicano Studies, University of California, Santa Barbara. Also: *New Scholar* 6 (1977).

Parke, John G. 1857. *Reports of Explorations and Surveys to Ascertain the Most Practicable and Economical Route for a Railroad from the Mississippi River to the Pacific Ocean.* Vols. 2 and 7. Washington, DC. Courtesy of Rio Grande Historical Collections, New Mexico State University Library, Las Cruces, Luke Lyon Papers.

Parmentier, Richard J. 1979. "The Pueblo Mythological Triangle: Poseyemu, Montezuma, and Jesus in the Pueblos." In *Handbook of North American Indians,* William Sturtevant, gen. ed. Vol. 9, *Southwest,* edited by Alfonso Ortiz, 609–22. Washington, DC: Smithsonian.

Parsons, Elsie Clews. 1929–30. *Isleta, New Mexico.* Forty-seventh Annual Report of the Bureau of American Ethnology. Washington, DC: Smithsonian.

———. 1939. *Pueblo Indian Religion.* 2 vols. Chicago: University of Chicago Press.

Paz, Octavio. 1961. *Labyrinth of Solitude: Life and Thought in Mexico.* Translated by Lysander Kemp. New York: Grove Press.

Rappaport, Roy A. 1979a. "On Cognized Models." In *Ecology, Meaning, and Religion,* 97–144. Richmond, CA: North Atlantic Books.

———. 1979b. "The Obvious Aspects of Ritual." In *Ecology, Meaning, and Religion,* 173–221. Richmond, CA: North Atlantic Books.

Reid, John C. 1858. *Reid's Tramp, or a Journal of the Incidents of Ten Months Travel through Texas, New Mexico, Arizona, Sonora, and California.* Selma, AL: John Hardy and Company.

Reynolds, Terry R., with Mary Taylor. 1981. *The History, Organization, and Customs of the San Juan de Guadalupe Tiwa, Las Cruces, New Mexico.* Manuscript prepared for the Native American Rights Fund, Boulder, CO.

Robb, J. D. 1954. *Hispanic Folk Music of New Mexico and the Southwest: A Self-Portrait of a People.* Norman: University of Oklahoma Press.

———. 1961. "The Matachines Dance—A Ritual Folk Dance." *Western Folklore* 20, no. 2 (April): 87–101.

Rodríguez, Sylvia. 1987. "Land, Water, and Ethnic Identity in Taos." In *Land, Water, and Culture: New Perspectives on Hispanic Land Grants,* edited by Charles L. Briggs and John R. Van Ness, 313–403. New Mexico Land Grant Series. Albuquerque: University of New Mexico Press.

———. 1996. *The Matachines Dance: Ritual Symbolism and Interethnic Relations in the Upper Rio Grande Valley.* Albuquerque: University of New Mexico Press.

Sallnow, M. J. 1981. "Communitas Reconsidered: The Sociology of Andean Pilgrimage." *Man* n.s. 16: 163–82.

Sando, Joe S. 1992. *Pueblo Nations: Eight Centuries of Pueblo Indian History.* Santa Fe: Clear Light.

Schechner, Richard. 1985. "Points of Contact Between Anthropological and Theatrical Thought." In *Between Theater and Anthropology,* 3–34. Philadelphia: University of Pennsylvania Press.

———. 1986. "Magnitudes of Performance." In *The Anthropology of Experience,* edited by Victor W. Turner and Edward M. Bruner, 344–69. Urbana: University of Illinois Press.

Schroeder, Albert H. 1979. "Pueblos Abandoned in Historic Times." In *Handbook of North American Indians,* William Sturtevant, gen. ed. Vol. 9, *Southwest,* edited by Alfonso Ortiz, 236–54. Washington, DC: Smithsonian.

Shadow Catcher: Edward S. Curtis and the North American Indian. 1993. Produced, directed, and written by T. C. McLuhan. New York: Mystic Fire Video. 89 minutes. VHS format.

Sheets-Johnstone, Maxine. 1990. *The Roots of Thinking.* Philadelphia: Temple University Press.

Siegel, Marcia B. 1977. *Watching the Dance Go By.* Boston: Houghton Mifflin.

———. 1979. *The Shapes of Change: Images of American Dance.* Berkeley: University of California Press.

———. 1991. "Rethinking Movement Analysis." Unpublished manuscript.

Simmons, Leo W., ed. 1963. *Sun Chief: The Autobiography of a Hopi Indian.* New Haven: Yale University Press.

Simmons, Marc. 1979. "History of Pueblo-Spanish Relations to 1821." In *Handbook of North American Indians,* William Sturtevant, gen. ed. Vol. 9, *Southwest,* edited by Alfonso Ortiz, 206–23. Washington, DC: Smithsonian.

Sklar, Deidre. 1985. "Etienne Decroux's Promethean Mime." *Drama Review* 29, no. 4 (T108) (winter): 64–75.

———. 1991a. "On Dance Ethnography." *Dance Research Journal* 23, no. 1 (spring): 6–10.

———. 1991b. "Enacting Religious Belief: A Movement Ethnography of the Annual Fiesta of Tortugas, New Mexico." Ph.D. dissertation, New York University, New York.

———. 1994. "Can Bodylore Be Brought to Its Senses?" *Journal of American Folklore* 107, no. 423: 9–22.

———. 1999. "'All the Dances Have a Meaning to That Apparition': Felt Knowledge and the Danzantes of Tortugas, New Mexico." *Dance Research Journal* 31, no. 2 (fall): 14–33.

———. Forthcoming. "Performance Observation Guidelines." In *Embodied Pedagogy,* edited by Sally Harrison-Pepper and Jill Dolan.

Snyder, Allegra Fuller. 1978. "Levels of Event Patterns: Dance in a Holistic Context." Paper presented to the Congress on Research in Dance, University of Hawaii, Manoa.

Sollors, Werner. 1986. *Beyond Ethnicity: Consent and Descent in American Culture.* New York: Oxford University Press.

Spicer, Edward H. 1962. *Cycles of Conquest: The Impact of Spain, Mexico, and the*

United States on the Indians of the Southwest, 1533–1960. Tucson: University of Arizona Press.

———. 1980. *The Yaquis: A Cultural History.* Tucson: University of Arizona Press.

Stern, Daniel N. 1985. *The Interpersonal World of the Infant: A View from Psycho-analysis and Developmental Psychology.* New York: Basic Books.

Stoes, Katherine D. n.d. Papers. Ms. 208. Rio Grande Historical Collections, New Mexico State University Library, Las Cruces.

———. 1937. *Las Cruces Sun-News,* December 12: 1–2.

———. 1939. "Tortugas Indians Revive Ancient Tribal Dance." *Las Cruces Sun-News,* December 10: 1, 3.

Sweet, Jill D. 1985. *Dances of the Tewa Pueblo Indians: Expressions of New Life.* Santa Fe: School of American Research.

———. 1989. "Burlesquing 'the Other' in Pueblo Performance." *Annals of Tourism Research* 16, no. 1: 62–75.

Taussig, Michael. 1987. *Shamanism, Colonialism, and the Wild Man: A Study in Terror and Healing.* Chicago: University of Chicago Press.

Tessneer, Marvin. 1973. "Unit Disavows Action in Suit." *Las Cruces Sun-News,* August 5.

———. 1974. "Judge Dismisses Suit Brought by Tortugans." *Las Cruces Sun-News,* October 16.

Tuan, Yi-Fu. 1977. *Space and Place: The Perspective of Experience.* Minneapolis: University of Minnesota Press.

Turner, Victor. 1967. "Betwixt and Between: The Liminal Period in Rites de Passage." In *The Forest of Symbols: Aspects of Ndembu Ritual,* 93–111. Ithaca: Cornell University Press.

———. 1969. *The Ritual Process: Structure and Anti-Structure.* London: Routledge and Kegan Paul.

———. 1973. "The Center Out There: Pilgrim's Goal." *History of Religions* 12, no. 3 (February): 191–230.

———. 1974. *Dramas, Fields, and Metaphors: Symbolic Action in Human Society.* Ithaca: Cornell University Press.

———. 1983. "Body, Brain, and Culture." *Zygon: Journal of Religious Science* 18, no. 3 (September): 221–45.

Turner, Victor W., and Edith Turner. 1978. *Image and Pilgrimage in Christian Culture: Anthropological Perspectives.* Oxford: Basil Blackwell.

United States Bureau of Census. 1980. General Population Characteristics PC(1)-B33 New Mexico; 1980 Census, General Social & Economic Characteristics, NM PC1-C-33.

Valdez, Frankie (pseudonym). 1987. Interview with the author (taped). Las Cruces, NM, May 17. (For copies of the taped interview, contact the author, c/o Department of Dance at the University of California, Irvine.)

Vandermasen, Reverend M. 1909. "Feast of Our Lady of Guadalupe as Celebrated by Indians in Las Cruces, New Mexico." *Rio Grande Republican*, December 10.

Vega, Lazo de la. 1956. "The Miraculous Apparition of the Beloved Virgin Mary, Our Lady of Guadalupe, at Tepeyac, near Mexico City." In *The Dark Virgin: A Documentary Anthology*, edited by Donald Demarest and Coley Taylor, 41–53. Freeport, ME: Coley Taylor.

Velez, Maria Teresa. 1983. "The Social Context of Mothering: A Comparison of Mexican American and Anglo Mother-Infant Interaction Patterns." Ph.D. dissertation, Wright Institute of Psychology, Los Angeles.

Vélez-Ibáñez, Carlos G. 1993. "Ritual Cycles of Exchange: The Process of Cultural Creation and Management in the U.S. Borderlands." In *Celebrations of Identity: Multiple Voices in American Ritual Performance*, edited by Pamela R. Frese, 119–43. Westport, CT: Bergin & Garvey.

Walz, Vina. 1951. "History of the El Paso Area 1680–1692." Ph.D. dissertation, University of New Mexico, Albuquerque.

Williams, Enyd. n.d. Audiotaped interview with Emma Narvaez. *Hosts to the World*, BBC radio broadcast. Produced by Ed Thomasson. Luke Lyon papers. Rio Grande Historical Collections, New Mexico State University Library, Las Cruces.

Index

Text:	10/14 Palatino
Display:	Cochin
Composition:	G & S Typesetters
Printing and binding:	Thomson-Shore
Index:	Laurie Reith Winship